Poverty in Rural America

Poverty in Rural America:
A Case Study

Janet M. Fitchen
late of Ithaca College

WAVELAND

PRESS, INC.

Prospect Heights, Illinois

For information about this book, write or call:
Waveland Press, Inc.
P.O. Box 400
Prospect Heights, Illinois 60070
(847) 634-0081

Dedicated to
the children of Chestnut Valley,
past, present, and future

This case study of poverty in the contemporary United States examines a problem that is widespread but little studied: run-down neighborhoods of intergenerational poverty scattered on the rural fringes of urban areas. Intertwining historical, economic, social, cultural, and psychological material and basing her work on a decade of participant-observation, the author provides a new understanding of the lives and actions of nonfarm rural poor people and identifies the causes of their marginal situation.

Beginning with a typical day in the life of one family, Dr. Fitchen illustrates in specific and personal terms the endemic problems – unsatisfactory employment, low and insecure income, social marginality, inadequate education, neglected health problems, substandard housing, and low self-esteem – that plague rural depressed areas. She describes the ways people perceive their problems and goals, the constraints they face, and the solutions they have developed, looking always for common patterns of thought and action – and an explanation of these patterns – that will be useful to students, practitioners, and policymakers. Among her conclusions are concrete suggestions for breaking the cycle of entrenched rural poverty.

I have made
a ceaseless effort
not to ridicule,
not to bewail,
nor to scorn human actions,
but to understand them.
—Spinoza

Contents

Part 4
Conclusion: Causes and Cures

Acknowledgments

This book reflects the influence and encouragement of many people over many years – more people and more influences than I can list here.

I offer particular acknowledgment to the many professors who have shaped and trained my mind as an anthropologist. At Vassar College, John V. Murra and Helen Codere not only introduced me to anthropology but also conveyed to me their love of it. Oscar Lewis and Edward Winter at the University of Illinois contributed further to my anthropological development. Years later at Cornell University, Robert J. Smith and Davydd J. Greenwood helped me to complete my formal training. They also provided the encouragement and critiques that were so important during the research and writing that preceded this book. In the later years of graduate school, I was assisted financially by a National Institute of Health Training Program grant, NIGMS 1256, for which I am grateful.

I also wish to express my appreciation to the many individuals working in poverty settings around the state and the nation who have shared their experiences with me. They work in a wide variety of circumstances as professionals, paraprofessionals, and volunteers. They attempt innovative programs and dedicate their energies to helping alleviate the problems caused by poverty. They have given me valuable insights.

I greatly appreciate the input of a number of friends who have read and commented on the earlier drafts of this book. Their questions and reactions helped me think and rethink my interpretations. In particular, Nina Lambert brought the perspective of clinical psychology and her own expertise to bear on an earlier draft, providing some thought-provoking discussions. Sandra Rosenzweig Gittleman combined her perception as a social worker and as an artist to create the illustrations that enhance this book.

All through the years of my involvement in this endeavor, my husband, Douglas B. Fitchen, has accepted this project as an integral part of my life, recognizing its importance to me and giving me the support I needed. Our children, John, Katie, and Sylvia, have grown up with this project. They have helped me immeasurably with their tacit backing, their willingness to let me follow my own interests, and, on occasion, with their willing labor. Young children's fingerprints still mark the index cards of bibliographies they so carefully alphabetized years ago. I also owe a personal debt to my father, Henderson Mathews, who was ahead of his time in encouraging me to ignore the restrictions of sex-role stereotypes.

Finally, I thank the people who have been directly a part of this study. They have shared their lives and thoughts with me. They have given me many, many cups of coffee, towed my car out of ditches and muddy places, made me feel welcome, given me new perspectives on life, and helped me grow. Most of all, they have provided me the opportunity to carry out the kinds of activities and observations I felt necessary for understanding their lives.

Janet M. Fitchen

Preface 1995

This preface is written for those who are presently studying poverty in rural America as well as future students, for those who are just beginning their inquiries and those who are advanced in their studies. For all students of rural poverty this book is a model of scholarship. It is a classic and its author has been a pioneer in the study of poverty. Janet Fitchen has been a role model for all who wish to understand poverty in rural America and for those who strive to teach those who desire to alleviate it. Tragically, Fitchen became a victim of cancer in April, 1995, at the height of her career. As a leader in the field she will be greatly missed, but fortunately much of her knowledge has been recorded in her writing.

Poverty in Rural America was Fitchen's first major contribution to our understanding of poverty, and many more followed. In the following paragraphs I hope to explain why I believe this book and its author deserve our recognition and continued attention. Shortly before she was stricken with cancer, Fitchen was planning a revision of *Poverty in Rural America*, in which she intended to incorporate an update of life in "Chestnut Valley" and add a chapter drawing on the insights she had gained from her continued research. Even though she was unable to complete this writing, Waveland Press decided to reissue the book. That was a fortunate decision, because now many more students will be able to benefit from her writing and insights.

Poverty is the lack of access to resources needed to have an acceptable standard of living or quality of life. In our "cash-economy" society, money is necessary to purchase goods and services that we cannot make or provide for ourselves. The person or family that has insufficient money is, therefore, lacking in needed resources and may be said to be poor, or living in poverty. But money is not all of what is needed to have an acceptable quality of life, to avoid being poor or to stay out of poverty. Satisfying material well-being is a part of it, and money is a means to that requirement. Meeting our basic psychological needs also is part of it. To satisfy these needs we must have the opportunity to participate in social groups — family, school, work, neighborhood, church — in a manner that meets our expectations and those of people who are important to us. Therefore, poverty is a lack of sufficient money, but it is also not being accepted and acceptable to important people in our lives, and it is a lack of opportunities to create and sustain a sense of self-worth.

Fitchen understood poverty in the fullest sense of the term. She knew that not having enough money can undermine people's ability to reach their aspirations for themselves and for their families, as well as limit their capacity to meet the expectations of others. She also knew that failure to achieve these aspirations and expectations often undermines a person's self-esteem and sense of self-worth. Frustration and depression result, which become a barrier to future opportunities. Moreover, others begin to perceive the person as a "failure" and to lower their expectations of the person who is struggling. Thus, a cycle of lowered expectations begins, which can lead to a self-fulfilling prophecy of recurring failures and continuing poverty. These reciprocal relations between psychological, social, cultural, and economic forces are extremely important to understanding how people "fall into poverty" and may stay there a long time — sometimes for a lifetime or perhaps several generations.

Poverty in Rural America is a classic study of several families in one community and of how psychological, social, cultural and economic forces have precipitated and perpetuated the cycle of poverty in their lives. Fitchen began her fieldwork in Chestnut Valley in the 1960s, and over the next twenty years she came to know each and every member of the families. "They practically became members of my own family," she once told me. She regularly visited them in their homes, listening to their hopes and dreams, consoling them in their failures and frustrations as well as celebrating their successes, and most importantly, earnestly listening to their explanations of events in their lives. This anthropological mode of inquiry is an antidote to the single-factor explanations of poverty, and to out-of-context descriptions of poor people's behavior and values.

As Fitchen says in the introduction to her book, "The people of this study, for the most part, are still poor. But they are much more than that. They are people who love and hate, laugh and cry, work and play. They are grandparents and parents, spouses and in-laws, children and babies, friends, adversaries, lovers, co-workers and neighbors. They are also people whose lives are fraught with problems and who cling to a precarious balance between hope and despair. Their actions in this difficult set of circumstances are generally misunderstood and often judged harshly by the surrounding society. And these negative judgments only make the situation worse, for they become causative agents that keep people down, that make them fail, and create the likelihood that their children, too, will fail."

From her participant observation study of Chestnut Valley, Fitchen gained insights and understanding of poverty among rural people. Her search for understanding was not confined to Chestnut Valley, however. She studied many other communities and rural people. Thus, over a thirty-year career of intense dedication to understanding poverty, Fitchen achieved a better grasp of the nature of rural poverty than perhaps anyone in the entire nation.

As a result of her dedication and tireless efforts, Fitchen has had a significant impact on the social science community. First, her research focuses on local expressions of and responses to pressures and changes of the greater society. Studying change in rural communities allowed her to explore ways that national and even international changes affect people's lives, their families and their communities.

Second, Fitchen developed a method for weaving together institutions and individuals as sources of information, allowing her to tap the perspectives of both. For example, in her research on residential mobility among the rural poor, she interviewed both family members of clients of the social service agency and the service providers to gain information about patterns of movement among the poor and about how this mobility affects the individuals as well as the service provider organizations.

Third, Fitchen's approach featured a sustained working relationship of reciprocity with local communities. For her, research is a collaborative affair. She sought the assistance and guidance of informants on what was important to ask and who to ask. As her research proceeded she returned frequently to the people and communities she studied to share her findings and to ask them to verify or correct her conclusions. Even the product of her research became a reason for further collaboration, as Fitchen gave local public presentations and engaged local service providers in brainstorming sessions aimed at finding better ways to respond to the changes, issues and problems identified by her research.

The depth of Fitchen's involvement with impoverished people — the income poor, the disenfranchised, the discouraged, and the powerless — allowed her to gain insights into the causes and consequences of poverty that could not be obtained any other way. She uncovered psychological, social, cultural, and economic dimensions and elements of poverty that challenge the superficial generalizations that occur when facts are abstracted from their human and social context.

In reading *Poverty in Rural America* you have the opportunity to "see" one of the leaders of ethnographic research and social science at work. Fitchen's research is in the tradition of anthropologists who depend upon direct involvement to garner insights into the lives of individuals and families, and into the workings of communities. From that base of information and insight, Fitchen was able to serve as an effective contributor to the academic literature that addresses poverty, as well as to serve as a policy advocate for the poor. She also made a path from her research to the classroom and from there to the offices of local, state, and federal agencies, helping everyone to gain a better understanding of rural people and communities whose quality of life is limited by their lack of access to essential resources.

The Spanish poet Antonio Machado wrote the phrase "*se hace camino al andar,*" which may be loosely translated as "we make our path by walking." These words might have been written to describe Fitchen's contribution to understanding poverty. By the way she walked through her career of studying the poverty of rural people and places, she made a path to follow for all those dedicated to the study of poverty. *Poverty in Rural America* is an appropriate place to begin our journey along the path made by Janet Fitchen.

Gene F. Summers
University of Wisconsin-Madison

Part 1

Introduction

1
A Day with Mary Crane[1]

About twenty miles north of town, out beyond the suburbs, a narrow side road branches off the highway. It follows along the base of the hill, then winds along the valley and crosses a stream. Flanking the roadside every so often are a worn-down farmhouse, a modest old house trailer, a converted-school-bus home, a half-finished house, and a tar-papered shack. A generation or two ago, there were farms along this road. But now the old fields are completely overgrown, shoulder high in goldenrod and blackberries, with a scattering of young pine trees and small groves of poplars. Only an occasional barn remains standing, sagging and empty. On the slopes behind these abandoned fields, trees and underbrush crowd inside the low stone walls that once enclosed grazing pastures.

Where the road again crosses the stream, a weathered church casts its protective shadow over the cemetery. Further along, the old schoolhouse stands, although it has long since been converted to a home. This was once the lively hamlet of Chestnut Valley, where church socials and school picnics drew a good crowd of families from the surrounding farms. Fifty years ago, there were two stores here, where people stopped in for daily provisions and daily gossip. There was a creamery and a blacksmith, too. But today Chestnut Valley is merely a collection of homes. People who live here now must drive more than fifteen miles to town to work, to shop, to attend school, to join a club, to see a doctor, or to seek help. And today, almost everyone who lives here is poor. The place is what some people call a rural slum, and it has a bad reputation in the surrounding county.

As the road curves on beyond Chestnut Valley, it rises steeply. There is a cluster of four homes huddled with their backs to the wooded hillside, their fronts close to the road. The first is a patched-up two-story house, its kitchen end sagging off to the side. Next is a small tar-paper-covered house; then a small old trailer perched atop cement block pillars. At the end of the cluster stands a larger, but older, trailer with an unpainted plywood entryway attached to the front. In the spaces around the houses, several old automobiles are parked. Partially hidden under the new snow are a car chassis, several

3

engines, fenders and other parts, and a tripod for hoisting out car engines. An engineless panel truck bulges to overflowing with tan plastic bags of trash, awaiting a spring trip to the dump. Firewood and assorted building and roof-ing materials protrude from snowy piles. Parked in front of one house are three snowmobiles, the cover missing from one, and an old garden tractor with a homemade snowplow attached to the front. Leaning against each home is a large kerosene drum. An abandoned, doorless refrigerator is stuffed with cartons of old clothing. A long laundry line behind the blue trailer flaps with the frozen pants and overalls of yesterday's washing. Along the road edge are some of the currently licensed cars and trucks, mostly quite old and obviously much used. The mailboxes beside the road are propped up on old oil drums, or hung from leaning wooden posts; none has a name or number on it to identify the people who live there.

The two-story house is the home of Mary and Bill Crane. It is an old house — it was already old and in poor condition when Bill lived there as a young child. Those were hard times; his father was not often home, and even-tually he just drifted away. His mother did all she could to keep food on the table and a roof over their heads. Bill remembers eating mostly potatoes, which they grew out back on the hill. Years later, after his mother died, Bill came back to live in the family house, bringing his wife and two small children with him.

Now, in 1971, Bill and Mary have four children and, as Bill says, "They're growing up like weeds in a potato patch." Peter is ten already, and Sandra is right behind him at nine. Ann is almost seven, and Tim, the baby of the fam-ily, just turned six last week. During the seven years the Cranes have lived here, the house has been fixed up a lot, with a strengthened foundation and new asbestos shingles on two sides. Just last summer, Bill spent his vacation, with the help of his kid brother, converting the attic space above the kitchen into a bedroom and joining it onto the upstairs of the main part of the house.

Bill, now in his mid-forties, is handy that way. He's always been good at construction work and good at fixing cars, too. But, as his wife, Mary, says, "His only problem is that he can never get one project finished up before he's working on another one." It has been five years since he began the plumbing project.

Mary, just thirty-five, grew up over on the east side of the hill. Her mother still lives there in the old farmhouse. One sister is at home, where she is rais-ing her baby. The other sister lives in a trailer in the back yard. Her step-brothers both live nearby. Mary's parents were originally tenant farmers, but the landowner sold his property to the state during the Depression. Mary's father managed to buy the house and a little plot of land around it. That took place during the last year he was sober and healthy, thirty years ago. Since then, Mamma has worked the night shift as a hospital janitor to keep the family going. Mamma's "new husband," Shorty, used to work in construction off and on, and now he's on a disability pension.

Mary's family and Bill's have known each other for years. In fact, Mary's grandfather, when he was alive, used to tell stories about when he and Bill's dad worked together digging potatoes and pitching hay over on the Smith farm. And Bill's oldest sister was married to a cousin of Mary's.

But Bill and Mary hardly knew each other as children. Bill was already sixteen and had quit school when Mary entered first grade in the valley schoolhouse. Mary went on to the consolidated high school, where she was a good student and hoped to be the first member of her family to graduate. In her sophomore year, Mary got a part-time job as a store clerk. Then, when a full-time opening came, she quit school, as money was pretty scarce in the family at the time.

A few years later, Mary began going with Bill. She used to ride home from work with him every night. Mary kept her job until she got pregnant and she and Bill got married. It was a difficult delivery for Mary, and the doctor was worried that there might be problems. The baby—they named her Melinda—was small at birth, and never gained much weight before she died, just short of three months old. That year, Bill worked in a factory in the city, but he hated it, so he quit and went to work for the county on the highway crew. For the last two years, he has been working for the state highway department.

Their married life has had its ups and downs. Drinking has been a problem, especially for Bill, but sometimes for Mary also. Several times Bill has gone off on a drunk for days at a time. Twice, after bad fights, Mary has packed up the kids and left home. But during the last couple of years, things have gone a bit better for them. Mary guesses that maybe by now, after all these years, she is so used to Bill's tirades that they no longer shake her up so much. Or maybe she is just too tired to do anything about the situation. Anyhow, what *could* she do, she wonders. Besides, their six months apart convinced her that, despite his faults, she really loves Bill—and she needs him. The children need Bill too, she thinks. They seem easier to handle now that the family is back together again.

Still, life is not easy. There has never been enough money to keep up with each day's needs—let alone to pay off the back bills. There are even some bills left from before Bill took his present job, when he was unemployed for most of two years. And it never seems possible to get ahead a bit. So many things have to be put off "until we have enough money"—like fixing up the house. Now that the kitchen attic will soon make bedroom space for the boys, they will have a living room again, and Mary hopes they can convert part of the space into closets, or perhaps build a front entry room for all the boots and snowsuits. It always seems as if there isn't any place in the house to sit down, as if every bit of space is taken up by furniture, clothing, toys, junk – and kids. And after all these years, there is still no running water in the bathroom. Mary wonders if there will ever be time when they will have enough money to be able to fix up the house the way they'd like.

Recently, Mary has been thinking that it would ease the money problems if she went back to work. This year, all the kids are finally in school. But so far, there hasn't even been enough free time for her to go look for a job, let alone actually go to work. It seems to Mary that it is all she can do just to cope with each day's living and family care. There is always something extra coming up that has to be taken care of. The house is almost always a mess; she is usually days behind in the laundry. But, Lord knows, she's sure no one could say she's a lazy person. Once she thought about taking on a night job at the hospital where one of her friends worked or working night shift in a factory, but Bill told her in no uncertain terms that she wasn't going to be taking any night jobs. As for daytime jobs, that would mean arranging for someone to watch the children after school, since Mary feels they are not safe at home alone. They are too much for her mother to handle though, so she'd have to pay someone. And what would she do about all the times a child stayed home from school? So, for this year at least, Mary has decided to give up the idea of getting a job. Maybe next year.

It is already February, only halfway through winter, and it has been a cold winter so far. The kerosene tank is almost empty for the fourth time. Christmas already seems long ago – although the payments on the new TV set will continue for months. There has been a fresh snowfall during the night, and drifts enshroud the cars and the still, dark houses along the road.

*   *   *

Mary Crane gets up quickly when the alarm clock goes off at 5:15. She immediately goes downstairs in her bare feet. She tiptoes past the living room couch where the two boys sleep and goes into the kitchen. She lets the dogs out the back door—it is still pitch black out there—and plugs up the crack with rags. She turns up the regulator on the heater and puts in more kerosene from the can. Going back upstairs, Mary tiptoes past the denim curtain that separates off the girls' room, where they share a bed. She gropes in her dark bedroom for her clothes, trying not to bump into the bed where Bill is still asleep. She dresses in the bathroom, throwing her nightgown onto the pile of clothing that covers the two old TV sets (a secondhand color set that had never worked right and a tiny portable they still hope to fix—Bill had traded some car parts for it). Today's clothes are the same as yesterday's: her husband's old pants and shirt and a navy blue sweater from the rummage sale. She had picked this sweater because it was big and long, covering the protruding bulges where her waistline used to be, before her last pregnancy. Mary leaves the toilet-flushing for later, since she forgot to carry up the bucket of water, and goes back down to the kitchen.

With the ceiling light bulb glaring bright, Mary rubs her eyes. She draws a pot of water from the faucet on the floor next to the pump, lights the stove, and puts the water on to heat. She also lights the oven, propping its door open to help heat the cold, cement-floored kitchen. She clears away the clean dishes and pots from the table, where they had been left to drain the night before, stacking them neatly in the wooden-crate shelves beneath the window. She fixes a cup of instant coffee and sits down with a cigarette, trying to arrange her thoughts after yet another bad night. Still yawning, she puts two eggs and the last scraps of bacon in the pan to fry, and goes upstairs to wake her husband.

Mary is reluctant to wake Bill. He is sleeping so quietly, so peacefully, compared to his violent temper of the night before. When he's sound asleep like this, his face seems still to have a young-boy look about it, despite the long scar from the motorcycle accident and the grey of his hair. That head must be aching now from all the beer last night. As Mary looks at him, she reminds herself of the decision she had reached before finally dropping off to sleep. This time she would pretend nothing had happened and hope the whole thing would blow over. After all, Bill had been going through a rough time recently, and his temper was so quick these days, he just couldn't seem to control it. But he has been cutting down on the booze. Maybe if she bends over backwards to be loving to him, and to ignore his yelling, things will smooth out again. Besides, for all his faults Bill has been a better husband and father than most of the other men around. At least he doesn't beat her up all the time like Betty's husband does. And he really loves the kids, even if sometimes it doesn't exactly look that way. So Mary taps Bill gently on the shoulder. "C'mon, honey, breakfast's ready."

Bill dresses quietly and comes down. He eats only part of the breakfast Mary serves him, saying, "Save the rest for Tim, he needs it more'n I do." Mary makes some toast in the new toaster Bill gave her for her birthday and, while he eats it, she makes and packs his lunch: two jelly sandwiches and a piece of leftover cake. "It's real cold out today," she says. "If I can get to town, I'll bring you some hot soup at noon. Will you still be working that section of Route 420?" Bill mumbles, "Yeah, I told you we'd be there all week. But your car probably won't start. And there ain't much gas in it. If you do go out, take an extra spare tire along—none of them tires on it are good for much." Bill gets up from the table, puts on his storm suit, pats Mary on the fanny, and sets out.

Mary fixes another cup of coffee, turns on the radio, and sits a few minutes. She massages her stiff neck and runs her fingers through her short brown hair. At 6:45 she wakes the children. Tim skips into the kitchen and eats the eggs and bacon his father left. "Your appetite's really picking up now with them vitamin pills," his mother beams. (Mary has always worried about Tim's being so small. He has hardly grown at all in the last year. Maybe it was just worms, but she sometimes wonders if he, too, has a problem with sugar diabetes.) Peter, always a good eater, fixes himself a big bowl of cold cereal and perches on the stack of tires to gulp it down. Amid yells of "Hey, you got my sock!" and "Mommy, where's my sweater?" all four children finish dressing and put on boots and assorted hand-me-down jackets. As they are about to leave, Mary notices that Ann's nose is still runny. "I think you'd better stay home today, honey. Your cold isn't getting any better." Ann whines that she wants to go to school anyway. At the same time, Tim starts fussing and whining, saying he doesn't feel good, asking if he can stay home. Mary decides that both of the younger ones will stay home today. She calls out her usual last-minute instructions to the departing older children: "You behave yourselves in school today. Don't cause no trouble." The two older children run out of the door as the bus pulls up at 7:15. The sun is almost fully up, but the morning is a cold one.

Already feeling tired, Mary sits down at the three-legged card table to work on a jigsaw puzzle she started the day before. The children turn on the TV and run around the house, then settle down to play with their toy cars. Soon Mary goes into the kitchen to draw water to heat in big galvanized tubs on the kitchen stove. She shoves the breakfast dishes to the far side of the table and pulls the wringer washer out of the corner. (Bill found this washer at the town dump, and it works a lot better than their old one, which now stands in the other corner, with a plywood board on top as a makeshift counter.) Mary goes through the bedrooms and bathroom collecting dirty clothes, throwing them to the foot of the stairs, and then kicking them into the kitchen, where she sorts them by color into four loads. "All that from just two days," she sighs. She puts the first load in, pours in a tub of hot water, sets the machine in action, and goes back to the living room to find a cigarette. She sits down to watch TV−part of a quiz show and her favorite soap opera−then reads through a daily prayer. After this interlude, she wrings out the first batch of clothes, setting them in a pile on the table for rinsing later on, and dumps in a second load.

At ten o'clock, Mary remembers she was supposed to telephone the pediatrician's office to see if the test results have come back. Throwing on an extra sweater, she goes out the front door and walks down the hill. She hurries past the tar-paper house with the barking dog. Bill recently had a fight with Gus. Just two days ago, the sheriff was called to the house on a complaint against Gus. Now, as Mary goes by, she keeps her eyes on the road, just in case Gus's wife is watching her from the front window. Mary would have liked to make the phone call from the Sloan's trailer, but no one would be home there at this time. So she goes on to Newton's. Barb Newton comes to the door in her bathrobe, looking half asleep. "Yeah, sure you can use it, Mary," she responds, "everyone else does." The trailer seems very hot inside, and smells of kerosene and urine. The baby, prancing around in diapers and an undershirt, gives Mary's legs a big hug. Mary places the call quickly. "No," she tells the nurse, "none of the other kids is having diarrhea. But Peter said he had more rectal bleeding yesterday." Assured that the doctor will send in a prescription, Mary hangs up, reminding herself to stop at the drugstore when she goes to town later. She thanks Barb for the use of the phone. Explaining that she must hurry home because of the kids, she departs.

As Mary opens the kitchen door, the children fall suddenly silent. Mary surveys the scene quickly, and shouts, "Tim, get off that ladder this minute before you fall and break your neck. You know what your father said. Stay away from that attic until it's finished. If I catch you up there one more time, you'll really get your ass whipped−and by your father, too." The children skip into the living room and begin jumping on the couch. "And keep off that couch, too," Mary warns, as she starts to put the second batch of washed laundry through the wringer.

Midway through the next batch of laundry, Ann and Tim rush into the kitchen. "I'm hungry, I'm hungry!" "Can we have a doughnut?" Mary's response is almost automatic. "No, you certainly can *not* have a doughnut. Wait 'til lunchtime." "But we want doughnuts *now*," they plead. "Well, you just can't have them now." Tim angrily punches his mother in the thigh. She swats his bottom; he screams louder, "I want a doughnut!" Mary covers her ears. "Oh, all right, go ahead and have your damn doughnut. But that's the only one you get, and you'd both better shut up and be good the rest of the day." The children quickly gobble up their doughnuts and run back to play.

Mary pours herself a cup of lukewarm coffee and lights a cigarette. It's almost time to go to town, so she heats a can of soup and pours it into a thermos. She makes sure the children are bundled up and grabs an old jacket of Bill's. As they leave, Mary pretends to lock the door, even though the lock is broken again—"Just so those thieving neighbors will think it's locked." She rolls a spare tire over from the side of the house and heaves it into the trunk of the car. They all hop in, she hooks the door shut with wire, and coasts the car down the hill until it starts.

Along the main highway, Mary stops to get two dollars' worth of gas and some cigarettes. When she reaches town, she stops at the children's elementary school to complain to the principal. She is angry because they have assigned Sandra to a special education class when, Mary believes, it's really the fault of the teacher that Sandra never learned to read when she should have. But Mary admits that, deep down inside, she is worried about Sandra. Could it be that the spinal meningitis had damaged the child's brain? Will she always be slow, like her cousin Cindy?

Mary drives across town and finds the spot where her husband's highway crew is taking its lunch break. "Hi, honey. Here's some soup." Bill takes the thermos and hands her his paycheck, after endorsing it while leaning on the car. "Did you get that wall paneling yet?" he asks. "Of course not. How could I? What would I use for money?" "Oh yeah. Well, now you can go get it. I'll maybe put the stuff up on the weekend. Then we can get the boys moved into that attic room. Maybe we'll have the living room to ourselves sometimes." Bill continues, "And I want you to get that gasket for the Plymouth and the registration forms from the motor vehicle bureau. I've got to get the Plymouth fixed and registered quick, 'cause I know my truck won't pass inspection—and the sticker ran out last Monday."

Mary heads for the bank, to cash the paycheck (slightly over $110 for the week). She goes to the drugstore and then to the supermarket. She fights off the children's requests for candy and bubblegum balls, and decides she probably can't afford to get the laundry soap this week. She looks up and down the meat counter, settling on five pounds of hamburger (on special this week). She remembers to buy a cake mix and a can of chocolate frosting: next Tuesday will be Ann's birthday. In all, the groceries come to $43.59.

As she pushes the grocery cart to the car, Mary is wrapped in thought. Should she maybe try to get on food stamps again? Two years ago, when her teenage sister Sue was living with them, Mary found that food stamps were a real help. She was able to buy more of the family's favorite foods then, and lots of whole milk. That was the year they bought two whole cases of canned peaches when they were on sale. But the family was declared ineligible for food stamps when Susan moved out again. Now, according to Mary's sister-in-law, there are new income guidelines and maybe the family would be eligible again. But is seems like a lot of trouble to go and get certified all over again.

Mary's thoughts ramble on to other money problems. How hard it is to make ends meet these days! Of course, it would help if they could get on Medicaid: the doctor bills are mounting and Peter is supposed to have more tests soon. And Ann's teeth are so badly rotted that it will take a lot of dentistry to fix them up. And there is still the back bill from the hospital for her own broken arm—the collection agency is after them for that one. But Bill refuses to let her apply for Medicaid. Ever since two summers ago when he got his new job, he has managed to make ends meet—sort of—on his own. He doesn't want to go back to the welfare department again, and he insists that Medicaid is the same as welfare. Mary reasons that it's mainly Bill's pride that makes him this way. He likes to think he can manage things himself. And maybe he could—if there weren't all those unexpected things to pay for all the time. Also, he got in a real argument with their caseworker at social services because she thought she could tell him how to spend his money—what to buy and what not to buy. Mary shudders as she remembers that day. She was really afraid Bill would haul off and hit the caseworker.

"Oh, well," Mary sighs aloud. In another month or two winter will be over, and instead of buying kerosene, maybe then she can squeeze out some money toward those medical bills. As for the water pipes up to the bathroom—well, that will have to wait some more.

Mary makes her next stop at the bakery sales outlet to buy day-old bread and doughnuts. Then, with the children happily eating bananas in the back seat, she drives to the lumber company. There she buys four wall panels—at half price because they are slightly damaged—and ties them onto the roof of the car. Next stop is a car parts dealer, to order the gasket. On the way home, she stops at the courthouse to pick up the forms to register the Plymouth. (She will fill them out for Bill, since he can't read too well.)

Just as they return home, Mary's mother pulls up in the driveway. She is driving the "Fordrolet," a vehicle Shorty put together from his old Chevy that was in a wreck and some Ford body parts that Bill gave him. "Well," Mamma calls out, "I didn't think this old heap was going to make it over the hill today. Clutch is shot to hell. Cripe, it's cold! You got any coffee?" "Sure, Mamma. C'mon in," Mary replies. "Soon's I unload the groceries, I'll make us a pot of coffee."

Susan climbs out of the back seat of Mamma's car. Although she and Mary are half-sisters and widely separated in age, they think of themselves simply as older and younger sisters. Sue bundles blankets around the baby and dashes into the house. Ann and Tim are delighted to see their little cousin.

Both children help unwrap the baby and take turns holding her in their laps and cooing at her. "Look, Aunt Sue! The baby can almost sit up now! Last week she couldn't do that at all."

Mary fixes a pot of coffee and the three women sit at the kitchen table talking. "Did your watch 'As the World Turns'?" asks Sue. "I think he's going to come back to her, I just have that feeling." "Hey, did you hear about Ralphie and them guys getting caught last weekend? And it was all 'cause of that damn dog." "Oh, by the way, don't forget you got to get your license for your dogs. I took care of Prince's license yesterday." "Say, Ellen was over to the house again last night. I just wish she'd make up her mind about that man. Personally, I think she ought to leave him for good." "Oh, have either of you seen Dottie recently? I heard one of her kids has been real sick—the doctors aren't sure what's wrong with him."

Meanwhile, Ann and Tim are playing on the floor with Donna, showing her their toys and trying to make her laugh. Mary watches the baby smile—and sadly remembers the baby she lost so long ago. Susan looks around the kitchen at the piles of laundry waiting to be washed or rinsed or hung up and sighs, "Damn! Looks like I can't use your washer today, huh, Mary? I threw the baby's laundry in the car just in case I could do it over here. Oh well, maybe Shorty will take me to the laundromat tonight." Mamma quickly puts down that idea. "My foot he will! It's Friday night, and he'll be wanting to be out with his buddies." "So," whines Susan, "what does he expect me to do, walk to the laundromat?" Mamma explodes, "Okay, Miss Smarts! Why didn't you think about that before you went and got yourself pregnant?"

Mary gulps down the rest of her coffee and gets up from the table. There's been so much quarreling and ugliness between Sue and Mamma and Shorty for so many years. Back when Sue got kicked out of school, Mary and Bill had taken Sue in because she needed a home away from her parents. Mary hoped she'd be able to help Sue straighten out. At first, Sue had really been helpful with the children, especially when Mary was laid up in the spring. But gradually she started drifting off. Then, when the baby was nearly due, Mamma and Shorty had taken Sue home again. Things were generally better now, but it upsets Mary to hear the old familiar digging, criticizing, and tearing down.

Now Ann and Tim start pulling and tugging on Mary's arm, complaining loudly of hunger. Mary, glad of the excuse to walk away from her mother and sister, goes over to the stove to heat up a can of soup. Mamma and Sue get up to leave. Mamma bundles up the baby, who has just fallen asleep in the corner of the living room. As they go out the door, Mary remembers to ask her mother to watch the children after school tomorrow, as she has an appointment for Ann at the dentist. "I was supposed to take her last week, but something came up and I couldn't make it."

At three-thirty, the school bus arrives. Peter and Sandra and four other children jump off, Pete yelling some taunt back to "Fatback" Newton, who is ambling down the road to his home. The children rush into the house, "Mommy! Mommy! Guess what?" Mary sits 'down on the couch, the four children crowded around her, to hear about the triumphs and tragedies of the children's school day. She listens and responds with real concern. "Well, don't pay no attention to what those other kids say. You're just as good as they are!" Mary looks carefully at the school papers they have brought home. Peter's spelling and arithmetic papers, though torn and messy, have long columns of "C" marks in red pencil, and at the top the words "very good" or a smiling face. Sandra's papers have more red "Xs" and frowning faces, but Mary consoles, "Never mind, honey. I'm real proud of you anyway. I know you worked hard on this 'rithmetic. Maybe next time you'll get more right. And that's a real pretty picture you made. Will you let me put it up on the wall here?" Ann and Tim, too, press for attention, and proudly tell their older brother and sister about the latest accomplishments of their baby cousin, Donna. Then, one by one, the children drift off into the kitchen to make themselves sandwiches, spread thick with the jam from last summer's wild blackberries.

Mary puts away the rest of the groceries, hiding the special Valentine cupcakes under an overturned pail on the windowsill. Distracted by loud noises from the living room, she rushes in to check. "Cut that out right now! Oh, you kids! Now you've torn my new curtains." (Mary had found the curtains at a rummage sale, and was especially pleased with the color – a perfect match for the begonias and geraniums blooming on the windowsill.) "Get out of here! Get out of this room!" She shoos them out. The boys run out to play in the snow; the girls scramble up the stairs. Mary stays behind to mop up the living room. The warm afternoon sun has melted the snow on the roof, causing a little stream of water to run down the newly painted living room wall and make a puddle on the linoleum. She mumbles something about Bill never getting around to fixing the damn roof, then goes out front to fill up the kerosene can. Coming in, she slams the door shut and sits down on the couch, absentmindedly starting to fold the pile of yesterday's clean laundry. Mary glances at the opposite wall, at the poster of a snowy mountain peak lit up in sunrise. Across the bottom of the poster is printed the "Serenity Prayer." "God grant me the serenity . . . ."

It is now four-thirty and Bill still isn't home. Mary wonders, "Why would he be late today?" Half an hour later, he pulls into the yard. He is greeted enthusiastically by the younger children. "Daddy's home! Daddy's home!" Tim shouts and dances around the living room. Bill knows the question in Mary's mind, and quickly explains. "I just stopped at the diner for coffee. I swear, the only thing I drank was coffee." Mary protests, "But I've had your afternoon

coffee ready here for an hour." Bill has no answer, and Mary drops the subject, not wanting to stir things up again. Bill leaves the room to go lie down in
their bedrooom. Twice he yells at the children to be quiet.

Mary goes into the kitchen to fix supper. The rinsed clothes are still in the
washtub; the clothing that never got washed lies scattered on the floor. She
kicks it aside, making one big pile next to the car engine that has occupied a
corner for the last six months. She clears off a bit more space on the kitchen
table, leaving the jar of peanut butter, a can of evaporated milk, ketchup, and
bread in the center of the table. She stacks the unwashed breakfast dishes
and coffee cups at one end of the table. Mary cooks a sauce of fresh ham-
burger, canned tomatoes, and onions, and pours it over spaghetti. She dumps
the puppy, the school books, and her husband's outer clothes off the four
chairs and sets plates on the table. One call to the children is enough. They
rush in, devour their spaghetti and sauce, eagerly drink their milk, and then
divide a can of peaches among themselves. Mary notices that Ann winces
from the pain of chewing her food.

Soon after six, the children are back in the living room. Sandra is glued to a
Western on TV. Ann is bawling because Tim has taken her wind-up car.
Mary yells at Tim to give it back, and swats him on the seat of his pants. She
dries Ann's tears on her sweater sleeve, and soon the two children are racing
their cars across the room. Peter lies sprawled on the floor, reading a school
book in the midst of all the noise. Mary suddenly realizes her own hunger and
goes back to the kitchen, where she dishes out a small plate of spaghetti for
herself. She sets the remainder on the back of the stove to keep warm for Bill.
When the water finally gets hot, she washes the day's dishes and feeds the
accumulated scraps to the dogs.

Bill wakes up, and Mary takes him his supper in front of the TV, the
children having been sent out of the room. Bill yells out to the kitchen, "Pete,
did you get them plugs cleaned on the Plymouth?" Pete answers weakly, "No,
Dad, not yet," and slams his book shut. He covers his ears with his hands,
hoping to shut out what he knows will follow – the usual tirade. "How come a
kid who's so smart in school can't do a goddamn little thing on a car? You'd
better get your ass out there tomorrow and get them plugs done or else!" Bill's
shouting is cut off by a fit of coughing. When he recovers from the coughing,
he remains silent.

Mary rubs Bill's chest with Vicks and pulls a blanket around his shoulders.
Bill coughs again, then says, "I shouldn't of gone to work today. This cold in
my chest is aching me somethin' awful. And my back is acting up again with
this weather." Then he brightens. "Well, I guess we'll be gettin' some overtime this week. On top of last week's overtime, it looks like we'll have enough
money to make it through this month." Mary doesn't tell him of her earlier
thoughts about applying for food stamps or Medicaid. Besides, counting the

overtime pay, they'd probably be over the eligibility limit anyway, at least for this month.

Soon Bill goes back up to bed and falls asleep. Around eight-thirty, the girls hug Mary and go up to bed. Tim is already asleep on the couch, still fully dressed. Peter stays up to watch another show with his mother, who curls up on the other end of the couch and dozes off. At ten, Mary turns off the TV and tucks blankets around Tim and Pete. She carries a pail of water up from the kitchen tap to flush the toilet. Undressing quickly, she climbs into bed beside Bill. She is asleep almost immediately.

Down the road, dogs are barking. A neighbor is leaving for work on the night shift. A snowplow churns its way along the road, past the darkened cluster of houses, headed back down through Chestnut Valley and out to the main road.

2
A Case Study of
Rural Nonfarm Poverty

Poverty persists in isolated enclaves in many regions of rural America. It is a vexing and tenacious problem, but one that has generally been overlooked. When brought to public attention, the problem has usually been misdiagnosed, and the patients have been held responsible for what is really society's illness.

In seeking to understand the problem and its tenacity, we can derive important perspectives from the men, women, and children who actually make up the category labeled "the rural poor." The individuals who grapple every day with rural poverty can, in fact, contribute much insight into this longstanding societal problem. If we were to observe them closely and elicit their perceptions, their hopes, their joys, and their despairs, we would finally see that the problem of rural poverty is not the result of inadequate people or insufficient ambition, as is so often believed. We would find, instead, that the problem of rural poverty is rooted in the sweeping changes that have transformed many parts of rural America over the past century, especially the decline of agriculture and the demise of the small rural community. We would also find that rural poverty exists in a total societal context, including not only economic but also historical, social, cultural, and psychological aspects that are interconnected.

The human problems found in rural poverty-stricken areas are societal problems, societally generated, rather than individual problems caused by individual pathology. The problems of Mary Crane and her family, for example, can only be understood as part of a wider context of time and space and causality. And the remedies must address the underlying societal issues rather than merely providing Band-Aid treatment for symptoms as they affect individuals.

To provide this contextual perspective on the problem of rural poverty, anthropological research has been carried out in a rural depressed community, fictitiously named Chestnut Valley. But this book is not a "community study" in the traditional sociological sense. The community itself is not the subject of

17

analysis, but merely the context, the backdrop. The book is primarily a study of the patterns of action and thought of a number of interacting, proximate, rural poor families, set against the background of their changing community environment.

This book is about the people – individuals like Mary and Bill Crane, their families, neighbors, and friends – who live out their lives in depressed rural enclaves. It describes their world, how they perceive it, cope with it, interact with it. The book is an ethnographic case study, taking one small enclave of rural poverty in upstate New York as a microcosm, as a sample for intensive examination. It is hoped that in-depth analysis of a cluster of interacting families in a particular rural depressed enclave can shed light on similar enclaves elsewhere in northern Appalachia, and on the rural poverty that blights other areas in the United States as well.

The Fieldwork:
Foundations for Understanding Rural Poverty

The idea for this project evolved in 1967, when chance contacts with several rural families forced a realization that poverty was a significant prob-lem in some rural areas, but that it was not well understood. The decision to do research among rural poor people was prompted by a conviction that anthropology can make a contribution to understanding contemporary American society and its problems.

In 1969-70, the setting was selected and basic household data were col-lected. At that time, the Chestnut Valley area contained thirty-five dwellings – twenty-three located fairly close together in a small residential hamlet and twelve scattered along a few miles of back roads heading out into the surrounding hinterland.

Thirty households were surveyed for basic data in 1969-70. However, since the focus of the study was to be on intergenerational poverty and related problems, ten of these households were excluded from further study because they were socioeconomically somewhat outside the main category of interest. This left twenty low-income households for further research; and it is this sample that forms the 1969-70 baseline for all quantitative data. (Some of the excluded people have been part of this study in various other ways. For example, they have served as important sources of historical background, giv-ing personal accounts of life in the community in an earlier time.)

The total population on which this study is based, however, is much larger than the twenty low-income families living in Chestnut Valley in 1969-70. Over the years, more than twenty additional households were involved in the study. One cause of the expansion of the sample was population increase and mobility. Between 1969 and 1975, there was a net growth of thirteen dwellings, mostly in the countryside. And during those six years, a total of fifty-five families lived in Chestnut Valley at one time or another. As people moved into and out of the area, the cast of characters of the study continually changed. Some of the incoming families were included in the study, and some of those who left were followed up in their new surroundings. Some families came into the area and into the study briefly, then moved out again. The sample was also expanded in another way. The naturalistic, flexible nature of

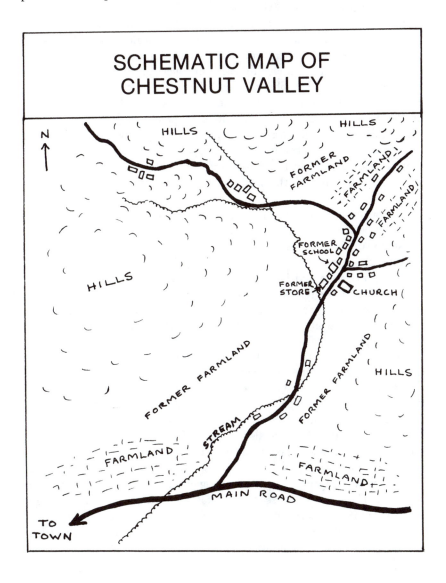

SCHEMATIC MAP OF CHESTNUT VALLEY

anthropological research put me in contact with many other rural poor people living elsewhere, some of them relatives and friends of the people of Chestnut Valley. These secondary contacts provided additional insights into ways that rural people cope with the problems of poverty.

In addition, the sample was intentionally expanded by brief periods of observation, community action work, questionnaires, and informal interviews conducted in other rural neighborhoods. These subsidiary studies were carried out to ensure that the main sample was neither unique nor idiosyncratic, to probe specific issues in a larger sample population, and to add breadth to balance the narrower in-depth observation of the main sample. Data from these one-time-only and short-term contacts added approximately thirty more families to the sample, although these thirty were much less central to the study. In all, the total number of households included in the study was just over seventy; forty were central to the research and, of these, twenty made up the baseline sample. (It is difficult to be precise about the number of households, since there was considerable fluctuation within and among households over the years. For example, a grown daughter and her children might at one time be part of her parents' household, and at another time live separately in a trailer in the yard, making it necessary to count hers as a separate household.)

The portrait presented in this book rests on a decade of observations, interactions, conversations, and co-participations. For about two years, field research was a continuous, everyday activity, though never the total live-in situation characteristic of traditional anthropological fieldwork. Interaction was fairly intensive and included many action projects as well as straight research. During the remainder of the decade, fieldwork was a varying, part-time activity: home visits tapered off to occasional, unplanned occurrences, returned to a more intensive level of daily interaction, then tapered off again, with only intermittent follow-up.

The fieldwork over ten years has yielded reams of notes recording observations, conversations, and impressions of each day's interactions. There are also more systematic forms of data, such as response sheets for topical questionnaires; newspaper clippings recording births, marriages, accidents, court cases, and deaths; tape-recorded recollections; and handwritten bits of life histories. Of course, there are also unrecorded forms of data: images, smells, sounds, and feelings stamped indelibly in the mind.

An important assumption of this research has been that the actors themselves are capable of providing significant insight into their own behavior.[1] There are, of course, some limitations to this position, and we cannot assume that actors are either conscious of, or willing to reveal directly, all their motives and thoughts. However, fantasy, rationalization, exaggeration, evasion, and wishful thinking are all valuable material. Statements affected by liquor and even purposeful lies are also significant and revealing data. The only problem in their use is that the observer must be able to distinguish them from "objective reality." For making this distinction, the long-term and in-depth nature of anthropological research is particularly helpful. The time span of association with informants, and the many different situations of observing and listening, reduced the risk of being naively taken in by conjured-up impressions the informants would like the social scientist to believe. Furthermore, as fieldwork progressed, there gradually developed a known context in which to place the verbal data, making it easier to separate fact from fancy, observation from hearsay, truth from gossip. As fieldwork proceeded, the remarks or actions of an individual informant became more understandable, even predictable, and could be interpreted in context, so that they became more reliable and useful as data.

Most of the observations that support this book took place in "naturalistic settings": conversing over a cup of coffee in a kitchen or living room; chatting on a doorstep or in a vegetable garden out back; while waiting in line for food stamps, or accompanying a woman to the welfare office or to a conference at school; while observing children in a school classroom or playing with them at home; while laughing together or wiping away tears. For the most part, these were spontaneous situations occurring in the normal course of daily life, daytimes and evenings, winter and summer, on Christmas Day or on any ordinary day.

Most home visits were unannounced drop-ins—spur-of-the-moment visits when I happened to be in the area. On all visits, even those that were prearranged, an element of unpredictability and surprise was always present. I never knew what to expect as I knocked on a door, nor what we might do or talk about that day. Even when I had a specific topic I intended to explore, it was often postponed because what was happening in the household at that time was much more pressing—and usually more interesting for research. Perhaps a woman had just been beaten up, and wanted to talk things out—or perhaps she preferred not to talk at all, or to talk about the weather. Often, a relative or neighbor had dropped in, and the intended interview session was postponed or interrupted by tacit agreement; on other occasions such a group setting turned into a fruitful session of people expressing their ideas for the future, their discontent with some aspects of the present. Sometimes a husband was unexpectedly at home, which either stifled conversation or greatly enhanced the usefulness of the visit. Perhaps a person was drunk or hung over, which could make conversation either impossible or very fruitful for research insights. Perhaps a new grandchild had been born, maybe a relative had just been thrown in jail; perhaps a man had just bought a new television set, or a child had been injured—these events always took center stage.

Happiness often needed sharing; worries and sadness often needed talking out; some situations called for action; some emergencies called for assistance in the form of transportation; and some events and moods had to be experienced alone, while others cried out for a listener. The unpredictability of people's lives became the unpredictability of fieldwork, its essence. The directions research took depended on whatever was going on at the place I happened to be at any given time. Although this necessary flexibility made the fieldwork less systematic, it also enhanced its value, as it afforded me the opportunity to catch the stream of life in its actual flow. I was compelled to notice the vividness, the urgency, and the sometimes exhausting pace of a life filled with unpredictable happenings and preoccupations. Additionally, unexpected situations provided insight and data that would hardly have been elicited through a more formal research method, capturing not only what people say they do, but what they actually do. No preplanned interviews could catch as well the unrehearsed episodes of daily life: the excitement when a young woman returns to her parents with her newborn baby; the tension of waiting to find out what the judge will decide; the diffuse strain that permeates a home when a fight is brewing; the obvious loss of self-esteem when a mother has injured one of her children in a heated test of wills; the reactions and interactions of people as the room where they are sitting suddenly catches fire; the anxieties over a sick child; the joy and pride of parents who have managed to get new Easter clothes for their children; the relish of men retelling the story of a close call with the police, a near-accident on a motorcycle, an outstanding car once owned. The naturalistic style of anthropological fieldwork is particularly suited to enabling the social scientist to "collect" such events as they happen, rather than trying to recapture them through questioning afterward.

The Analysis

Problems

Compiling these diverse observations into written description is a difficult task in itself, but it is only a part of the job, only one step removed from raw data. The important next step is to search for recurrent patterns or themes in the observed data; to extract generalizations from myriad recorded actions and behaviors. For example, family time-lines were constructed to summarize the significant events in the life histories of individual families; these time-lines were then compared for common denominators. Beyond the search for patterns or themes, there is the work of analytical interpretation; seeking out the structural, cultural, and psychological factors underlying the patterns of statements and actions. Through continued contact with many people from the original sample populations, I have been able to test hypotheses against new data, to reject or refine generalizations, and to ask some of the people for feedback on my descriptions and interpretations as they have been developed.

One difficulty throughout the analysis of data has been that it is not easy to generalize. Each family and each individual is in some sense different from all others. Low-income rural residents exhibit the same wide range of behavior that the people of any other socioeconomic stratum do. In any walk of life, some people are quiet and reserved, others are talkative and loud, even vulgar; at any economic level, some women are immaculate housekeepers and other women keep a sloppy house; in any social stratum, there are homes in which children receive open demonstration of affection and homes where little human warmth is exhibited. It is difficult, then, to generalize about the people, or behaviors, or "home life," or values of a socioeconomic stratum. Even more difficult—and potentially more misleading—is the attempt to compare two socioeconomic levels on the basis of such generalizations. Therefore, great caution must be exercised in seeking commonalities and relationships.

In the course of the decade of observation and analysis of rural poor families, some regularities and patterns have emerged, however. These patterns rest on several underlying factors. To begin with, there is a foundation of similarity arising out of ethnic uniformity ("old-stock Yankee"), and out of shared participation in the local version of contemporary American culture (including both the rural, northeastern version and the generalized national version as seen on TV). Superimposed on this base, the constraints of poverty and marginality faced by all of the families of this study appear to operate in fairly regular and predictable ways to yield fairly similar outcomes. Hence, there seem to be common patterns of behavior and action that arise out of the common situation of social and economic marginality.[2] Thus, although individuals and families do vary, and people are indeed very complex, it is possible to draw some generalizations concerning patterns among the rural poor without doing violence to the uniqueness of each individual.

Another difficulty in this particular kind of research with people is that, as informants have occasionally reminded me, there are a lot of things I do not know about the individuals and the neighborhoods under study. This is still true, despite the several years of interaction and observation. At times I have been disturbed that the more I knew, the more I was aware of how much I did *not* know. However, the complete details of every individual's personal life are not essential to the analysis of general social patterns, and are often quite irrelevant. We can attempt to develop an analysis that is valid and complete enough so that if a previously unknown fact were to come to light, it would fit into the analysis and the predictions already presented. Therefore, there is no need or justification for the social scientists to push, dig, and cajole for every detail of a person's life.

This reluctance to pursue people ruthlessly and relentlessly, to mine them for personal details, is part of a general ethical concern for the needs and rights of the people a social scientist studies. The research and writing of this book have been guided by the ethical principle that the informants on whom it is based should in no way be harmed by either the research process or the publication of the study. Furthermore, people should be made aware that they are, in fact, under study. As soon as my initial activities went beyond casual interaction to become a purposive research inquiry, I told them of my plans. No previous acquaintance took the opportunity I offered to sever the relationship at that time, and only a few appeared to become more guarded in their conversations. From that point on, all potential new informants were told at the outset that I was doing a study to see how low-income people in the rural area get along, the problems they face, the solutions they devise.

In publishing anthropological studies, privacy is usually protected by the use of pseudonyms for communities and for individuals. But this is not always a sufficient safeguard. At times, generalized analysis has to be substituted for colorfully descriptive factual reporting, to insure protection of identities. (For example, in the discussion of causes of marital problems in Chapter 7, no "biography of a marriage" could be included to illustrate the seven sources of stress that are described. Similarly, though fieldnotes chronicled the illnesses and injuries occurring in two families over the course of a year, the data could not be published in that raw and revealing form.) Occasionally, some particular details of a nonsignificant but identifying nature had to be omitted or altered. Thus, in the description of "Mary Crane" and her days's activities, some background facts have been blurred, some details have been altered, and some pieces have been borrowed from observations made in other households. This produces a blend, necessitated by the commitment to protect privacy. However, where details have been altered, the replacements spliced in have come from other observations made in similar situations, and thus they are consistent with, and likely to have occurred in, this case. Mary Crane's day is fact, not fiction, but it has been slightly altered for ethical considerations of informant privacy.

If the risks to the people studied are minimized, the investigator need not wait for a lifetime to pass before sharing the observations with the rest of the world. If research is to have any practical use in formulating more effective policy and programs, as the Chestnut Valley study is intended to have, its results must be communicated. Several informants have actually encouraged me not only to probe their situations, but to help bring a new understanding of it to the rest of the society. It is my sincere hope that their expectations in this regard may in some measure be fulfilled.

Limitations

The analysis presented in this book is based on a very small sample of people in one particular location. Because of this, it did not seem appropriate to pursue the collection of highly quantified data for testing hypotheses. For example, the reader will find that the role of alcoholic beverages is referred to at several points in this book, but no quantitative material is given. With the small size of the sample, it did not seem worthwhile or significant to attempt to collect precise data on frequency and quantity of alcohol consumption. Furthermore, such probing might have jeopardized rapport with people and posed some ethical problems as well.

To the extent that this study generates research questions that it does not sufficiently examine or answer, it should be seen as a plea for further research. Systematic research on much larger samples of populations in poverty would allow us to make reliable comparisons among different samples of people, would enhance our understanding of poverty in general, and would be useful for designing appropriate policy and programs. However, one caveat must be included here: research on "the poor" can be useless and misleading if we do not also have comparable research on "the nonpoor," and on society in general, to provide a context and a basis for generalizations. Too often social scientists – and the public – have made comparisons of "lower-class behavior" and "middle-class behavior" in which the former was researched but the latter merely assumed; in which "real behavior" of the poor is compared to "ideal behavior" of the middle class.[3] The paucity of empirical research concerning other segments of society has led to some unfortunate, misleading, and pernicious statements about "the poor." So, while hoping that this study might generate future research questions, I do not mean to suggest that research should concentrate only on poverty-stricken populations.

A further limitation of the analysis presented in this book is that it relies on data that did not derive equally from all informants. In anthropological fieldwork, as opposed to random-sample surveys, data are gathered from situations and informants where the investigator has best access. Approximately thirty hounholds were only briefly interviewed, and so were known only partially. Of the remaining forty households, some were visited much more often than others. Some homes afforded more up-close observation; some informants spoke more easily, candidly, perceptively. Close personal ties developed with some individuals and families, while relationships with other families remained more formal and distant. The most complete and in-depth data came from a half-dozen families who were intensively involved in the study for long periods of time. As a result, the analysis does not reflect all individuals or households equally, although I have tried to seek balance by using the insights from more closely observed informants as clues to what to probe with other people.

The main effect of this fieldwork bias will be noticed in the predominance of women and children – their words, their actions, and my interpretations of their situations. In fieldwork, I had greatest access to women, not only because of our shared sex roles, but also because of our shared interest in children. Additionally, during many of the hours I spent in homes, women and children outnumbered men. Some men were only briefly around and available for conversation; some husbands would find an excuse to leave the house soon after I arrived. Although I came to know most of the men, and knew some of them well enough to learn a lot about and from them, generally I knew the men in their capacity as husbands, fathers, brothers, or sons of the women I knew. Wherever possible, I tried to correct the feminine cast of the research, for a holistic case study of rural poverty must be done from the point of view of both men and women. Occasionally I bridged the obvious distance between male informant and female investigator by observing and listening in situations where men interacted with other men and boys, and quite often there were husband-and-wife conversations to join. But most one-to-one conversations with men were somewhat formal situations, perhaps because some of the men continued to believe that I was really a spy for the welfare department, or connected in some way with the schools. Despite the effort, the balance of observations, conversations, and activities—as reflected in field notes—was clearly on the side of women and children. Perhaps, however, this emphasis has merits of its own.

Chestnut Valley and Beyond

Even the qualitative, small-sample analysis presented in this book can be generalized beyond the immediate research population. There seem to be striking similarities with rural poverty in other localities, and to some extent also with situations of urban poverty. One can find these similarities in ethnographic studies of other American poverty situations.[4] Similarities have also become apparent through probing the experiences of social science researchers, applied social scientists, human service personnel, and others who have worked among poverty-stricken populations in many areas of the United States.[5]

It is hoped that the observations presented here may help readers to understand a variety of poverty situations elsewhere in America. However, it would require much careful study to assess the degree to which any of the conclusions based on research among white rural poor people in the northeastern United States are applicable to other rural poverty locations, let alone to urban poverty, or to poverty situations with different ethnic or racial variables. The question would be: to what extent do the generalizations derived from this case study in northern Appalachia hold up in the mountains of southern Appalachia, the delta of the Mississippi, the Indian reservations of the Great Plains, the Mexican-American barrios of the Southwest, or the ghettos of the eastern cities? Despite variations in location and details, an inheritance of economic poverty and social marginality is likely to produce many similar features, no matter where it occurs in our affluent late-twentieth-century society. But until much research is accomplished, caution must be taken in applying conclusions based on one population to other populations with different parameters.

In addition to a substantive understanding of poverty, the book should also have transferability in that it presents a model of inquiry. The holistic approach of anthropology is a multifaceted perspective that views a societal problem from the combined points of view of historical forces, economic situations, social structures, cultural values, and attitudinal factors. Additionally, the anthropological tradition stresses the need to see a situation from the point of view of the people who are in it. Thus, it directs the investigator to seek out and listen to people's own statements of their aspirations and experiences. This anthropological mode of inquiry is an antidote to single-factor explanations of poverty and to out-of-context descriptions of poor people's behavior and values.

Why This Book?

This study grew out of the concerns of the 1960s, when the American mainstream and the U.S. government discovered a fact that many Americans had known firsthand all along—that, sprinkled in the midst of affluence, there was also serious poverty.

Over the years since this study began, the public's interest and the government's commitment to overcoming poverty have gradually tapered off and faded away. Unfortunately, it cannot be said that poverty, too, has become a thing of the past. It hasn't.[6] And because it hasn't, there is still a need for studying and analyzing the problem, and for sharing the perceptions gained in that endeavor. That is the reason for this book.

The people of this study, for the most part, are still poor. But they are much more than that. They are people who love and hate, laugh and cry, work and play. They are grandparents and parents, spouses and in-laws, children and babies, friends, adversaries, lovers, co-workers and neighbors. They are also people whose lives are fraught with problems and who cling to a precarious balance between hope and despair. Their actions in this difficult set of circumstances are generally misunderstood and often judged harshly by the surrounding society. And these negative judgments only make the situation worse, for they become causative agents that keep people down, that make them fail, and create the likelihood that their children, too, will fail.

Better understanding, in itself, is therefore necessary and important as a first step to overcoming the problem of poverty in rural America. To furnish a new understanding is the main goal of this book, and it is an expressed desire of the people whose actions and words have contributed so much to the study.

If people would try to see what it's like from our point of view. . . .

This search for an understanding of poverty in rural America begins in Part 2 with an investigation into the historical forces that brought it about in the first place. In Part 3, separate chapters present ethnographic description and analysis of economic patterns, marriage and the family, patterns of childhood, relationships within the neighborhood, and relationships with the wider community. Part 4 integrates the different threads of the book by delineating the ongoing causes that perpetuate rural poverty, and by suggesting some remedies that could break the generation-to-generation cycle.

Part 2

Historical Background

History: The Trends of Time

Introduction

Over the course of the last hundred years an economic and social blight has slowly penetrated parts of the rural northeastern United States, insidiously attacking the small farming communities of upland plateau and hill regions. The blight began as an economic illness, causing agricultural decline; it later progressed to a social decay, causing the collapse of rural communities. The blight proceeded unrelentingly, with much the same inexorable sweep as was the case in the chestnut blight, which struck the same region and wiped out whole hillsides of stately and useful trees. And just as the succeeding growth was a paltry replacement for the chestnut trees, so the new institutional substitutes emanating from the growing urban centers were never able to compensate for the losses that had occurred in the rural upland areas.

A major long-range effect of this socioeconomic blight has been the tenacious problem of rural nonfarm poverty. Therefore, an understanding of historical forces must necessarily precede an analysis of the contemporary problem of economic poverty and social marginality in the rural areas. And so, we turn now to an examination of the intertwined forces of economic and social history as they were played out in this particular locality.[1]

1800 to 1870

Settlement, Development, Consolidation

Chestnut Valley lies in one of the later regions of New York State to be taken over by white settlers. But once development began, it proceeded quickly, compressing in a short period the same general phases that occurred more slowly in other upland areas of the Northeast.[2] In the first two decades of the nineteenth century, settlers came in rapidly, mostly from eastern areas of New York State and from New England, with some from Maryland and Virginia also. (Among these early settlers were the great-great grandparents of several of the older people now living in Chestnut Valley.) Farmers of greater financial means bought up large tracts of land in the flatter valley areas, while those of more limited means and those who came somewhat later were restricted in their choice of location to hillsides and hilltops. The new residents quickly cleared the forests, developed farms, made roads, built houses and stores, and established schools and churches. In-migration continued until about 1855, when the population reached a peak that was not regained until more than a century afterwards.

Chestnut Valley, like many other hamlets in the region, grew and developed as a small crossroads center, a nucleus of services and people at the center of a surrounding hinterland farming area. In the 1860s, the hamlet was able to satisfy most of the service needs of its residents. The maps of 1867 show that there were twenty-four buildings, about equally divided between residences and business establishments. There was one general merchandise store that also housed the post office; there was also a shoe store, a cabinet shop and harnessmaker's shop, and a doctor's office. Nearby were a tannery and a shoemaker, and there was a mill down along the stream. There were two Protestant churches, each with a parsonage, and one cemetery. (Within a decade, however, one church disappeared from the maps.) In addition to the one-room schoolhouse in the hamlet, two other schools were located in the nearby countryside. The area served by the hamlet was roughly three to four miles in diameter, and included about forty farms.

As in many other upland areas of the Northeast, the period around the Civil War marked the apex of early development and growth of the small agriculture-based community. After that, the number of people and dwellings, the amount of land under cultivation, the number of businesses, and the possibility for prosperity all began to diminish.

1870 to 1920

Gradual Decline of Agriculture

In the closing decades of the nineteenth century, agriculture in Chestnut Valley began its slow decline, just as it did elsewhere in the northeastern upland plateau. The decline was related to national trends: rapid expansion of more productive agriculture in the Midwest; development of modern systems of long distance transportation (first the canals, then the railroads); and the beginning of mass marketing of farm products in an increasingly urbanizing nation.

The severity and extent of agricultural decline in any particular locality was largely determined by local soil and topographical factors. Except for a few valley floors, the predominant soils in the Chestnut Valley area are categorized as marginal or submarginal for agriculture. They are mostly low in nutrients and highly acidic, and contain stones and clay. These soil characteristics, combined with the common slope of 8 to 15 percent, make the land vulnerable to erosion.[3] The rough terrain imposes further limitations on farming: problems of water supply for hilltop farms; lack of running streams large enough for mills; long distances over rough roads to the mills and markets of larger villages.

In the earlier period of subsistence farming on newly cleared land, these limitations of geography, topography, and soil were not particularly restrictive. But in the late nineteenth century, they became significant impediments to further development of local agriculture. It was not so much that the natural resources had changed (although soil fertility had probably been depleted through several decades of use), but that the conditions of agriculture had changed.[4] New technology, agronomic patterns, transportation facilities, and marketing techniques were revolutionizing agriculture in other regions of the United States and in the better suited parts of the Northeast, but they simply could not be utilized here. These poor-soil hill farms were not responsive to the new technology and were difficult to adapt to efficient large-scale production for emerging mass marketing systems. Furthermore, the small-scale family farm, providing the family's sustenance and a limited cash income, was hardly able to generate the cash savings needed for investment in modern agriculture. Those farmers who could afford to do so got out of "back hill farming" in this region, either migrating to modern farms in the Midwest or moving into urban occupations in nearby, growing cities. Those who stayed, and the new farm operators who came in to buy up the hill farms when others left, could only adapt by attempting to find small niches where there was a demand for products that they could successfully raise despite the problems of soil, topography, and limited capital.

The predominant pattern in the first decades of the twentieth century was the small-scale family farm, which supplied products for home consumption, either by people (milk, eggs, beef, lamb, poultry, vegetables, and apples) or by animals (barley, oats, and wheat). Surplus products—cream, milk, veal, grains, and later hay and potatoes—were sold or traded locally. Few, if any, products were produced solely for market. The poor-soil farms were not heavily capitalized, substituting family labor or cheap farmhand labor for cash investment, and bringing a very low cash return to the farmer.

One elderly woman recalled her father's farm as it was about 1910.

> My father had grown up on that farm, and later he bought it from his father. There were 260 acres, but a big part of it was woodland and too steep to farm. My father was a good farmer. He had a hired man to help him, and my brothers, of course. My mother and sister and I didn't do much farm work, as we had work of our own to do.

My father kept around twenty cows and usually three horses and a flock of sheep. He raised a variety of crops, mostly grains to feed the animals, and food for the family. He raised pretty much the same crops his father had. He had grown up knowing which crops did best and on which part of the farm. He didn't have to learn that in books.

The cows were for our own use, and also we took milk to sell to the creamery in the Valley. We raised the bull calves born on the farm to sell as veal calves. What few things we needed to buy, my father often got by trading calves or lambs or potatoes directly. Of course we never had to buy such things as coal for heating, as we cut all our own wood. My father would figure on just two trips a year to the County Seat to buy what he needed, to have our teeth fixed and our eyes fitted. Mostly we provided for ourselves and our needs.

People worked so hard in those days. They didn't expect to get much money. All they wanted was to live comfortably, to provide their family with food and clothes and a place to live. We had a good life, but it was a struggle.

Acquisition of a farm or a farm operation was relatively open during this period.[5] Some men were able to take over or inherit working farms from their families, but purchase was even more common. A young man could save his earnings from working as a farm laborer (either year-round or seasonal), then expand this capital with loans from relatives to enable him to purchase a farm. Renting and share-farming were also common paths toward the goal of eventual farm ownership. These systems allowed a young man to accumulate savings and at the same time to build up a herd and machinery, so that when he eventually purchased his own farm, he would already have the livestock and equipment.

From 1870 to 1920, there was a steady increase in the rate of turnover of ownership of farms, and an increasing mobility of farm families within the area. In a fairly clear pattern, both tenants and owners moved through a succession of slightly better farms, with first-time owners taking over the least desirable locations as the former owners or renters moved up to slightly more productive farms, or left farming entirely. Toward the end of this period, the buyers included families coming back from the Midwest to obtain inexpensive hill farms.

In addition to turnover and mobility, this period also shows an absolute decrease in the number of people engaged in farming. Some farm families moved off the land to nearby towns and cities, and some farm-raised young adults left for urban areas, in both cases giving up agriculture. Thus, the "excess population" was being drained off the land. Most farmland was not actually abandoned, however, since land belonging to absentee owners could be rented or share-farmed by nearby farmers, who frequently used the barns and even the abandoned houses for storage of crops. But some of the most marginal farmland was let go, growing up in brush and scrub trees, evidenced by the fact that whitetail deer began to reappear in the area around 1915, after having been totally absent during the period of most extensive farming.[6]

Despite these trends, farming was still the community's economic base at the end of the period, as it had been at the beginning. But the base was not healthy. On the whole, the farms were generally of low productivity, and few farmers were making a significant cash profit after meeting family consumption needs. Older farmers whose sons had moved away to the cities wanted only to get through their last years on the farm. Younger men who remained on the farms could expand their acreage through inexpensive rental of extra land, but they could not expect to prosper. The limited cash profits meant limited cash available for capital investment, and many farmers were locked into such financially uneconomical patterns as the continued practice of producing their own feed grains. The lack of cash combined with factors of poor soil quality, difficult topography, and difficult farm-to-market transport—and all these factors prevented farmers from wholeheartedly entering into market production.[7] Subsistence farms continued in this area long after much of U.S. agriculture was becoming fully market-oriented.

Changes in the Nature of the Rural Community

Reflecting a period of change in agricultural patterns, the social community, too, was undergoing change and redefinition. Mobility and turnover on the farms affected the social composition of the hamlet nucleus that formed the center of the farming hinterland. The population of the hamlet remained steady and then increased slightly, as some farm families moved inward from their difficult farms, more than counterbalancing those hamlet residents who had left for the larger towns and cities.

During this period (1870–1920), the overall trend in the region was that people of the open-country farms and of the smaller hamlets began to turn outward to more distant communities for more of their service needs. Flourishing villages, towns, and small cities offered a diversity of business services, government functions, and educational facilities, and these became ever more accessible with modern transportation. The service-dependence on outside communities increased steadily, especially in the early decades of the twentieth century.

Concomitantly, the commercial activities of the hamlets contracted and their volume of trade diminished. By 1920, Chestnut Valley showed a markedly reduced array of services. Two grocery stores remained, two blacksmiths, one wagon shop, a shoe shop, and a creamery where farmers brought their whole milk to be separated, leaving the cream to be made into butter. (Soon afterward, the creamery was closed, replaced by a skimming station, so that farmers had to cart the separated cream to a cheese factory elsewhere.)

Nevertheless, as social communities, the smaller hamlets and their associated open-country hinterlands continued to show considerable strength and cohesion. Throughout the period, the Chestnut Valley community provided social life and social identification for its residents. As late as 1920, a variety of formal institutions united the hamlet with its hinterland in a yearly round of activities. The church had an active ladies aid society, with a membership of about thirty-five, including farm wives as well as residents of the hamlet. The farm bureau and home bureau met regularly in the community. The hamlet school was also the center of a variety of practical and festive events for the public. In 1920, few local people looked to the growing urban centers for their entertainment or social life. This hamlet-and-hinterland social unit was a viable, active community.

1920 to 1950

Severe Agricultural Decline

The dominant theme during the decades after World War I was gradual abandonment of farming as the economic base of the community and as a livelihood and way of life for its families. Many of the poorer farms were unwanted: the older people who had struggled through their last years on these farms died; and their sons and daughters turned to more promising futures elsewhere. Since farms in these marginal agricultural areas were not competitive in market production, they had benefited only minimally from the wartime and postwar agricultural boom conditions.

The price of good local farmland fell to under ten dollars an acre, while some went down to two dollars an acre, putting it within reach of people of quite limited means. From distant cities came industrial workers, some of them first-generation immigrants from eastern and southern Europe, ready to invest their meager savings from years in American mines and factories, hoping to fulfill their dream of becoming independent farmers on their own land. Some purchased their land sight unseen from real-estate catalogues, or viewed under a blanket of snow. "When the snow melted, we found that it was mostly stones and clay." Other new buyers came because they had been squeezed out of competitive midwestern agriculture, attracted by the low prices and the possibility of smaller scale farming. Some families moved to Chestnut Valley after having given up marginal subsistence farming in a similar but even less promising region elsewhere in the Northeast. Typical of this latter pattern is a family with six children who came in the late 1930s from a farm in the western part of the state, "a small farm with ramshackle outbuildings and a bedraggled house with sooty walls and plank floors."

Turnover on farms became particularly rapid in the late 1920s, with both population exodus and in-migration superimposed on the older pattern of mobility of local families from farm to farm within the area.[8] Within six to ten years, a piece of land might be bought, worked, given up as hopeless, and, if possible, sold again. Each new owner struggled until he, too, sank into debt. For those who stayed in agriculture, farming remained, as it had earlier been, a labor-intensive operation in which subsistence production was predominant, capital investment limited, and cheap family labor crucial. It was hardly a profitable venture and many local farmers were poor and in debt.

At the same time, many of those who gave up their low-production farms entered the urban labor market at a disadvantage, often in debt and unable to offer marketable labor skills. They continued to live in their rural farmhouses because it was less costly to do so, but even when they stopped farming, their financial situation did not improve substantially. Thus, by the 1930s, there were impoverished rural nonfarm people as well as impoverished farm people.[9]

In hindsight, it was a period of sharp agricultural decline, but at the time the severity and irrevocability of that decline were disguised or not fully perceived. Land continued to be worked, and people continued to live on farms and to eat from them. But it became progressively harder to break even in farming, and the degree of modernization fell farther and farther behind that of other regions. More farmers met their cash needs by taking on outside work. Highway work, carpentry, or factory work became the sole source of cash for some families. The farm operation was scaled down to production solely for home consumption, and the wives took over much of what remained to be done on the farm: caring for the chickens, a cow or two, a couple of pigs, and a vegetable garden.

A few farmers attempted to adapt to the changing situation by intensifying their farming, specializing in certain cash crops. Often this was a short-term solution, feasible only as long as market prices remained high, competition was weak, and the farmer had good direct access to a retail market. It was during this period that timothy hay, well suited to local soil conditions, became a major cash crop as well as a farm-consumed item. Hay was sold to commercial middlemen who traveled from farm to farm with equipment to bale it to be shipped off, particularly to New York City. (The main consumers were the horses of the city's equestrian police force.) But the farmer received a diminishing share of the market price, and the demand decreased dramatically. Similarly, potatoes became a major cash crop for a time, and were shipped out to the coal mining areas of Pennsylvania. But this market, too, succumbed to competition from other growing areas and to the fall of market prices. Eggs, also, were briefly a market-production item for some farmers.

The Depression years, with prices bottoming out between 1930 and 1934, and remaining low almost until 1940, caused a decrease in the already meager market production in the area, since the proceeds from crop and dairy sales hardly met the cost of production. According to the local newspaper correspondent in 1932, the Chestnut Valley potato crop was going to buyers for twenty-five cents a bushel, down from $2.25 or more in 1920. An elderly farmer remembers when it wasn't even worth hauling the potatoes to town. As a consequence, some families discontinued production for the market. But retrenchment to subsistence farming is, in a sense, a disguised form of agricultural decline, a retreat back to an earlier kind of farming, even less profitable, even less modern.

During the 1920s, some of the least productive land was removed from agricultural use, simply abandoned to the natural succession of weeds, brush, and scrub trees. But there was still a great deal of low-productivity land being farmed. Long before the Depression made it worse, agricultural economists were concerned with the problem of unprofitable agriculture on unproductive land in some regions of New York State. The experts argued that the physical characteristics of the local soil, particularly its poor water-handling capacity, would make this hilly terrain only minimally responsive to such new techniques as the application of agricultural lime and chemical fertilizers. Furthermore, the region still lacked the improved roads and marketing facilities deemed essential to the survival of local agriculture. Hence, the best solution appeared to be to remove the unsuitable land from agricultural use entirely.[10] In the 1930s, the state government carried out an extensive program of buying poor agricultural land (largely submarginal, but including some marginal land) in the central and southwestern part of the state.

Around Chestnut Valley, the state bought a considerable amount of poor quality hilly farmland that was lying unused. Many of these parcels had been sold at least once in the previous decade, or had only recently been acquired by inheritance or foreclosure. Neither absentee owners nor neighboring farmers found it worthwhile to work the old fields, and few young men were willing to take over the marginal operations still extant. In most cases the land was sold eagerly to the state for as little as two dollars an acre. Where houses remained, unoccupied by owner or tenant, they were dismantled by the owner and reconstructed in a nearby hamlet, or added to a farmhouse somewhere else, or even pulled down or burned down by the state. By 1935, much of the submarginal land had been removed from agriculture and had begun its transition to state forest areas, which it remains today.

Individual Histories of Withdrawal from Farming

The gradual and cumulative abandonment of farming is illustrated over and over in the life histories of individual farm families. Elderly residents of Chestnut Valley recall in detail the difficulty of eking out a living from a marginal farm, and the slow process by which they adjusted to changing times. Their nostalgia for the past is definitely tempered by their vivid memories of the all-consuming struggle. As one man put it, "People may talk of the good old times. Well, they weren't. They were the bad old times." The struggle and the gradual withdrawal is revealed in three individual life histories, briefly summarized below.

In the first passage below, an elderly woman who grew up on a farm in Chestnut Valley describes the gradual transition out of farming during her own generation. It is a typical example, starting with a farm that had been settled by her forebears before 1840, and ending with the sale to the state, almost a century later.

After I finished my schooling, I taught three years in the schools of the neighborhood. Then I married and left home. My husband worked as a hired man on a farm ten miles away from my family's farm. He worked there two and a half years, but didn't earn much. Then he worked on a farm nearer where he grew up. But still, he wasn't getting much pay for such hard work. He didn't seem to be getting anywhere. Then he quit and worked a while for the railroad. Finally, he went into carpentry. He started as an apprentice and he worked hard, learned quickly, and advanced well as a carpenter. In 1920 we moved from his family's place to this village.

My older brother lived home until he was thirty years old. He farmed with our father, just like our father had farmed with his father. Then my brother got married and began farming up the road on the next farm. But he just couldn't make it on his own. Father helped him out sometimes with some of the harvesting. Then there were some hailstorms and other things that hurt his crops. So he just gave up farming. He and his wife and their first two children moved to the city {thirty miles away} where he got a job in a factory. {The brother's piece of land was then bought by a neighboring farmer just starting out.}

Then my father died, at the relatively young age of sixty. He just killed himself working on that farm. He had worked so hard on that land, that stone heap! He only just eked out a living. We often said that if he'd picked some other region to settle in, life might have been a little easier for all of us. After he died, my mother wanted to move off the farm. She gave it to my brother. She asked him to take the farm off her hands. He used to come up from the city where he was living to plant some crops on the farm. He'd haul the crops all the way back with him to sell in the city. That was pretty hard. Then he let others use the place for farming. Then, when the state offered to buy the land, my brother sold it to them.

In the passage below, a brief summary of the contours of one man's life illustrates a fairly typical history of farming through the first half of the twentieth century. Mr. Clark, born before the turn of the century, is like many other marginal farmers who struggled most of a lifetime before giving up the farm. Clark recalls his father vividly.

"My dad was a potato farmer, a very good farmer . . . terrific ambition. I remember how he'd almost lather like a horse under the harness; and he wouldn't walk, he'd almost trot."

Clark's father was a tenant farmer, moving through a succession of farms in the township, generally operations small in size and potential. He kept a few cows, once as many as twenty-five, as well as pigs, chickens, sheep, and always several workhorses. Clark's father rented additional land nearby, and concentrated on potatoes (up to twenty acres) and hay. He also raised a variety of grains for the farm animals. At times they had a regular hired man, who was given the use of a tenant house as well as produce and firewood. Normally, extra help would be hired only for the short duration of potato digging.

Clark grew up as his father's main help. He says, "I was practically raised in a potato field." He took the milk to the creamery and the potatoes to town, and did all kinds of field work. His schooling was intermittent, with several moves to different school systems, as his father moved from one farm to another, but he loved to read. He also took part-time jobs occasionally. Later, Clark went to work independently as a hired man on a series of different farms in the area. Then, with his new bride from the farm next to where he had grown up, Clark went into farming on his own.

He rented a series of farms, generally small-scale, diversified operations on relatively poor soil and hilly, remote parts of the community. He could put almost no cash into his operations, except for the small rent. But his labor investment was high. He raised a variety of crops (buckwheat, oats and barley mixture, and hay) for his small herd of livestock (eight cows, three horses), and sold buckwheat for what cash he needed. He felt he could not make a go of it if he bought feed, as some farmers did, particularly as he was not selling milk as a source of cash income.

The Depression years found Clark, his wife, and children living in a house that had been abandoned, getting along with the help of relatives and what little work he could find with other farmers. They moved again to a nearby farm, and then in the mid-1930's, they rented a farm on the same hill where Clark had spent several boyhood years. After a few years of renting, the owner offered to sell him the nearly 200-acre farm for $800, including the house, barn, and grain crib. As Clark says, "Even in those days, that was really a bargain." So he scraped up the money from relatives and became a farm owner. He built up a herd and sold extra calves. He kept about a half-dozen cows, and took milk to the separator in the hamlet, where the cream was sold and the skim milk brought home for calves and pigs. He also raised veal calves to sell.

Clark was typical of those farmers with meager cash resources who could not make the necessary investment to get themselves into the more profitable market of selling whole milk to dairies. "The barn wasn't in any shape to sell milk. It had to pass inspection—and this old rattletrap barn wouldn't. It would have cost a lot of money to fix it up to be allowed to sell milk."

Clark and his wife and children continued a diversified operation, in which they raised virtually all their food and the feed grains for the animals. Although he sometimes planted potatoes on a fairly extensive scale, generally Clark's farming was marginal in size as well as profits. He never invested in mechanized farming, continuing with horses all along. Eventually, though, Clark made enough money from selling small amounts of cream, eggs, and potatoes to pay back his loans.

By the end of World War II, some of the children had left home, moving into nonfarm employment, and Clark's ability to work was severely curtailed by poor health. No longer able to keep the farm going, the Clarks sold the place. With the proceeds, they bought and renovated a rundown house in the hamlet, and Clark's wife took a job in the city.

A few farmers, however, were able to keep above the break-even point. They took advantage of falling land prices to acquire additional land for expanding their operations. Good land could be purchased for about ten dollars an acre in 1920, while poorer land went for between two and five dollars an acre, and marginal farmland could be rented for a dollar an acre. Thus, with a little increased investment derived from profitable farming, from hiring out, or from loans from relatives, some farmers could manage to enlarge and modernize their operations during a period when others were just barely hanging on or giving up. The career path of a farmer who not only hung on to his farm throughout his lifetime, but managed to make it a paying operation, reveals the combination of factors that contributed to success.

Mr. Block was nearly an adult when he came to Chestnut Valley in the early 1900s. His parents had moved here from western New York to take over a farm that had belonged to a cousin. After working for his father and then working a few years as a hired hand, and with the help of loans from family, relatives, and neighbors, plus a bank mortgage, Block was able to buy one hundred acres adjoining his father's farm. He later took on a share-farm operation (half the proceeds to the owner, half to Block, with free use of land and buildings). Subsequently, he purchased this farm, thus owning outright two adjacent farms. He kept a small herd of cows (about eight) for the sale of milk and calves, and grew buckwheat and oats-barley mixture for market. Block's well-kept account books show that he always knew which parts of his operation were profitable, which ones not. And so he shifted from one emphasis to another, specializing now in potatoes, now in eggs. When possible, he expanded his holdings until he was managing quite a large farm, by local standards. However, his enterprise had a greater proportion of crops to dairying than was the case among other similarly prosperous farmers in the area. He purchased modern harvesting machinery as it became available, often paying off the cost and turning a profit by hiring out himself and his tractor and machinery to do harvesting for other non-mechanized farmers. He continued to expand his operation until he reached middle age. Then he began to scale down the operation and took on some part-time carpentry work. As old age approached, and with no children desiring to take over the farm, Block further reduced his crop acreage, eliminated his livestock, and began to live off his savings.

These individual life histories and the aggregate history of the community reveal that the period from 1920 to 1950 was one of severe agricultural decline to the point where farming no longer formed the economic base of the community. Operating farmers comprised a small and decreasing fraction of the community, and they were mostly elderly.

Demise of an Active Social Community

In terms of population size, the total hamlet-and-hinterland community of Chestnut Valley decreased steadily from 1920 to 1950, as more people moved away from farms, and fewer families came in to replace them. However, the population loss was mostly from the open country. The hamlet center ac- tually increased, particularly in the 1930s, as there was a move inward from hinterland to hamlet. Older people who had finally given up the family farm moved to the hamlet to be near relatives and friends. Additionally, some young sons and daughters of farm families took urban jobs but did not want to live either on the isolated farms or in the city, choosing instead the in- termediate situation of the rural hamlets. Inexpensive housing was available in the hamlet where, for example, closed-down shops could be converted into homes.

In the early 1920s, the community thrived as a social entity. Community identity and pride were strong. The hamlet-and-hinterland community had a cohesion built out of history, supported by the framework of formal institu- tions, and reinforced by ties of kinship and marriage, and by informal social relationships. The variety and vitality of Chestnut Valley's activities and organizations during the peak years of the early and middle 1920s is revealed in the weekly "correspondence" sent from Chestnut Valley to the newspa- pers of nearby county seats. In addition to the many items reporting births, marriages, illnesses, and deaths, the notes about people's visiting and travel- ing and the vicissitudes of their farming, the weekly news columns also pre- sent a picture of a high level of organized activity.

- The church was active, with regular services and a resident minister. A Sunday school was organized, and church socials were well at- tended. (By 1930, several churches from the township were con- solidated into a larger parish organization, sharing an itinerant minister, but there seems to have been no diminution of local church activity until many years later.)
- The ladies aid society of the church was active, meeting monthly in Chestnut Valley homes, with close to forty members.

- A cemetery association supervised the church's cemetery.
- A meeting hall above a store was used for "political meetings and entertainment."
- A Red Cross auxiliary was formed.
- A county library truck delivered books to the school and to the home of a widow who served as community librarian.
- The home bureau (sponsored by Cooperative Extension) held monthly all-day meetings in women's homes, with demonstrations by the extension agents, and occasional tureen suppers. Membership and attendance varied from twenty to fifty women. The home bureau held periodic wiener roasts at the church, to which the community was invited.
- The farm bureau and home bureau combined with the ladies aid society to sponsor activities and education programs in the church. Open to the whole community, the morning programs and evening movies drew a crowd of sixty to eighty.
- There was a men's baseball team that played the teams of other villages of the township.

Perhaps the most important institution in the community was the local school. The elementary school in "the village" (as the hamlet center of the community was proudly called) had twenty or more "scholars" attending, with a succession of young women teachers from the community. There was also one school in the nearby countryside, the second having closed its doors in 1920 because there were "only four legal-age children" in its district.

The school was active in sponsoring public community activities. There were "Christmas exercises," to which the public was invited, and yearly Halloween socials – which were held in the church parlor but sponsored by the school, with proceeds going toward the purchase of books for the school. There were public meetings to decide on questions of district consolidation (at that time, consolidation meant one one-room school combining with another), and public meetings to elect school trustees. These meetings were usually followed by "a social event," with ice cream served. Many families attended, "including children."

Older students had to leave the community if they were to attend high school. They boarded out in rather distant communities, but their progress and their visits home were followed in the local news column, their graduations attended by a host of proud relatives from Chestnut Valley.

There were various public health services available in the community. Occasional free clinics were held at the church, sponsored by the Red Cross or the tuberculosis association of the county. Two doctors from nearby villages and three nurses served at the clinics. A diptheria immunization clinic was held at the school for all children of the community.

Such was the tenor and level of organized activity in the hamlet-and-hinterland community of Chestnut Valley at its high point in the mid-1920s. However, by the late 1920s and all through the 1930's, the character of the community was changing and the rate of change accelerating. As a social community, Chestnut Valley suffered severe and protracted decline. The combined forces of urbanization and modern auto transportation made it increasingly difficult to hold people's allegiance to their home locality, difficult to ensure active participation at the local community level. Some people were attending and joining more active social groups and voluntary associations in the larger villages or in the urban area. But it was not only the pull of the rising urban community that undermined the rural community's social life. Basic transformations resulting from agricultural decline were also having a marked effect. With less farming, there were fewer informal get-togethers of farm families. And as informal interaction decreased, participation in formal organizations declined too. With little money available among hard-pressed farm families, there was little to spend on community social events. In addition, demographic factors took their toll. The high turnover of population and the presence of "outsiders" apparently made it difficult to maintain the sense of community: old-timers felt that the newcomers didn't integrate well. And an aging population structure, resulting from exodus of many young adults, further diminished participation in and decreased the vitality of community organizations. The social community was being eroded.

The World War II era seemed to place a temporary restraint on the pace of social change, and even gave some new purpose and life to old organizations. In 1945, the community retained the school, the church, one general store, and some organized groups. But Chestnut Valley had been able to hold on to only a small portion of its former cohesiveness and social animation, and only a small fraction of its young people. And thus, the community as a social entity had no strength to fight off the sweeping forces of the early 1950s.

1950 to 1970

The Final Collapse

The visual landscape of the rural Chestnut Valley area has changed remarkably. In 1920, according to photographs and local memories, clusters of farm buildings nestled around farmhouses, and big expanses of fields were neatly outlined by hedgerows of trees and interspersed with well-defined woodlots. Only a few areas were receding toward their wild state at that time. Now, in the 1970s, there is a motley mosaic of overgrown fields, brushy pastures, and young forests, with only a very few fields still under cultivation. A few forlorn hay barns stand alone in weedy fields, and along the back roads isolated cellar-holes are surrounded by a green carpet of myrtle, overgrown lilac bushes, and a line of front-yard maple trees.

Only four farms are still in operation, primarily dairy farms, renting additional land elsewhere for hay and corn. (This compares to about forty farms, each quite small in acreage, a century before.) More fields revert to weeds each year, and a diminishing acreage is tilled. Farming now plays a minor role upon the landscape.

Some of the old roads are totally abandoned, and some have no residences along them. By 1960, only eighteen of the original forty-two open-country homesteads that dotted the Chestnut Valley landscape in 1870 still had a usable house standing on the site. But countering this trend, some new dwellings have come in during this most recent period. Beginning in the mid-1950s, a few houses sprouted up along the back roads; by 1970, there were several new clusters of homes, mostly substandard houses and old trailers.

The townships surrounding Chestnut Valley all experienced significant population growth in the 1950s, mainly as a result of encroaching suburbanization. Several townships regained their 1850 population peak by 1960, and have continued growing since then. The Chestnut Valley area has also experienced population growth, but to a lesser degree and from different sources. The people who have come to Chestnut Valley recently are not middle-income suburbanites, but generally low-income rural families with insecure employment histories and low-skill jobs. Often they have come from other declining rural areas, and frequently they have come because of prior ties of kinship and friendship to the people of Chestnut Valley. Like the in-migrating farmers of a generation before, these people have come to this particular spot because the land and housing are relatively inexpensive and the cost of living is low. The major recent growth in Chestnut Valley's population, however, has been due to natural increase of the resident population, as the adult sons and daughters of the poverty-stricken families settle their trailers on their relatives' property and raise their families.

In the hamlet of Chestnut Valley, as well as in the countryside, the visual landscape has changed. The aging houses have suffered wear and tear outpacing upkeep and repair. While only a very few houses have been built in the last half-century, the former schoolhouse, shops, and stores have been converted into residences, or have burned or been torn down.

It is the "social landscape" of the community that has changed most, however—almost beyond recognition. Since 1950, the effective social community has almost vanished. Chestnut Valley, once a viable rural community, has become the victim of urban centripetal forces. It is now totally without formal social, educational, religious, or service institutions, and no longer possesses even a small grocery store. The one-room school was closed in the early 1950s, its pupils bused away to consolidated urban school districts; the church doors are only rarely opened by an itinerant minister; the last grocery store gave in to the competition of suburban shopping centers; and the former local farm and home groups and other social groups have died out or been merged into consolidated township-wide or county-wide organizations.

As the formal institutional structure of the rural community was dismantled, the informal social interaction was also affected. Without the base of ongoing formal institutions, such as the elementary school, even informal interaction became difficult to maintain. Informal social patterns were also undermined by the decline of farming, since the traditional social-agricultural interactions of working and celebrating had fallen into obsolescence. Additionally, informal social patterns crumbled as the population became increasingly burdened with old age or with the daily problems of poverty – or with both.

Today, Chestnut Valley is a vague concept in terms of geographic boundaries. It has no identity as a post office address, a named telephone exchange, a school district, or a local government. And it is no longer considered a socially meaningful entity. As one person said, "There is no longer a community here at all, just people." There is little to unite the scatterings of residents in the hamlet and along the roads of the hinterland. No longer is farming the common interest it once was, providing for daily and seasonal patterns of conversation and communal action. No longer is there an annual round of activities to give meaning and regularity to interaction. No longer are there public places and public activities for the entire community.

Many people spoke of their perception of these changes, their sense of loss.

> These days there's no community feeling. Nobody cares what each other does. It used to be very different. Families would get together. Especially in farming – borrowing machinery and helping each other with the haying. And we had sewing bees and hymn sings and card parties and dances in each others' homes. And neighbors all helped out in emergencies. If you got burned out, all the neighbors would bring you things, help you start over, even let you live with them. And at funerals, we'd all help the family prepare the house and the food. Nowadays, nobody cares. Neighbors don't help each other in emergencies. You have to go to the welfare or the Red Cross or something – and that just isn't the same.

In former times, the people of these rural areas were geographically isolated from the growing, modernizing urban centers. As modern transportation improved, they turned increasingly to the cities and towns for services, goods, jobs, and schooling, although their social needs could all be satisfied within their own local communities. But in the end, this local social community crumbled. Rural people were unable to prevent the eventual disintegration of the social fabric of their small community. The blight that afflicted Chestnut Valley had struck not only at its economic base, but had eaten out its social core as well.

4
History:
Differential Adaptation to Change

The salient point of this history is that two trends coincided and exacerbated each other: agricultural decline and social collapse. Within this historical context, we can see specific factors that brought about economic poverty and social marginality in the rural upland area.

Differential Economic Adaptation

Changes in the economic base of the rural area had different effects on people; some were better able to cope with and adjust to these changes than others.

Those who faced changing economic conditions from a position of strength were able to adapt successfully. From interviews, life histories, and family account records, it appears that the factors fostering successful adaptation included absence of debt, availability of some cash resources, access to relatives who could make loans, possession of a reasonably good farm in the family, access to farm machinery and starter herds from relatives, personal qualities such as practical knowledge and astuteness in making farm decisions, and, of course, luck. On the whole, those who came out on top were those who had the resources and the flexibility to risk innovation, to expand their farming operations, to specialize and modernize. These farmers were able to survive price drops and natural disasters—such as crop failure, barn fire, or disease in the milk herd—that might completely wipe out a marginal, debt-ridden farmer. For these more secure farmers, the main limitations forcing eventual withdrawal from farming were ill health, old age, or the lack of sons willing to take over the farm.

However, many farm people were left behind by the changes of the 1920s, 1930s, and 1940s—left behind and trapped in poverty. Partly this was a matter of insufficient farm management skill. Several people have indicated that hard work alone was simply not enough.

My brother, even though he was raised on a farm, couldn't run a farm on his own. He was smart enough, but it just wasn't his nature to run a farm. He could do the work all right, but he couldn't plan the farming, couldn't run it on his own.

My son was a hard worker, a good worker. But he couldn't make a go of it. He simply could not do the planning, make the decisions.

People were also left behind because the timing of their transition out of farming was unfavorable. Those who opted out earlier were able to sell their land for a good price and enter the urban economy solidly. Those who clung longer to their rural subsistence-scale operations (because they wanted to or because they had no alternative) found that by the 1930s their farms had become almost worthless, as no one wanted to buy run-down farms. But their skills were almost useless in the urban economy, and there was already a glut of would-be workers looking for scarce jobs. So the marginal operators remained stuck on their farms. They exhausted any cash reserves they had, retrenched to subsistence farming, and went further into debt. Since the demand for agricultural labor had diminished sharply, men were no longer able to supplement farm income or save toward buying a better farm through the traditional pattern of working for other farmers. Unable to get out of debt, unable to get out of farming, and unable to get their money out of their farms, many families were locked into dead-end farming at subsistence levels or below.

Similarly, small-scale entrepreneurs lost money and time trying to readjust their doomed rural businesses to changing conditions of the local community and the national economy. They invested borrowed cash and extra years of family labor to keep a small local shop or store going, only to realize later that the local trade area could no longer support their enterprise. But by that time, it was hard to get a toehold in the business world of the urban center.

For many rural people at this time, the lack of capital, of education, and of experience in nonagricultural jobs made adaptation outside agriculture at least as hard as adaptation within it. Men who did enter the urban job market often remained trapped in low-level jobs due to their lack of appropriate skill and training, and were vulnerable to displacement by mechanization. Some farm laborers and part-time farm operators (both owners and renters) who could not make ends meet on the farm took manual jobs with local highway departments as a part-time supplementary source of income. Gradually road work became a full-time replacement occupation.

The general effect of this period of sweeping economic changes was that a significant proportion of rural people were unable to make a successful transition. People who were already slightly behind at the start fell farther behind. For some local families, poverty became a lifetime condition, rather than a temporary state along the path to success. Residents remember the hardships of the late 1930s.

> There was nothing to eat but potatoes – and only a few of them. Since our mother was sick, we fed the potatoes to her. Us kids got the water they were cooked in – our potato soup.

> I remember seeing my mother crying because Dad was gone and there wasn't any food in the house. I remember seeing Mom doing all the farm work, doing man's work, wearing an old pair of man's shoes. Some years Dad would settle and get a good job, carpentry work or such, and we'd have a few decent meals and clothes.

The differential success of adaptations in the 1920s and 1930s has had long-range implications. Most of the residents of the Chestnut Valley area who adapted successfully during that period have lived out a life of relative security; their children and grandchildren are integrated successfully into the work force of the urban center, full participants in the organized activities and material rewards of modern life. On the other hand, the children and grandchildren of the residents who found the earlier transition most difficult are today still attempting to cope with and adapt to a situation that demands more capital, skills, and risk-taking flexibility than they have available. Both then and now, the people with the fewest resources at hand (good farmland in the earlier period; or money, education, or sociopolitical position now) tend to have the fewest and least attractive options for adapting successfully to changing conditions. The limited economic adjustments of one generation have, in turn, placed limitations on the ability of the next generation to gain better access to resources from which new adaptations could be made; and so, poverty begets poverty.

Social Differentiation Without Exclusion

In social aspects also the sweeping changes affected people differently, and tended to produce social differentiation in the local population. But in the earlier period, this did not mean social separation and exclusion.

It is apparent that in the 1920s there was already some differentiation on the basis of prestige or status. From the lists of officers of the formal organizations of Chestnut Valley in that period, it is fairly clear that there were certain prominent families who more or less ran the community. The same names appear over and over in the records as officeholders in local township government, the church, the school, and community groups. But newspaper accounts and elderly people's recollections also reveal that attendance and participation in the organized social life of the community was fairly broadly based, rather than limited to the prominent families.

Similarly, in private visiting patterns, although there were social distinctions, apparently no class of excluded people existed. This conclusion is supported by the recollections of older residents, and also by the weekly newspaper columns, which kept track of who attended a Saturday night social at which farm, who visited whom for Sunday dinner, who was indisposed, and so forth. In these informal aspects, also, there was a circle of top families, interrelated by marriage and associated in frequent visiting.

The factors conferring high standing appear to have been: length of residence in the community, reputation of one's relatives, and prestige of previous generations of the family. But prestige criteria did not significantly restrict participation in the social life of the community. People who were not from "an old family" or "a respected family" might never attain the highest prestige, but they could be, and were, active participants in the social life of the community. Even the economic differences that existed between families did not divide people socially into clearly defined, noninteracting groups.[1] Times were hard, and most people had to struggle. Furthermore, in the self-sufficient family farming that characterized the area for so long, economic differences were not readily apparent in material consumption or style of living.

There were, indeed, a few families who were clearly poorer than most and whose reputation was generally not good. Their economic position is revealed in their patterns of working for many years as low-paid hired men, or in renting a succession of very small, marginal farms, never advancing far up the agricultural ladder. They were also found in such lower-level agriculturerelated jobs as blacksmith's assistant. It is clear from recollections of people from both ends of the spectrum that some of these families were often the subject of whispered derision and jokes, or the objects of pity. They were people who, according to the higher-prestige people, "didn't amount to much." Sometimes their intelligence was called into question; often their drinking was cited. But it is also apparent that even these people were very definitely a part of the community, both in thought and in action. Those of lower status participated along with everyone else in the regular activities of work and play, education and worship.

Frequent social interaction among people, no matter what their prestige or wealth, was partly the result of the cooperative nature of traditional agricultural work patterns. Farmers "changed works" at peak harvest periods, with a group of several farm operators helping each other out. Both temporary and regular hired men would accompany their employers and participate fully in both the work and the celebration of its completion. It was a time of con viviality, as well as a time of fever-pitch work. If a hired man did his share of the work at such times, his presence was valued and his reputation as a worker might help to outweigh any other aspects of his standing in the community. In fact, a series of newspaper items shows that the whole community several times intervened with the legal authorities to have a young man let off lightly for a driving-while-intoxicated charge. Behind this action was the fact that the individual had earned a reputation as a good farmhand, and he was needed. It didn't matter that his family was not among the higher-prestige group.

The cohesion among families in the community, regardless of economic and status differences, was also a result of mutual interdependence. Neighborly help in time of crisis, companionship among isolated farm families, and lending of farm and household implements were real necessities. Fortunes and reputations were secondary to neighborliness; being a helping neighbor was a quality that bridged other distinctions. Because family emergencies and disasters small and large were common facts of life, no one could be so secure as to be above participating in this kind of reciprocity, no matter how he might feel privately about a particular neighbor.

The pattern of hired farm labor also contributed to keeping open the social interaction among families of different status, preventing a stratum of poor and rejected people from settling out on the bottom. A young man with no farm to inherit, or an older man who had been unable to do well in farming on his own, could find a secure position working for some other farmer. Often he and his family lived in a tenant house or in a part of the main farmhouse. His worth was judged by his hard work and faithfulness. His limited financial circumstances or the reputation of his parents hardly diminished his and his family's participation in the Saturday socials and harvest celebrations of the neighborhood.

The most significant differences between the poorer families and the rest of the community show up in the education and school experiences of children. Already in the 1930s, in the one-room school, some children were ridiculed. A graduate of the elementary school, looking back some forty years, recalls one family with three pupils in the school.

> It was whispered that their mother had left them, that their father was a drunkard, that the children were left to fend for themselves.

Some of the children from "unfortunate homes" are reported to have been shy and awkward in school, others pugnacious. Some attended only sporadically and were older and bigger than their classmates. Other children were somewhat separated not only by their poverty but also because of the recency of their arrival in Chestnut Valley, where it seemed everyone was related to everyone else, except for the newcomer families. A written recollection of a child's first days at the Chestnut Valley schoolhouse is vivid.

> The kids, strangers, made me feel funny. They stared and giggled, all friends and neighbors and cousins, except me. I was self-conscious in my once-bright polka-dot dress. It was faded now and didn't meet their approval. I slunk down, trying to hide under its sort of grey big collar. I was conscious of a hole in my sock. I felt like crying. No cousins, no friends, no nothing. I wanted to go home.

Beyond grammar school education, the better-off families sent their daughters and most of their sons to high school. The earlier pattern had been to send the "scholar" to board with relatives in a large town where he or she could attend high school. Later, bus transportation made it possible for students to attend high school on a daily basis while living at home, and more children were able at least to begin high school. Many of the children from the more successful rural families completed high school and some undertook further education. Eventually, they became schoolteachers, skilled workers and craftsmen, urban businessmen, or modern farmers—most of them secure socially as well as economically.

On the other hand, the families of limited economic resources and lower reputation rarely sent their daughters to high school; their sons, in some cases, never finish grammar school. The subsequent career profiles of these children tend to be confined to unskilled labor, interrupted work patterns and, in most cases, poverty.

It also appears that marriage patterns and the consequent social ties and residential location began to separate some groups of families from others. By the 1930s and 1940s, the sons and daughters of Chestnut Valley's more prosperous families were marrying people who had grown up in other, more thriving communities, people whose careers and futures were integrated into the growing, modernizing, urbanizing society. Almost none of them settled down in Chestnut Valley. During the same period, many children of the poorer families were marrying people of marginal backgrounds similar to their own, people from nearby run-down rural areas. Most of them settled in or near Chestnut Valley.

Despite the economic, social, and educational differences among residents, it seems clear that in the period from 1920 until close to 1950, there was no clear-cut clustering of an intergenerational group of derided and despised families living in poverty. True, there was obvious poverty, but "poverty" was neither a social identification nor a derogatory epithet. As one person said,

It wasn't so bad being poor in the old days. A lot of people were poor then, and you weren't an outcast just because you were poor.

Separation of Social Worlds

The subsequent loss of a local community has changed this picture drastically. No longer is there an integrative, cohesive community that can combine the full range of economic differences into a regularized round of activities and an inclusive sense of shared membership. The collapse of the local social community has brought about a cleavage of the population into almost completely separate groups, based on economic and social standing.

Furthermore, the replacement of the local rural community by the distant urban-suburban conglomerate has had markedly different effects on different families. The families who managed to stay above the margin economically, who operated reasonably profitable farms or took on fairly good part-time jobs, also tended to adapt well socially to the new urban-based community. They were integrated into formal organizations and informal networks that spanned a much wider geographic area. As rural depopulation set in—and each hamlet could no longer support its own granges, churches, and ladies' clubs— groups from scattered communities consolidated into single, larger units, often township-wide. The families who were on top economically tended to participate fully in these new, larger units, and thereby established a wide range of social ties. Additionally, they maintained close interaction with brothers and sisters, sons and daughters who had moved out to a wide geographic circle centering on the urban nucleus. These rural people developed networks of relatives, friends, and associates that became increasingly far-reaching. This expanded world became the new focus of their social life, replacing the decaying and insular rural hamlet-and-hinterland community. Even though they continued to live in the rural areas, these families developed wide horizons and a feeling of belonging to a larger, more varied, and more urban community. Their special activities and interests, anchored elsewhere, were more important to them than their home locality, and thus they were able to insulate themselves from the deleterious effects of the decline of the rural community.

For other families in the Chestnut Valley area, however, the range of identification remained significantly more restricted. The very people who were unable to keep on top of the economic changes of the 1920s were the ones most severely affected by the loss of local community. For them, incorporation into the urban community has been much slower and less satisfactory. As new urban institutions took over from rural community organizations, the poorer rural residents were not able to transfer their participation or to forge new social ties. Their relatives, friends, and prospective marriage partners are still mainly concentrated in the depressed rural enclaves, either within the immediate neighborhood or in nearby, similar neighborhoods. The poorer rural people have not been able to enter or to embrace the wider social world: they have not joined, nor do they attend, the educational, fraternal, religious, or voluntary associations of the urban center or its suburban satellite communities. In short, their social connections are restricted and do not integrate them into the new, wider community that has replaced the former rural hamlet-and-hinterland community (see Chapter 10). In this sense the rural poor are now without a community.

Summary: History, Geography, and Rural Poverty

The social and economic history of the Chestnut Valley area reveals that rural poverty has been a fairly long-term phenomenon, and elucidates some of the reasons for its concentration and distribution in a region such as the Southern Tier of New York State.

Historically, the limitations of the natural resource base (that is, the unsuitability of local soil and topography for modern agriculture) have been a contributing factor, producing a succession of unprosperous farmers. In the 1920s, the definite correlation between poor soil and poor people had a close cause-and-effect relationship. Marginal land, by definition, could only support marginal farms, and these brought but meager profit to the families who worked them. Some farmers never made it very far up the agricultural ladder of success before the ladder was taken away by the forces of national and regional economic change. With little formal education and few employable skills, they entered the lower levels of the urban labor market and remained there. They tended to continue to live on family land, sacrificing proximity to jobs for the availability of inexpensive housing on the family homestead and a preference for rural living. Thus, they remained both poor and rural: they became the rural nonfarm poor.

Another important source of the present nonfarm poor population was migration into the area from nearby counties. People occupying marginal positions in their own depressed rural regions came to this area because the urban job situation appeared brighter here. They selected Chestnut Valley as a place to live because of the low cost of land and housing, and because they married into its families.[2]

What all of the chronically poor nonfarm people in the rural area have in common today, then, is that their parents or grandparents made an unsatisfactory transition from agriculture or agriculture-related occupations, in which insufficient resources, unfortunate timing, and large-scale economic trends all worked against their making an advantageous adaptation to nonagricultural pursuits.

The socioeconomic differences that existed at the time this region of the state was being transformed from agriculture have not been erased by time, however, but have become crystallized, firmed, and passed on to successive generations. In the late 1970s, the region was still faced with severe rural poverty, and there is a remarkable correlation between the distribution of chronically poor people and the distribution of poor soil. Why should this be so? The rural poor people of today are not in farming any more, so their limited economic position can no longer be attributed to poor soil quality. By what other mechanisms, then, does the unsuccessful adjustment from agriculture in the 1920s and 1930s continue to affect the families of the 1970s? Why or how have the deficits of earlier adaptations been handed down to subsequent generations? The answers to these questions must be sought at the intersection of the past and the present. The questions will be probed specifically in the concluding section of the book (Chapter 11), where we will seek explanations for the continued persistence of the problems of economic poverty and social marginality that afflict such rural areas.

*   *   *

These two historical chapters have set the stage, have sketched out the backdrop of history. It is on this stage that the actors of today, the families and individuals who populate this book, play out their lives. It is against this backdrop that their actions, life patterns, thoughts, and words can be understood. The spotlight throughout the remainder of the book will be on the chronically poor people who currently live in and around Chestnut Valley.

Part 3

Ethnographic Description
and Analysis

Economics:
Supporting the Family

Introduction

This chapter and the next one examine the ways in which chronically poor rural families manage their various resources toward meeting their needs. The focus is on the means by which a household supports and supplies itself, and on the feelings, ideas, and underlying themes that shape people's economic actions.

A basic assumption of the chapters on economics is that poverty is a much more complex and far-ranging phenomenon than is indicated by the annual income levels specified by the government as "the poverty line."[1] Poverty is not just an income somewhere below a federal guideline; it is an economic situation, an economic niche, and, often, an economic forecast. And poverty has social, psychological, and cultural concomitants as well.

A second assumption is that the economic actions of poverty-stricken people must be examined, not just with reference to dollar incomes, but in terms of people's total economic situation and the larger social, psychological, and cultural context in which economic poverty is embedded. To understand poverty, we must not only record what people earn, but also what they spend; not just their economic actions, but also what they say about their actions; not just what they do in the economic sphere, but also why they do it.

This analysis of economic patterns in their real-life context will challenge some beliefs about poverty commonly held by the wider society. In general, Americans tend to believe that people remain in poverty for the following reasons: (1) they don't work, (2) they spend money foolishly, and (3) they don't aspire to a better life. These popular "explanations" reflect the common stereotypes that poor people are: (1) lazy, (2) spendthrift, and (3) lacking in ambition. And the same stereotypes underlie much of our government's approach to dealing with the problem of poverty. Hence, there are policies requiring "welfare mothers" to take jobs (reflecting belief and stereotype number 1 above); programs teaching "proper" money management to low-income housewives (based on belief and stereotype number 2); and attempts to expand the horizons of the "culturally disadvantaged" (because of belief and stereotype number 3).

Observations and analyses of economic patterns in this one northern Appalachian microcosm of rural poverty challenge the validity of these stereotypes. In fact, the following observed patterns clearly contradict the three parts of the general stereotype.

- Most of the people studied do work — long, hard hours at jobs that give them in return little personal satisfaction and little income.
- Most of the people studied are very clever in stretching what money they have and compensating for the money they lack.
- Most of the people studied do, indeed, have hopes and aspirations for improvement — for their own lives, if possible, but especially for their children's lives.

If the underlying stereotypes are wrong, then the policies and programs based upon them are not likely to be effective in solving the problem of long-term rural poverty.

Making a Living

The Working Poor

The rural families of this study can appropriately be called "working poor," in that most households have at least one gainfully employed member most of the time, but in most cases income generally hovers around the poverty line.

Data from the 1969-70 survey of twenty low-income households indicate that in nineteen of the households, either the husband or the wife was working, and in one case both. In eighteen of the households, men were employed in autumn 1969, though as the 1969-70 winter wore on, the male wage earners in two of these households lost their jobs, due to construction layoffs in one case, injury in another. In the autumn of 1969, there were four households with employed women, although two of these women were laid off in early 1970. In only two of the twenty households were there adult men who had been unemployed for a long period of time. In only one case was there no employed adult.

There is virtually no employment in the Chestnut Valley area, and most workers drive at least fifteen miles to work. The biggest single type of employment for men is with the highway and maintenance crews of the state, county, town, and city. The urban factory assembly lines also provide employment for both men and women. Other employers include the railroad, a metal fabrication plant, a trucking firm, and construction firms. A few men are self-employed in construction or salvage work. The women are most fre' quently employed by hospitals and other health-care facilities, as well as by motels and educational institutions, all of which regularly need unskilled labor of a janitorial nature, and which accept a high turnover of employees. Both men and women tend to cluster with particular employers, due to the fact that people make their job contacts through their personal contacts: the net' works of relatives and neighbors serve as informal employment agencies. Fur' thermore, certain employers are known to be more apt to hire low-skill and/or short-term workers.

The people are also "working poor" in another, broader sense; although they are poor, work is a basic part of their concept of living, important in their thoughts as well as their actions. For themselves and for their children and their neighbors, they believe in work as the respectable way to support oneself or one's family, and they judge a man harshly who could work but does not.

The belief in the value of work is part of a long tradition. In an earlier time, being a good worker was more important as a criterion of an individual's worth than was his wealth. Men and women built reputations through their work performance in the appropriate spheres of activity in the farm-based community. Hard work as a farmhand was a prime means for a boy from a family of low economic position to gain personal respect and accep' tance in the local farming community. Hard work was also essential for climb' ing the ladder toward economic advancement. Today, in the post-farming era, people still invest years of effort following through on their commitment to the work ethic. Being a good worker, which is interpreted locally as being steady on the job and working hard at it, still is a matter of pride and some recognition.

Despite the high rate of employment and the strong commitment to work' ing, most of the twenty households nevertheless remain poor. Fifteen households out of the twenty had a income on or below the poverty line, which in 1970 was just under $4,000 for a family of four. Income from employment is not only generally low, but also insecure and variable. While a single month's earning might indicate that a family belongs in an income bracket above the poverty line, over the course of a year or several years the income may average substantially below poverty levels. People speak of their earnings in terms of the weekly or biweekly paycheck, rather than in terms of annual income, partly as a reflection of this variability. In 1969-70, men were bringing home $85 and $92 per week for highway crew work; by 1971-72 they were clearing $104 and $111 per week. If these earnings had been steady throughout the year, the annual take-home incomes of these men would have been between $4,400 and $5,800. This would have placed their families above the poverty level only if there were four or fewer members in the households and income remained at that level all year. In most cases, the income adjusted for family size was borderline or below, with respect to the official definition and guidelines. Construction workers at the time were bringing in nearly twice as much as factory employees and road crew, but they faced regular winter layoffs and other slack periods of reduced income.

The income figures on which poverty is officially defined are gross income figures, but obviously the household lives on its take-home pay, after deductions for withholding taxes, Social Security, and health insurance. In many cases, the actual amount of the paycheck is further diminished by additional deductions. Some employees may have part of their wages garnisheed for past debts – a kind of after-the-fact installment plan. Some workers purposely have extra money withheld from their paychecks to receive a federal income tax refund in April – an unofficial payroll savings plan.

Occasionally, but unpredictably, income is boosted by overtime pay, which may increase take-home pay up to 20 percent. Overtime is viewed as a periodic and necessary financial lift, enabling a family to catch up on back bills or make some long-postponed purchase. In periods of economic recession, however, factories and highway departments cut back on overtime, leaving workers without this cushion and giving them, in a sense, an effective cut in wages.

> We were just scraping by. We were even doing okay. But now, without overtime, it seems like we always come out short.

In some cases, there are also periodic across-the-board pay raises, but these have hardly kept pace with inflation in the cost of living.

> My husband got a raise, but then they upped the insurance and cut out his overtime. So we're right back where we were, except that the price of food and things keeps going up.

Women take jobs as a temporary substitute for or supplement to their husbands' irregular, seasonal, or low-paid employment. In households where women are employed, the woman's job is apt to be the main source of income. Of the four employed women in the 1969 sample, one woman's husband was not living at home, two had husbands who were not working, and one woman's husband had a sporadic job history, though he was employed at the time. In seven other households, the wives had an intermittent or fairly regular history of employment, although they were not currently working.

Any overlap period of double income in the family is looked on as a means of catching up on back debts, maybe getting a little ahead, or earning enough to cover some particular target item, such as monthly payments on the purchase of a house or trailer. When the goal is reached, the woman may quit her job to stay home with the children, or perhaps to have another baby.

Men at Work

Working for a living is considered important – both as an economic strategy and as a measure of a man's worth. But often the world of work does not provide sufficient rewards, either financial or social. Commitment to work and dogged persistence in work is not, in itself, enough to raise a family out of poverty. In case after case, a man has worked quite steadily at a grinding, low-paid job – showing up on time, doing what is required, maintaining a fairly good attendance record – and still, ten, fifteen, or twenty years later his family is just hovering above the poverty line.

One reason for this long-term limited earning power is the nature of the regional and local economy. The demand for low-skill employees has not expanded in recent years, and fluctuates with the national economy, sometimes shrinking markedly. Thus, job security is low. The pay scale remains low, compared to the regional cost of living; and advancement opportunities are limited. The faltering growth rate of the national economy in much of this period, particularly noticeable in the decline of the northeastern regional economy, has taken its toll among lower-level employees. They are at risk for unemployment and underemployment, and are caught in the bind of inflation.

The world of work also fails these men in another way: intangible rewards for the jobs they perform may be as low as the cash incomes earned. Factory work, a job on the highway crew, institutional maintenance, and janitorial work do not usually provide either social connections or social status. A man's co-workers are apt to be people he already knows, people in the same socioeconomic position. Although a man who works hard and steadily at a job usually gains some self-respect and recognition from his co-workers and family, his accomplishment is not easily demonstrated or validated in the community. The kinds of employment available are low in prestige – menial tasks that carry a low status and pay too little to allow the worker to purchase a socially approved life style. Thus, hard work brings little social reward and little recognition, as well as too little money.

Some of the jobs men hold do have some definite advantages, however. Highway crew work, for example, though it yields relatively low pay, does offer some job security and the opportunity for overtime work in winter. The nature of the work itself also holds advantages for men who have the physical strength and prefer to work outside. Especially if the job involves operating a truck or other machinery, there is an opportunity for demonstrating personal skill, power, and bravery: men speak proudly of dangerous situations, near-misses, and clever escapes on the job. Additionally, the multiplicity of municipal highway departments (state, county, township, and city) provides an opportunity for a man to be hired at the same kind of job in several different jurisdictions. He can move laterally from one municipal employer to another, since the job skills are transferable. There is also the attraction of having one's friends, relatives, or neighbors as employment contacts and co-workers. But the advantages of these jobs may now be diminishing. Political and economic pressures to control highway maintenance costs lead to reduction or elimination of overtime, and to the institution of more bureaucratic practices in the hiring and administration of highway departments.

Men's attitudes toward their long-range employment future tend to be restricted. A man sees that his co-workers are no better off, and obtain no greater rewards, even if they have been on the job a long time. The possibility of changing jobs offers little encouragement, as he sees that his former co-workers and neighbors have not found things much better in other employment situations. Neither significant promotion nor job-changing for the sake of advancement is common enough among neighbors, friends, and relatives to serve as a model or incentive. And few opportunities exist for learning the skills or proving the capacity to advance. Thus, a man does not see his job as a rung on a career ladder that he can climb upward toward increasingly more satisfying and more remunerative jobs. Rather, he expects only to stay where he is or to step sideways. Furthermore, men perceive job security as more important than advancement. A man who is just making ends meet feels he cannot take the risk of seeking a better job because he might not find one, or the one he gets might turn out not to be what he wanted, or he might not be capable of keeping it.

Better to stick with this lousy job than to be caught with no job at all.

Personal job advancement is also limited by psychological factors. The men of these pockets of poverty are handicapped occupationally by a legacy of diminished self-esteem. They have grown up watching their parents struggle with debt-ridden farms or in grinding, dull jobs that yielded insufficient monetary or personal rewards. They have known their parents' heavy feeling of failure in the world of work. Their own experiences in the competitive world of education and urban employment have further convinced them that failure is the expectation and often the fact. From their observations and experiences of failure, whether firsthand or vicarious, they form limited expectations for their own job futures. They seek, and have found, mainly those jobs that offer the least room for personal initiative and the least expectation of personal development. These low expectations, in turn, become active forces inhibiting advancement in the job world, no matter how strong the commitment to work.

The interaction of limited expectations and limited achievement in the job world is exemplified by the cases in which an employee turns down an offer of a job promotion (from work crew to leader, for example) in which he would be given responsibility over subordinate workers and some limited decision-making authority. The employer regards the promotion as a real chance for a man to get ahead; thus, when the employee turns down the offer, the boss concludes that the man has no desire to better himself. But this pattern is really much more complex. The level of common laborer is considered safe because hard work and good attendance will usually produce adequate results and make failure unlikely, thus providing job security. But in any role involving decision-making and supervision of subordinates, hard work would be only one of several ingredients, and would not by itself guarantee successful performance. Such a job is usually regarded as too much of a risk to the individual.[2] If a man were to advance to a higher position and prove unable to perform adequately, his own personal abilities would clearly be called into question—a risk that a man with low self-esteem is hesitant to accept. Any job with a managerial or supervisory role over other people may seem particularly risky because it requires the very skills about which men may feel least confident. To accept a position of authority over others is thought to invite jealousy, resentment, and certain criticism.

> My husband wouldn't want to be in the middle that way. He'd catch heck from his boss above him and he'd catch heck from the guys below him. No, he'd rather be one of them [the crew of laborers], even if he has to pass up a higher salary.

Thus, many of the men adapt to the security of being steady laborers among their bottom-rung peers rather than advancing to higher positions where they would be faced with decisions to make, and caught between superiors and subordinates. In the lower echelons, a worker avoids further erosion of his personal sense of self-worth by insuring that if something does go wrong, the blame will not fall on him, since he only did what he was told. These considerations also seem to explain, at least in part, the typically lukewarm response expressed both in action and in words to various government-sponsored job training programs that have been proposed or established.

A few of the men have not only failed to advance in their jobs, they have become so discouraged about their lack of success in supporting their families or so burdened by other problems that they eventually lose even their basic commitment to work. Some have worked at a single job for as long as ten to twenty years before surrendering to a growing alcoholism or mental-health problem that eventually causes them to lose their jobs and permanently drop out of the world of work. The life histories of these men usually include a physical disability—perhaps an accident or injury—as the factor that tipped the scale from work to alcoholic unemployment. In the preponderance of cases, however, men exhibit almost dogged determination to work—to get a job or to continue on a job despite its meager rewards, and when they find themselves out of work, most exhibit restlessness, edginess, and self-doubt. Among older men who have worked for most of their lives, this situation causes distress, but among young men who have had little experience in the world of work, prolonged unemployment may have a considerable effect on their future functioning; they may give up trying to get a job more easily than men who have had at least some positive work experiences.

There is a circular feedback operating here. The constraints of being locked into low-status jobs, the lack of advancement, the limited personal involvement, development, and pride—all these combine with the low pay to reinforce a man's already low self-esteem. And low self-esteem tends to further restrict a man's potential performance in the employment sphere. Additionally, the meager earnings and lack of advancement on the job may restrict a man's satisfaction in his performance as husband and father. This results in further strain on the family, which in turn causes and perpetuates other problems, including the undermining of job performance.

Thus, while most men exhibit a resigned persistence about the necessity of work, the overall impression they give is that they are more tied than committed to their particular jobs. For most, the job is merely a job, a respectable though inadequate source of income. It has rarely been possible for men to "work themselves out of poverty" or to earn their way to higher social status.

Working Women

For women, the same general picture of low-level jobs with limited returns holds true. But for women the negative aspects of work are not nearly as strong as they are for men. Fewer women work; they work for fewer years; and they experience less employment-related and personal failure. Women's comments reveal that they have less ego-involvement in their role as income earners than do men. For women, the job is an extra role they assume, in addition to their basic role as mother, wife, and homemaker. Working is not mandatory for their role fulfillment or self-esteem. The money that women earn either supports the family (if there is no income-earning husband) or buys the extras and treats (if hers is the second income). In either case, what is noticed is how *much* she brings home, not how little, as may be the case with a man.

For all of the women who are employed, or have recently been employed, money is the primary reason they give for working. It simply makes life easier if the wife has a regular income, even though relatively low, to supplement the low or insecure income of the husband. Often, too, women state that they prefer working to going on welfare. Besides, if the husband is living at home, welfare support is not usually available, even though his income or his unemployment or disability benefits may be inadequate for family needs.

There are also important secondary reasons why women work or want to work. Employed women, in most cases, have the right to determine how their earnings are spent. Some women find that having their own source of income reduces the friction between husband and wife over how money is spent. If a husband won't allow his wife to spend his earnings on certain items for the house or children or herself, her only recourse is to try to get a job so that she may spend money to satisfy the needs she perceives as important.

Employed women also seem to gain considerable satisfaction from their social interaction with other workers on the job. To a much greater extent than men, women's talk about their jobs tends to center on interactions with co-workers—discussions at coffee breaks, the problems other women on the job are having with their husbands and so forth. And some employed women are simply seeking to get away from the house. Some women clearly keep themselves employed, despite complaints of how hard it is to manage everything and how tired they are, because they do not want to stay home—either in an overcrowded house full of small, noisy children or in a quiet, empty house when the children have all reached school age.

The secondary reasons for working are revealed most clearly when women who have generally been employed are not working, perhaps due to layoffs, the closing down of a factory, injuries, disabilities, quitting, or the birth of another baby. They express dissatisfaction, and exhibit restlessness and sometimes depression, indicating a sense of both social and psychological loss. On the other hand, a woman who has finally obtained a job after being on welfare expresses renewed pride and confidence in herself. The following comments, made by women who were actively looking for work (utilizing both the state employment bureau and informal inquiries among working friends and relatives), indicate some of the reasons and the urgency behind their desire to go to work.

If I could go back to work, we wouldn't be just hanging on like this.

I really have to get out and *do something*. I'm just going nuts here—all alone all day with nothing to do. [All her children are in school or grown and moved away.] I've even taken up crocheting. And I'm so disagreeable—I take things out on the kids when really it's just that *I* get on my nerves all day. Right now I'd do anything, any work, even if it would be against the doctor's orders. [The doctor said that she should not take a job requiring any lifting or even standing on her feet all day, due to a back injury.] As it is, I do all sorts of errands for my married daughter and other people—just to occupy myself. I'm really raring to go! It's been so long since my accident. I'd be so happy! Things seem to go so much smoother when I'm working. I get along better with the kids, and with myself too. And the housework—why I can whip through this trailer in minutes if I have something else to do.

I've got to get me a job. I can tell it's really time now for me to get working. I find myself beginning to give up, and then I know I really better get out and get a job. Something, anything, even volunteer, if it has to be. The thing is, there's so much wanting doing around this house, but never any money to do it, so I can't get at any of the improvements and projects I want to do. So after a while I just give up. Why, this last Saturday, I just stayed in bed all day. When that happens, I know I got to do something quick. I'm so dying to get a job. I'll take anything. If I catch myself in time, keep myself from giving up altogether, get a job so's I can be out doing something and getting some money for all the things we need, then everything will be okay.

The women who have not been employed recently give a variety of reasons for not working. Some say they can't take a job because of problems of transportation and lack of child-care arrangements. However, it seems that these are not always strong deterrents, for most of the women find various ways to solve these problems *if* they really are able to work and *if* a job is available. Rides can be found with neighbors, babysitting with relatives or neighbors. Frequently a women may work night shift, using the family car while her husband is home with the children, or she may work during the day, with her husband on night shift and thus available for after-school care until the mother is home. Furthermore, since the most common pattern is that the woman goes to work when her husband is out of work, transportation and child care may actually not be serious obstacles because the car is available and the husband can be at home.

More significant deterrents to women taking or keeping jobs have to do with attitudes and beliefs about women's roles, and with the relationships between husbands and wives. Some husbands openly disapprove of or actually prohibit their wives from working. Some wives report that their husbands would be jealous of the competition, particularly if the husband is out of work or earning very little. A number of women also report that their husbands believe a woman should be home with her children. One man stated emphatically, "I'm the husband. She's the wife and mother. I didn't marry her so that she could go out and work." His wife said, "No, I'm not thinking about working now. I can hardly keep up with what I've got here at home — four kids, grandma, and a husband that's more trouble than any kid. How could I work too? In a few years, maybe I'll think about working. Right now, there aren't any jobs anyway. So why bother to even think about it?"

Many husbands and wives agree on the division of roles, preferring that the husband work if he can and the wife stay home at least as long as there are young children and maybe until they are teenagers. This feeling seems often to be a reflection of the adults' own sense of having had insufficient mothering when they were children. If at all possible, they want to provide a mother in the home for their children.

Other facets of the husband-wife roles and relationships also discourage women from working. Some women don't work because their husbands express considerable suspicion about allowing their wives to associate with other men. The job would provide an opportunity for women to play around or get involved. Some husbands do not trust their wives to resist such temptation. Additionally, some women do not want to take jobs because they feel that their husbands are too lazy to work unless it is absolutely essential to the family's existence. As the saying goes, "He's the type of husband that, if his wife will work, he won't."

In some cases, or at some times, the woman's low self-esteem also acts as a deterrent to employment, making her doubt that she could get and hold a job. This is particularly true for those women who have been out of the job world for an extended period to raise children. Another deterrent to work is the exhausting demands of keeping house and taking care of the family in a situation of substandard facilities and inadequate equipment. Women who feel overwhelmed or constantly behind in their housework think that it is unrealistic to take on an outside job.

Another deterrent for women is their longstanding health problems: unhealed injuries or illnesses of long ago; exhaustion from continuing overwork and undernourishment; lifelong medical conditions such as diabetes; ignored gynecological problems; and, frequently, "nerves." While these health problems are generally below the acute level, they tend to drag on for long periods, sapping the energy and wearing down the spirit. Women with such conditions find it hard to think in terms of managing a job and the family too.[3]

Despite these deterrents, many women do try to take on a job. A few manage to make a go of it; others give up the attempt, deciding to wait a few years for their situations to change. For a number of women at various points in their lives, the ideal situation as they see it would be part-time employment. But the compromise of a part-time job (or piecework at home) is rarely available in the local employment area, so that a woman must work full-time or not at all. Consequently, women work when the situation at home permits it and when extra income is most needed; and they quit when the strain and inconvenience of working outweigh the monetary or other benefits. Later, they go back to work again; then they quit again. Thus, as individual work histories show, over the long run women have created their own version of part-time employment through their start-stop work patterns. They are likely to continue this intermittent employment pattern in the future, as a way of adjusting the world of work to their own needs and situations.

"Being on Welfare is No Picnic"

Another important source of support is welfare or public assistance. Most of the households studied have had welfare help at some point. At any given time, about one-quarter of the chronically poor families of this study are receiving assistance. In 1970, in the base sample of twenty low-income families, five were on AFDC (Aid to Families with Dependent Children). In 1974, four families were receiving AFDC. Of these four households, the husband was absent in one, in another the husband's self-employed earnings were irregular. In the third, the husband's earned income was too low to cover both household needs and support payments to his children living elsewhere, and the wife was not receiving child-support payments from her former husband. In the fourth household, the husband's alcoholism was too severe for him to obtain or hold a job.

Other households receiving AFDC have included at least one unmarried woman with a baby living as a subunit in her parents' home. In other cases, households have received payments from the welfare department designated for a specific individual in the household, perhaps a foster child or a retarded or disabled relative released from a state facility. But this support is not AFDC and not regarded as welfare.

The pattern observed over the years is that families go on and off AFDC (or in a few cases, home relief) as their situation warrants, using it as a necessary last resort in extended periods of nonemployment or absence of the husband-father. Very few of the entire group of families studied have been on public assistance for long periods of time. (Thus, although two or even three generations of a family might have received welfare support, it is by no means a situation of continuous welfare dependence, which is the usual public stereotype.) In many cases, welfare is merely a supplement to some other income source, rather than the sole support. In no case has welfare brought a family above the poverty level.

Among the low-income rural families, there is clearly a stigma attached to being on welfare. Families who are receiving or have received assistance are sensitive about it and do not talk about it unless there is a particular problem. This stigma seems to be felt more among the older people than the young adults and new parents. However, even on the school bus, children occasionally taunt each other about being on welfare, repeating derogatory comments and allegations they have heard at home. Adults openly discuss the welfare status of their neighbors, frequently exaggerating the amount another family receives and criticizing the way it is being spent.

Living on welfare is definitely considered second-best to earning an income, which is preferred for both financial and social reasons. This becomes apparent, for example, when a man is "temporarily" laid off and has used up all his unemployment benefits, but does not accept "going to the welfare" as a satisfactory answer because he really wants to go back to his job, to earn the family's support and to earn his own self-respect.

A particularly strong objection to being on welfare is its potential control over individual and family actions. People fear—with some justification and some exaggeration—that "the welfare" (meaning the official personnel of the department of social services) will take away their house or land, will force them to sell their cars, will dictate how they must spend their money, and may even take away their children.

Being on welfare is viewed as undesirable particularly because it cuts down the flexibility of individuals to cope with their own situation, because it restricts their options. For example, an unemployed, disabled man might want to spend money buying another wrecked car, so he can fix it up and sell it at a good profit. If his family is on welfare, he is discouraged from generating this extra income, he is not free to make his own spending decisions, to act when the time is right, to maneuver. Likewise, a wife wants to be free to accept a wandering husband back and attempt to keep him, even if it means using some of the meager welfare-budget household funds to satisfy his personal whims. But she does so at the risk of losing her welfare benefits.

In the day-to-day living on the borderline between just barely getting by and not making it, the freedom to act quickly—to make changes in family arrangements, to move to a new location, to spend half the food budget on something else—is an essential adaptation to poverty living. The various restrictions and constant need to keep caseworkers informed of one's doings are thus felt as particularly oppressive. (For example, the requirement that a recipient inform the department of social services before he or she moves to a new location and the paperwork involved are a particular nuisance, and people sometimes get into trouble for not following these regulations.)

These negative feelings about public assistance are superimposed on the traditional rural value of the individual family providing for its own needs. Particularly among older people, reluctance to turn to the government for help is often quite strong. This reluctance, combined with the threat of losing independence and swallowing pride, makes some older people hold out against requesting public assistance, even when their needs are great. The same beliefs inhibit some potentially eligible families from applying for food stamps or medical assistance because they see these programs as part of the welfare system.

Of those who have been on welfare, most do not consider it an adequate or a satisfying means of supporting a family. Recipients may complain that one gets too little money from welfare—and too much supervision.

They are always trying to give you less than they are supposed to.

In return for what they hand out, they meddle in your life, urge you to leave your husband, pressure you to move away.

You have to tell the caseworker every time you do anything.

They try to tell you just how you should spend every penny they give you.

On the other hand, the same people also complain about the large number of "lazy cheaters" who soak up welfare money when they really could work. And some recipients, while they state that they do not like being on welfare, are openly appreciative of its support at a time when no other alternatives seemed possible. On the whole, people want a welfare system that will help struggling families like themselves adequately when needed, and without humiliation. But they see welfare as second-best, an inescapable necessity sometimes, but not the preferred means of long-term family support.

Other Sources of Support

Over the long run, the income level in many households is just barely enough to support a family from one payday to the next. Rarely is income sufficient or secure enough to enable a family to get out of debt or to build up a reserve toward anticipated or unexpected future expenses. But people do have various means of occasionally augmenting household income. At times, earnings may be boosted by putting in overtime, by taking on additional after-hours jobs, or by the wife's working. Household income may also be increased by participation in government programs such as food stamps, Medicaid, and Supplemental Security Income.

There are also important unofficial ways in which people devise substitutes and supplements for employment income and public assistance. They constantly draw on their resources of personal ingenuity and social contacts to obtain small, irregular cash income, goods, and services.

One temporary source of support is other people. Occasionally young men out of school but only sporadically working will continue to draw from their parents' provisions, or will append themselves to the household of a neighbor or girlfriend. A young woman with a baby or small children but no child-support payments from the father may be supported by her parents, either instead of or in addition to collecting public assistance. Although the provision of such support is regarded as part of parental or grandparental responsibility, depending on others is not respected as a long-term means of providing for oneself or one's children.

Junk cars provide a small and intermittent income. Some men invest considerable time, skill, and energy in buying, repairing, and selling or trading used cars and car parts, as well as motorcycles, snowmobiles, home appliances, and other items. This activity does not bring in any steady income, and the amounts for each transaction may be small ($15, $50, $100 or more may be cleared as profit, if labor is not counted), but it provides extra money now and then for general living expenses or for extra expenses such as house maintenance and car insurance. The profit from this enterprise may be col-lected either in cash or directly in goods needed or desired by the family: a "new" heater or water pump, a TV, or building materials may be obtained through repairing and trading cars or supplying car parts.

There is no evidence that illegal activities have formed any significant basis of financial support, and they are definitely not perceived as an acceptable means of making a living. While illegal activities have been engaged in by some people at some times as a means of obtaining material goods or cash, the game-law violations and the petty larceny, theft, and breaking and entering charges listed against some of the men at various times are mostly the result of youthful pranks or drunken vandalism. They often involve the playing out of hostilities between neighborhood families or specific individuals, but they are not economic activities: they are neither a way of life, nor a way of making a living.

In considering contributions to household resources, it is important to recognize the role played by wives, even when they are not employed. In most cases, it is the woman who spends the time and energy making the trips to town, filling out the forms and going to the various offices to boost family income with food stamps, Medicaid, or public assistance. Women also con-tribute to balancing the household budget by minimizing cash expenses. Women spend considerable time in such activities as going to rummage sales to get cheap clothing; fixing appliances, the house, or the car to avoid repair bills or replacement costs; gathering and preserving wild or garden produce; and doing numerous errands that would require a husband's taking time off from work (such as registering motor vehicles). Women may also earn either cash or goods by doing favors for neighbors, such as giving rides to town and babysitting.

If the family is keeping a disabled or retarded relative or a grandchild, there may be public assistance money coming into the household for that in-dividual, even though the husband may be earning a stable income. It is the wife who does the housework and care required by the extra individual, and so she is, in effect, bringing in a very small income from the government for the work she does in that connection. In all these ways, even women who are not employed are effectively making a substantial contribution to the household's balance of income and expenses. But this contribution is not usually thought of in economic terms by the woman or her husband, and usually goes unrecognized.

Supplying Family Needs

The Cycle of Getting and Spending

The other side of the coin from earning is spending. It is popularly assumed in American society that people remain poor because they are spendthrifts, wasting money foolishly on luxuries rather than sticking to basic necessities, spending without plan, and making no provision for tomorrow. However, a closer look challenges those old stereotypes. What look like unplanned, unconnected expenditures may actually be part of a pattern, a strategy for dealing with the perpetual problems of too little money to cover the household's needs.

Many people are paid weekly on Friday; others are paid biweekly. Welfare checks come once a month in most cases. If the husband is the primary earner, he usually retains control over his paycheck, periodically doling out small amounts of cash to his wife "for groceries." If he earns extra money (from selling fixed-up cars, for example), it is assumed that he is entitled to spend this cash as he wishes. The wife has control over the small amounts of money she acquires, and in most cases she uses such discretionary money to buy clothing and treats for her children. In the case of regularly employed women, the paycheck usually goes toward major recurrent expenses, such as house payments and/or groceries.

The prevalent overall pattern of spending in most households is a payday-to-payday cycle of getting and spending money and being out again by or before the next payday. But in most cases it is not a haphazard cycle. A common pattern of disbursement of income is to pay one or two regular bills each week of the month. The first week's paycheck may go for rent, or for major grocery shopping, or for buying food stamps.[4] The second week, the electricity bill may be paid and perhaps the telephone bill, if there is a phone. The third week the heating fuel bill may be paid, and/or perhaps the second batch of food stamps purchased. The fourth week an installment on a loan or an overdue bill might be paid. In this way, a family just makes it through a month of bills to begin the cycle all over again. Whatever money is left over from bills goes for groceries, for gasoline, and for other household and family needs. One housewife described the tightness of her budgeting system as follows.

> When a month has five Fridays in it, we're really in luck, because there's one paycheck where we don't have to take a big chunk out of it right away to pay a major bill. So we can splurge, like buying a few extra groceries or a new jacket for one of the kids.

Thus, money is spent almost as soon as it comes in, and the night before payday finds a family with little food in the house and little gasoline in the car.

Where the Money Goes

FOOD generally constitutes a major portion of a family's budget. For families not on food stamps, the weekly cash outlay for food ranged, in 1969-70, from an occasional low of $20 for a family of five when money was very tight, to $80 or more for a family of six. Most noteworthy is the considerable variation among families and within any one family at different times, depending on the amount of cash available.

Most women shop in the large urban supermarkets once a week or bi-weekly, picking up extra items in between at small roadside grocery stores closer to home. In some cases, lack of sufficient storage space and refrigeration necessitates small-quantity buying. Women vary considerably in their shop-ping skills and economical buying habits, but many are real experts. The kinds of food purchased vary considerably from one family to the next. Family tastes, cooking facilities, and the predilections of the homemaker seem to be more important than monthly income in determining the types and varieties of food purchased. However, macaroni products, potatoes, beans, and bread predominate in all households, and when income is lower than usual meat purchases may be eliminated for a week at a time. Families on food stamps generally find that the stamps make a real difference, providing a benefit value ranging from a few dollars to about half of the household food costs. Food stamps also appear to reduce somewhat the fluctuation in the amount of money a family spends on food and the quantity of meat and vegetables purchased.

HOUSING COSTS in these rural areas do not usually constitute a major expense for most families. People have worked out various strategies for keeping down the cash cost of housing to an amount they can generally manage to pay. Many families live "rent-free," perhaps in a house that has been in the family for generations, or in a very modest house that was built or purchased inex-pensively enough to be paid off quickly. One family of seven paid $1,000 in monthly installments to buy their house in the early 1960s, fixing it up over the decade with investments of time and money. Although the house was still substandard, the family was no longer burdened by monthly rent or mort-gage payments. This situation is quite common. Renting a place to live is recognized as causing extra financial strain, and only four out of the twenty families were renting homes in 1972. Rents ranged considerably: one family with three children still at home paid just over $100 a month for a large but run-down house; a family of nine paid $155; two families (ten people) shared a large, dilapidated, isolated farmhouse for $35 a month. A family of four paid $60 monthly on a land-contract for a trailer and a lot that they would own in two years. In a few cases, meeting rent or land-contract payments or property taxes puts too much strain on the family budget. The wife may take a job ex-pressly for the purpose of meeting housing expenses, or the family may move to cheaper quarters.

Increasingly common as a low-cost housing solution is the trailer. Many of the lower-income families, particularly, live in trailers they have purchased, usually secondhand at least. A family may pay less than $1,000 over a year

or two, and can set the trailer rent-free on relatives' land, thus minimizing the monthly cash outlay for housing. This practice gives rise to a familiar sight in the countryside: an old farmhouse with a trailer parked beside it. Trailers are installed either on a relative's land or on a separate lot, rather than in a "mobile home park," for economic as well as social reasons. (In a park, one must pay rent for the lot, must pay for septic and water privileges, and usually must have an impressive-looking mobile home, not a beat-up old trailer.) In 1970, six out of the twenty low-income households in the basic sample were living in trailers, ranging from a very small old-style one in disrepair—really cramped for a family of six— to a large, modern mobile home. The latter was much admired by the neighbors, but it lacked a septic system and a well, and was extremely crowded for its family of ten, despite a wood-frame addition on the front. The percentage of trailers has steadily increased over the decade.

HOME HEATING is apt to be a large, recurrent expense during the long, cold winters (heating season often lasts from mid-October through late April). Fuel is most frequently kerosene, purchased in small amounts and frequent intervals at a combination grocery store–gas station along the main highway. (Some families have switched to regular bulk kerosene delivery to avoid the nuisance of frequent purchasing and the risk of occasionally running out. However, most cannot afford to pay a large bill all at once, and thus cannot take advantage of discount rates on quantity purchases.) Some houses have consistently used wood stoves, and more now are converting to wood due to the high cost of other fuels and the low cost of wood—which is cheap if one obtains a permit and cuts and hauls it himself from nearby state forests.

Whatever the source of heat, some houses are uncomfortably cool and

Whatever the source of heat, some houses are uncomfortably cool and drafty. The most common situation, however, is uneven heating: the main room is so warm that small children run around in diapers and undershirts; the rest of the home so cold that the space is hardly usable in winter. A fan dangling from an extension cord may be hung above a space heater to blow some of the heat into another room. Rags and newspapers are used to cover leaky windows and stuff cracks in doors. The odor of kerosene pervades many houses and trailers. A number of families use the kitchen stove (usually fueled by bottled gas) as an auxiliary room heater.

CLOTHING expenditures are regulated by the amount of money available at any particular time, with a definite seasonal peak before the start of school and cold weather in the fall. Clothes that are bought new come mostly from the discount stores in the shopping centers fifteen or twenty miles away; a family trip to such a store may be a big Friday night event. A large part of the wife's and children's clothing, however, comes from rummage sales around the county. Free, used clothing comes from relatives, friends, and official organizations like the antipoverty programs. Women generally neglect their own clothing needs: the lack of a warm coat and waterproof footwear for the mother is the most frequent hallmark of an overstrained family budget. She considers these items for herself extras she can do without until more money is on hand. But clothes for the children must be provided, not only to keep them warm, but because the mother wants her babies and school children to appear as well dressed as possible.

APPLIANCES AND FURNITURE needed for family living are acquired from many of the same sources as clothing. Most are at least secondhand. An inventory of some houses reveals a surprising number of articles gleaned from the municipal dumps—furniture, appliances, pots and pans. (However, as prog-ress marches on, the old town dump is frequently replaced by a modern, regional "sanitary landfill operation" that greatly limits scavenging because it is far away, patrolled or locked up, and constantly being covered over with earth or other fill.) Some furniture may be donated by acquaintances, traded from relatives and friends, or occasionally bought new or nearly new on time payments. In the past, some families were able to purchase a refrigerator or beds with extra help from public assistance. Almost every family has a television set, perhaps very old and in poor working order, perhaps new. For the house itself, supplies to repair it or to make improvements are obtained by trading, or bought wherever they are cheapest, even if it means traveling a considerable distance, buying unmatched lots, seconds, and material that is not precisely suited to the job.

OTHER HOUSEHOLD AND PERSONAL GOODS are obtained wherever they can be had cheaply. They are often secondhand; if they are new they usually come from discount stores. Toys for children, especially for Christmas, may involve considerable expense, as mechanical and up-to-date television-advertised toys are frequently desired. Parents may begin purchasing children's presents in September, taking out bits of money from the grocery allotment to be sure the children will get the presents they want. But sometimes a child receives toys donated by the Salvation Army or gleaned from the county's dumps.

RECREATION consumes a variable amount of money in different families at different times. Some families go for long periods with almost no money spent on recreation. Many families own snowmobiles for winter recreation, some own a motorcycle, and a few have owned a motorboat for fishing. These items are usually acquired at least secondhand, and prices paid have ranged from $100 for an old snowmobile up to a rumored, but unlikely, figure of $1,000 for a boat. Most such items require money for replacement parts as well.

Some men regularly spend money going out on the town with friends from work, or male relatives, though most drinking takes place at home. Some husbands (and a very few wives and children) regularly go to stock car races. Women rarely spend money on recreation for themselves, unless it is in the company of their husbands. Few families take vacations; at most they take a short trip to visit relatives or to see some major tourist attraction.

MEDICAL EXPENSES are a continuing problem for some families. A few families have outstanding medical bills from years ago; others incur bills that they can only pay off in installments. People purchase over-the-counter and prescription medicines at discount drugstores, and obtain professional services mostly from private doctors and the hospital emergency room. (Relatively few utilize the free well-baby clinics sponsored by county health departments.)

Some financial help comes from insurance plans connected to employment, and from state Medicaid or the federal Medicare program for older people. But families sometimes incur medical costs when they have no insurance, and usually have to pay some portion of costs even when they are covered. There is often confusion about medical insurance or assistance – what it covers, when it expires, how far back it is effective, and whether the family is currently eligible. Medicaid is available to people with incomes below a certain level, even when they are not on welfare, but fluctuating incomes and recertification problems leave many families without coverage. When a family is on welfare, Medicaid is almost automatically available, though it is not retroactive to cover previous medical bills, and does not pay the full bill.

SAVINGS from income are meager, for after meeting various current and past expenses, a family is usually out of money, if not in debt. Occasionally, however, some families are able to come out with a little money left over at the end of some week or month. Small amounts of money may be put away for some particular future goal.

Like I say, there's the future to think about. We'd like to get this house finished so it will be a good place to live in. And we'd like to help the boys towards their future. Our oldest one is starting high school now. He's a good student. Maybe he'll want to go to college. We'd like to help him out the first year if we could.

In some cases, small amounts of cash may be set aside from each paycheck to meet anticipated fixed expenses, such as property taxes or car insurance. Sometimes, however, those little earmarked funds have a way of being spent as petty cash.

When the tax bills come around, somehow there is nothing left in the tax jar.

As we have seen, a few families successfully save by a system of using excessive income tax withholding as a kind of self-imposed, forced savings plan. They regularly plan far ahead which home improvements or other expenditures will be made with the spring refund. Very few families have savings accounts in banks, but a few have checking accounts and use these mainly for accumulating and withdrawing small savings, rather than for regular bill-paying. Many families have bills on account with the merchants or loan agen-cies of the city, usually for such things as tires and car parts, heating fuel, and medical services. Some feel it is important to have such accounts and to keep them paid up to maintain a good credit rating for future borrowing.

Conclusion

Money problems are constant in most of the families and periodic in the others. Conversations frequently turn to the money problem.

> Right now we're kind of stuck for money. We're just making it by. Like, we just keep up with the bills. I just got a new drum of kerosene and paid the phone bill, and our money's about all out. So I couldn't get the one more roll of insulation we need to finish off the bedroom. So, we'll have to wait till next week before we do any more work on that room. *If* there's any money next week.

The stress and worry about getting by is ever-present, but is heightened at certain times. Early winter is often a particularly bad time because of all the expenses of warm jackets and boots for the children, high fuel bills, perhaps a new battery for the car so it will start in cold weather, and the big expense of Christmas presents for the immediate family. All of this comes at a time when some employed men (in construction, especially) face a layoff period or a cut-back in work. As cold weather approaches, women become noticeably more concerned over the insufficient money for meeting family expenses. Marital strains, which seem to be especially prevalent at this time of year reflect the financial squeeze. Occasionally, the strain is sufficiently overwhelming that a man simply can't continue, and will go off on a drunk or in some other way lose his job, throwing the family into even more severe straits, and perhaps forcing them to revert to welfare assistance for a period. But women also feel this seasonal pinch deeply, since the items that must be acquired are within the realm of purchases normally made by women.

> I'm not sure how we're going to get through the next few weeks. We haven't got much food, and the fuel tank is almost empty already, with winter not even begun yet. And I'll have to get things like boots for the kids soon, too.

This chapter on economics has studied where the money comes from and where it goes. In analyzing the income side of the ledger, the observed pat-terns seem clearly to contradict the notion that people are poor because they don't work and don't want to work. Again and again, the commitment to work has been apparent: work as a way of supporting oneself and one's family; work as a way of gaining the material things one wants in life; work as basic to a man's self-esteem. This conclusion holds true not only for the twenty low-income families in the original sample, but also for the bulk of the fifty other low-income rural families who have been observed and interviewed over the years.

Likewise, the analysis of spending patterns contradicts the public's claim that the rural poor remain poor because they waste whatever money they have by spending it foolishly with no thought for tomorrow. In fact, the low-income people of this study appear quite adept at stretching the available money to make it cover as many of their needs as possible – yesterday's, today's, and tomorrow's.

6
Economics:
Patterns of Spending

Analysis of Spending Decisions

Money management on the margin of poverty involves constant maneuvering in an attempt to satisfy many competing goals with too little money. Spending behavior in this context is not random, however, but patterned and fairly predictable. The patterns arise out of the needs and goals that people are attempting to satisfy, and from their feelings about those needs and goals.

This chapter explores the social, cultural, and psychological factors that impinge on and shape economic behavior. People, whether poor or affluent, are not economic robots, spending money purely for primary subsistence needs or financial gain. Families in poverty, just like nonpoor members of American society, use their available financial resources for a variety of purposes, including the satisfaction of psychological, social, and status drives. Spending patterns, therefore, cannot be understood simply in terms of dollars and cents, but must be seen in the larger context of people's multifaceted lives.

Almost any expenditure of money involves a decision, and that decision, in turn, rests on values, goals, and perceptions held consciously or unconsciously by the decision makers. In order to uncover these social, psychological, and cultural factors, a most useful approach is to study a number of spending decisions made by different families, and to observe a series of spending decisions made by a single family over a period of time. We can record what was purchased, and what was thereby not purchasable. We can probe the decision makers for explanations of the factors that go into making a decision; we can follow up on people's reactions.

In seeking to identify the underlying values and goals, the most useful decisions to analyze are those that occur when the family has less money than usual because of a loss of income or a large, unanticipated, and unavoidable expense, or the family has more money than usual, either from intentional saving or from a windfall. Analysis of spending decisions made in these circumstances reveals priorities in terms of which needs are taken care of first, which are postponed or given up, and what extras are obtained when possible.[1]

A Specific Spending Decision

Although many families plan their finances ahead and attempt to save toward a desired acquisition or a needed improvement, savings mount slowly and are sometimes sidetracked from the originally intended purpose. Ordinary living expenses nibble away at meager savings; competing goals push in ahead; or the money is suddenly reassigned to some other desired or needed item.

To illustrate the working of these phenomena and to indicate some of the noneconomic factors influencing economic decisions, a typical example drawn from actual cases will be described in detail.

A family had decided that, at last, it would try to get a reliable water supply by having a well drilled. Under the advice of a worker from a county agency, the wife had been setting aside small amounts of money from the household budget toward this goal. Now, in Feburary, she had nearly $100, from months of extra-careful grocery shopping, neglecting her own need for a warm coat and a pair of shoes, and saving what she earned babysitting for a neighbor's child. The husband planned to add to this amount his recent overtime pay of about $100. Later, he would put in any additional overtime pay and the $200 or so he expected from an income tax refund. The financing of the additional $200-to-$300 anticipated cost of the well-drilling was uncertain, although they had talked of taking out a loan. They hoped to have the work done in the spring.

The next time the agency worker returned, she was surprised and dismayed to see, parked on the front porch, a snowmobile. The wife hastened to explain this turn of events, admitting that, in fact, they had spent most of their savings on the snowmobile. She felt guilty and defensive because the family had failed to follow through on what they and the worker had so carefully planned. Their savings were now badly depleted, and the well-drilling would have to be put off again. As the wife said later, "I felt very small, almost like a little child who had been naughty."

After this episode, discussion with the family revealed that the sequence of events was more complex than could be judged directly from the mere presence of a snowmobile on the porch instead of the thumping of a drilling rig in the back yard. In fact, the snowmobile was secondhand, having been offered to the family quite unexpectedly at a bargain price of $300 by a co-worker of the husband. The offer came at a time when the family had most of the cash available, with the difference payable in car parts. The opportunity gave them the prospect of obtaining a long-desired item that could provide enjoyment for the whole family and satisfy the children's requests and nagging to be able to participate in a recreational activity highly prized by their schoolmates and neighbors. Both parents felt that, for one of the children in particular, it would be a benefit to be able to participate in snowmobiling and snowmobile-bragging with his friends, as he was currently going through some adjustment problems in school.

At the time, the certainty of possessing a snowmobile was perceived by the couple as a far greater advantage than the somewhat unsure possibility of eventually putting in a well—after many more months of scraping and saving. Furthermore, the prospect of having to take out a loan for the balance of the cost of drilling was of some concern, since the last time they had gone into debt it had been a long, slow process to pay it off.

And so the decision was made. The entire family was excited and pleased. The husband felt particularly proud that he was able to provide this much-desired item for his children. The wife shrugged off the fact that she would have to continue hauling water from the spring out back. "I've been doin' it so long, might as well keep right on."

Financial Management with Limited Finances

To understand such a decision, and many similar decisions made in the face of limited income and definite needs for substantial improvements in living conditions, it is necessary to consider the whole context of factors surrounding and underlying economic decisions.

A family such as this one is perpetually operating on a small income, but is nonetheless faced with making a large number of spending decisions. Decisions have to be made frequently, usually as a series of separate decisions involving rather small amounts of money, each one considered in terms of the financial picture and the family situation at the particular time. Since the money available is limited, and inadequate to cover all demands on it, the family must exercise a temporary limitation of consumption in one area to permit expenditure in some other area. One woman explained it very well.

> You have to stop and figure out, and you have three alternatives. You decide you can go without some things and save up until you have enough money to get the thing you're wanting. Or you can keep living the same as usual and go in debt to get the thing. Or you can give up the idea of getting it.
>
> Going way in debt for something is bad. We've done that before, but we don't want to get in that bind again—always shelling out most of the paycheck on a lot of back debts. So, for us, we try to give up some things to save up for something else we really want. But usually we're operating so close that there's not much we *can* give up.
>
> So, sometimes we have to decide that the thing we wanted is out of the question for us now. Like, for example, I sure would like to get the materials so my

husband could add a new room onto this house during his vacation this summer. I've wanted it for a long time. But now I see that it's not going to be possible because we can't afford it. So, okay, that's that.[2]

To the extent that a family is able to make ends meet, it does so by constant financial juggling, not satisfying some needs in order to satisfy others. Certain living expenditures can be temporarily cut back more easily than others. The biggest sacrifice is usually made in the realm of housing and household equip- ment, reflecting in part male dominance in making spending decisions. While better facilities and furnishings are indeed desired—particularly by the wife, who spends much more time in the house—they are often assigned a lower priority or repeatedly postponed. The purchase and installation of a flush toilet, for example, may be put off again and again. In part this is because a toilet would hardly bring the enjoyment, pride, and prestige that would come from possessing a snowmobile. Also, installing the toilet might be useless without other major improvements, such as an indoor water supply or a sep- tic system, and these cost so much that the occasional bits of money squeezed out of regular income are only a drop in the bucket. The long period of scrimp- ing necessary to save up for them may be perceived as unrealistic.

Sacrifices of quality and quantity are also made in other spheres. The food budget in most households is flexible enough to absorb temporary reductions. When money is particularly short, a housewife may use her total supply of reserves and staples, serving meager meals of odds and ends for a few days. She knows that eventually she will have to spend extra money to replenish her basic food supplies, but in the meantime, she has released some food- budget money to take care of some other need. Even in the food budget itself, there is room for trade-offs to adjust to a reduction in available money. In a particularly tight week, a housewife will buy mainly cheap and filling foods (potatoes, bread, macaroni products, beans), omitting the extras she might like to purchase (meats, fruits, soda pop, and other family favorites). She may switch to powdered milk or Kool-Aid as a money-saver, may eliminate desserts entirely. Detergents, cleaning aids, and paper products may be postponed week after week after week. Coffee and cigarettes, however, are seldom put off if the family uses them, though the day before payday may be particularly difficult if a household is down to its last cup of coffee, its last pack of cigarettes. A housewife may also alter her techniques when money is particularly tight: one woman reported cooking all meals outdoors on a wood fire during a six-month period when there was not enough money to pay for cooking gas. Clothing expenses may be similarly minimized and put off to allow for other expenditures.

Despite the necessity of frequent, short-range decision making, people also think in terms of spending money to fulfill long-range desires—usually involving improvements in housing conditions and provisions for the children's future welfare. But it is difficult to scrimp and save for a vaguely defined future goal when other, more pressing needs are constantly arising.

Practicality and pragmatism force concentration on feasible, short-range solutions. Both men and women pride themselves on their ability to devise inexpensive substitutes. Their overall goal in managing money is to maximize the family's chance of getting through today with a modicum of happiness and a minimum of pain. What cannot be bought today can be substituted for or put on the "hope list." Thus, instead of new chairs for the living room, slipcovers become the substitute goal; but if the money earmarked for slipcovers has to go toward emergency car repairs, the wife throws away the mail advertisement for the $15.98 slipcover-set special, and sews patches on the old couch and chair.

Flexibility

The examination of a number of spending decisions reveals that the crucial factor is flexibility. Flexible spending appears to be essential for coping with poverty, an adaptation to uncontrollable fluctuations in a generally meager income. In the ordering of expenditure priorities and in the amount of money spent for any one priority, an attempt is made to maintain flexibility. The primary strategy is to keep fixed costs to a minimum, particularly fixed cash costs. When a paycheck or AFDC check arrives, fixed costs are usually paid first, since nonpayment would result in trouble with a bill collector or termination of services (heating fuel, rent, electricity, or car insurance may be cut off). The remaining money is allocated among nonfixed costs (food, clothing, recreation, home improvements). People attempt to minimize fixed costs as much as possible so they can maintain the maximum flexibility to decide how to spend their money. Flexibility is basic to the entire process of managing money on an income that is both insufficient and insecure.

Flexiblity in making spending decisions also serves important psychological needs. People seem to enjoy being in a position to decide how to spend their money. They talk about decisions before and afterward, and they show off their acquisitions with pride. The zest for making purchasing decisions and for trading or "wheeling and dealing" among relatives, neighbors, and co-workers is in clear contrast to the observed pattern of shrinking from decision-making roles in the public arena of the employment world. Spending decisions offer the individual the opportunity to prove himself or herself in a situation of relatively little risk to self-esteem and considerable chance of ego-enhancement.

Unfortunately, this same flexibility may also have the negative effect of giving credence to the public's claim that poor people have erratic spending habits and do not plan or budget. Closer observation shows, however, that while spending patterns are flexible, they are not haphazard. Over and over, spending decisions reflect a balancing of a set of needs or desires against the constraints of financial reality. Observed over time, spending decisions reveal consistencies and common themes.

Themes Underlying Spending Decisions

From the analysis of the context and nature of many spending decisions, five basic themes emerge.

Sense of Material Deprivation

One long-run legacy of a childhood of severe poverty may be a certain acquisitive orientation to material items, perhaps a heightened quest for "things." Memories of material deprivation in childhood, of having to do without, of being ridiculed in school for the lack of or shabbiness of certain possessions, are frequently mentioned by adults. These memories apparently foster a situation in which acquiring things becomes important to one's sense of security. These adults may be quicker to buy, perhaps more ready to satisfy a whim, and susceptible to commercial advertising for all sorts of products.

Ironically, this sense of deprivation seems to leave some people unsatisfied even with the things they do acquire. The much-desired item is purchased, perhaps sacrificing needed winter clothing or house repairs, or incurring a husband's or wife's anger. But once owned, the magic fades quickly, the promise of happiness remains unfulfilled—and the quest is on for something else, more, better. Thus, the feeling of material deprivation often remains unassuaged, a nagging appetite never really satiated.[3] (Certainly, this spiral of spending and disillusionment is not peculiar to the families in this sample; it appears at all economic levels in American society, and is part of the basic economic system, played upon by the hucksters of consumerland. But for people who are poor, the money spent to satisfy a craving for possessions makes a more serious inroad in the family budget.)

The material deprivation factor seems to explain a number of the observed actions and attitudes toward the acquisition of things. Some individuals—women especially—are known to be collectors or "squirrels," filling their houses with boxes of free, used clothing, stacks of magazines, dozens of used rugs, and discarded chairs—far more than could ever be utilized by their families. Husbands collect cars, car parts, television sets, appliances, and hardware, partly for the same reason—an insatiable appetite for amassing possessions. Other examples come readily to mind. A housewife may begin in early October to purchase the various parts of a Thanksgiving dinner, to be sure she will have a complete dinner, with all the trimmings, when the time comes. A mother accepts a teenage daughter's clothing splurge, even though it used up some of the welfare money intended for the daughter's baby, because she recognizes that the daughter "has to have something special now and then to feel good about herself." A child, uneasy about the family's food supply, keeps opening the refrigerator door, not to take any food, but just to make sure there is food in it.

The need to assuage deprivation feelings through acquisition may underlie many purchases. The fear of being without, the sense of material deprivation—these may haunt an individual throughout life.

For the Sake of the Children

Like their more affluent counterparts elsewhere in the community, the parents in this study clearly want their children to have more of the good things in life than they had. But there is a difference of degree. Most of the low-income parents experienced a severely impoverished childhood, and thus exhibit a particularly strong urge to provide for their children what they were not able to have. This urge becomes an almost obsessive drive in some cases, and is closely related to a syndrome of low self-esteem and transferrence of goals from self to children, as well as to the sense of material deprivation. Parents may attempt to fulfill this desire in nonmaterial ways, such as in their determination to provide a "good home life with both parents." But if couples are unable to maintain harmony under the stress of overwhelming problems, material gratification may be offered as a substitute and an expiation of parental guilt. (Again, the situation and the reaction to it are not unique phenomena of low-income people—it merely hurts more when "guilt money" is harder to come by.)

The emphasis on providing material items so that the children will not be subjected to the same feelings of deprivation that their parents experienced varies from one family to another, and from time to time. It is particularly strong in relation to Christmas and to the child's experiences in school. It clearly affects some fathers; it frequently and deeply affects many mothers. It lies behind a decision to spend a rather large sum of money to purchase a "luxury item" such as the snowmobile cited in the earlier example, or a brand new television set.

The desperate hope that one's children will find success and happiness—or at least fewer problems—in life underlies many purchases. One woman expressed it succinctly.

> Poor people often get over their heads in debt because the salesman can sucker you into buying something for the benefit of your children. The pitch he gives you is, "You don't want to let your children go without. Your children need this. Their school work would improve if they had that. They need this." The poor

person falls for this pitch every time because he wants these better things for his children.

As a result of their susceptibility to sales tactics stressing their children's well-being and future success, a few homes have complete sets of encyclopedias (although school personnel often believe that the homes these children grow up in contain no books).

Making a Good Deal

Another consideration underlying many economic decisions is the concept of "making a good deal." With financial resources severely limited and demands on them always in excess of what can be met at any one time, balancing money supply and want-satisfaction requires a constant search for ways to get something for less than normal cost. If a man is offered a good deal on an item that his family has wanted or needed for some time, he may seize the chance, even though it precludes his obtaining some other thing that was actually a higher priority. There is an apparent and expressed reluctance to pass up a good deal—a fear that if you do not take advantage of it when it comes along, you might never again have the opportunity to acquire the desired item.

Just what constitutes a "good deal" depends somewhat on the object or service in question, but low cash price is central. A good deal may be offered by a regular commercial outlet, as in the case of a close-out special on merchandise, or a generous trade-in allowance, or favorable credit terms. If an item is offered by a personal acquaintance who is respected and assumed to be honest about the value of what he sells, the likelihood of the purchase is even greater. Not only is the acquaintance's price apt to be lower than store prices, but the prospective buyer feels a sense of confidence that he will not be cheated. Since not all such private exchanges turn out satisfactorily however, a man weighs his past experiences and his trust in the seller before making the deal. He does not want to be "taken," since this not only wastes his money, but also reflects badly on his judgment. If a man has the money, if the deal looks good, and if other pressing needs can be put off without incurring too much discomfort for the family or displeasure from his wife, he will try to take advantage of the offer. The wife, for her part, will stress the "good deal" aspect as a counter theme to her own disappointment at not having been able to buy whatever item it was that *she* held in priority.

In dealing among friends and acquaintances, there is also the added factor of reciprocity. A man might accept an offered item because he knows that the seller needs cash quickly. By making the purchase, he is insuring that when he is in a similar bind, he can raise cash by selling something to the same man. Thus, a good deal among trading men provides a kind of insurance policy along with the purchased item.

A Matter of Timing

Because of the large number and frequency of separate spending decisions, timing is particularly important. For each decision, the conditions at that particular moment are crucial. People know from years of experience that, for the most part, you can only buy when the money is available. Although installment payments and credit loans are used occasionally, both for essentials and to acquire lower-priority items, the availability of ready cash is a much more important factor in a decision to purchase. It is the timing that often determines whether a purchase is made: if cash is on hand at the same time that an offer of a good deal comes along, a purchase is likely to be made.

Maintaining Optimism and Harmony in the Family

A family's perception of its own well-being is also an important theme underlying spending decisions. While a person may categorically state that happiness can't be bought with money, he or she may nonetheless use money to purchase items that will relieve personal unhappiness or family discouragement, even if the relief is only temporary. (Here again, this is not a pattern unique to low-income people.) As people save toward a high-level goal, as in the case of the well-drilling, the savings may mount up so slowly that the goal begins to seem impossibly out of reach, and discouragement sets in. At such times, with some cash savings on hand, a person is vulnerable to any offer of a good deal on almost any other item. By opting to take up the offer, a man can gain a material item that may bring some immediate pleasure to his family and some recognition to himself as a good provider and a clever dealer. He will rid himself of the burden of discouragement caused by the fact that his higher-order goal seems always out of reach. In any case, for a stress-filled family enduring a long winter in a crowded house, a snowmobile and a working television set make important contributions toward family harmony.

Thus, spending money on desired items that are not absolute essentials is a phenomenon that serves a definite positive function in its contribution to mental health. If the family were to save only toward long-range goals and spend only on "necessities," discouragement could become overwhelming. A wife is often keenly aware of her husband's sense of discouragement and failure as he struggles to satisfy family needs and wants. If he jumps at the chance to buy a used snowmobile or another cheap car, she tries to hide her disappointment, telling herself that if this makes him feel better, her new furniture can wait. Additionally, she may fear that excessive discouragement might lead her husband to drinking. And she emphatically feels that the consequences of drinking to escape discouragement are far worse than the consequences of his spending money on a frivolous but harmless item. So she puts up with, and expects to continue to have to put up with, this pattern of spending. Although such expenditures may cause marital arguments, several women have explicitly commented that it is necessary to be able to spend money occasionally on things that will keep their husbands' and their families' spirits up, to get the family over a potentially dangerous period of discouragement.

*   *   *

These five themes underlying spending decisions have been discussed in terms of a male decision maker because this is the predominant pattern. However, the same underlying themes, operate in the smaller spending decisions made by women, whether the money they spend is earned by them or by their husbands.

When women do the family grocery shopping, for example, their selections reveal their determination to restrict total food expenditure, their need to adapt to fluctuating amounts of grocery money, and their desire to provide what they consider good food. Women are attracted to weekly specials and other bargains, and tend to stock up whenever extra money is available, for timing, flexibility, and making a good deal are important to them also.

Women are also conscious—more conscious than their husbands—of the fact that spending decisions are a means of satisfying the social and psychological needs of family members. They are aware that their spending decisions can make their children happy or please or placate their husbands. Buying—or not buying—treats for the children, for example, is recognized as an important part of the relationship between parent and child, an expression of love, an expiation of guilt, a reward, a bribe, or a punishment. (Again, this pattern is certainly not peculiar to poor people.)

The importance women attach to this spending role is clearly indicated when they are denied the role. A woman whose husband does the shopping (not uncommon, especially if she doesn't drive) may feel, or even say, that her role as wife and mother is somewhat diminished by the lack of opportunity to make spending decisions. She has one less card to play in the daily game of family interaction.

In households where the woman is the sole economic decision maker, the same underlying themes are apparent—although the goods purchased may be different. For example, few women on their own would purchase a used car if they already had one usable car; and items for the children and the house may take greater precedence than they do with a male decision maker. In most cases, the so-called "female-headed household" is really a subunit of a larger household—temporary in duration and incomplete in structure—and the spending decisions usually involve smaller amounts of money. A single woman living with her parents and supporting her children from AFDC or a paycheck has little discretionary money and almost no chance of accumulating cash, no matter how she scrimps. Women heads of households may differ from male decision makers in that they may attempt to compensate for the fact that their children are growing up without a father. Typical examples of this compensatory spending include the regular purchase of candy and expensive toys as treats for children, or routinely falling for cute and stylish (but relatively useless) children's clothing.

The Net Result

General Consequences of Economic Patterns
and Underlying Themes

Over time, the patterns of spending described in this chapter have certain predictable consequences. The long-range economic picture for a family following these patterns would be one of consistently consuming all available resources on "just living" or "just getting by," without making any clear progress toward higher goals of improving the standard of living, and without gaining any real relief from the constant anxiety and strain of living at the break-even point. In fact, this is exactly the way the decade since 1969 has turned out for many of the people of this study. A few changes and some tangible improvements have indeed been made, such as additions to and modernization of houses and trailers. But the struggle to get by has consumed nearly all of the available financial resources, and has left most people still at the break-even point.

It is precisely this lack of observable "improvement" that is so readily condemned by the larger community. Outsiders ask why the rural families are unable to improve the appearance of their homes, to raise their living standards. Why are they unable to get out of poverty? The answers to such questions are usually shaped by general stereotypes about poverty and the poor.

> Those people either do not know how to live or do not care how they live. They aren't smart enough to manage their money. They are unable to save up for needed improvement. They go on buying sprees, wasting their money on unnecessary and luxury items. They don't care about the future. If they want something new, they get it now—to heck with the future.
>
> No will power. No judgment. If they had to work for the things they get, they might realize the value of a dollar.
>
> They just go on living the way they do without a thought to their future. They'll never amount to anything because they have no aspirations.

Over and over again, the outside community finds its general stereotypes about poor people confirmed in superficial glimpses of the material standards of living in the run-down rural areas. But the larger community is jumping to conclusions, leaping from the visible results of successive economic decisions to imputed moral and mental characteristics, concluding that these people are poor because they are inadequate, both as earners and as spenders of money.

The analysis of the patterned economic behaviors presented in these chapters does not support such allegations. A study of the patterns and underlying themes of people's economic behavior provides new answers to challenge the familiar stereotypes and character defamation. This method can be applied to understand a variety of observed actions that might otherwise be interpreted incorrectly through the condemning lens of stereotypes. The next few pages will examine two common aspects of the rural poverty scene—substandard housing and junk cars—by utilizing the same approach of looking at the total context of factors lying behind particular actions.

Substandard Housing

During the research, special attention was paid to housing, not so much in terms of the condition of the dwellings, but as a way of exploring the needs, problems, desires, and values of the residents. In probing for and recording people's comments about their housing situation and their decisions concerning housing, much was learned about the nature of spending decisions with regard to housing. (For this substudy, the sample population was expanded—lengthy interviews were conducted with a dozen other families not included in the main part of the research and informal discussions with other families living in substandard housing in various rural locations nearby.) The results of the housing study are summarized below.[4]

Those who live in rural pockets of poverty express or exhibit the following main concerns or goals with respect to their housing: (1) to provide shelter for household members, (2) to minimize the cash cost of housing, (3) to be assured of a place to live in the future, and (4) to maintain flexibility to modify living arrangements and adjust housing expenditures to meet fluctuations in family size, household needs, and availability of cash. In these dominant housing goals, we see again the importance people attach to keeping cash costs down and keeping cash expenses flexible to meet changing needs and fluctuating resources. Comfort, convenience, and appearance are of secondary importance—they might be listed as goal number five. Middle-class concerns such as the value of the dwelling and its location for enhancement of social status, or for investment potential, are rarely mentioned.

Given the perpetual shortage of money, it is not easy to meet the four basic housing goals. Over the years, people have developed a variety of strategies to enable them to do so. The most common, time-tested, cost-cutting methods of achieving these housing goals are listed below.

1. Acceptance of housing that is inexpensive because it is substandard or deteriorated or inadequate. (All twenty dwellings of the original sample would have been classified by government census as substandard; eight were significantly below standards.)
2. Acceptance of housing that is inexpensive because it is located in an undesirable, low-priced neighborhood.
3. Willingness to compromise and make trade-offs between ideal preferences and real prospects; to settle for the security of a modest place one can afford rather than the comfort—but insecurity—of a more costly place.
4. Upgrading housing by piecemeal patch-up, repair, and expansion whenever time, materials, money, and optimism are available. (No house is regarded as finished; it is always in a state of being repaired, improved, expanded, or changed.)
5. Attempting to own rather than rent, to gain the security of occupancy and to avoid a fixed monthly outlay for rent. (All four of the renting families in the 1969 sample viewed renting as only temporary, ownership as much preferred.)
6. Use of informal arrangements for financing housing. If one's home is borrowed, purchased, or rented from relatives or friends, payments tend to be smaller, may be paid irregularly whenever cash is available, and can often be paid in goods or services instead of cash.
7. Clustering of houses or mobile homes close together on a single lot, to avoid buying and paying taxes on extra land and to facilitate pooling of facilities. Clustered homes may share a septic system or well, may use a single electrical hookup to save installation charges, and may share appliances such as a telephone or washing machine.
8. Reliance on relatives and other neighbors in active patterns of exchanging services, trading equipment, and providing emergency or overflow living space.

By a combination of these eight strategies, rural people with limited incomes and few prospects for greater prosperity in the near future manage not only to keep a roof over their heads, but also, importantly, to provide themselves with a home in the social and psychological sense. And they do this inexpensively enough so that their limited income can be stretched to meet other family needs.

There are drawbacks to these strategies, however. For one thing, the resultant housing quality leaves its occupants shortchanged in terms of comfort, space, convenience, and sometimes health and safety. Second, the housing is vulnerable to public scrutiny. Critical passers-by and visiting personnel from community agencies and institutions see the piles of building materials in the

yard beside a ramshackle house and remark only on the poor condition of the house and the mess and squalor of the yard. The passer-by is not aware of the perpetual process of repair, upgrading, and modification to adapt to current needs. The passer-by doesn't realize that those building materials, obtained perhaps in trade last fall, are waiting to be joined by some more materials when a little cash is available and will eventually enable the husband to build the new front entryway that his wife has been wanting. The public only condemns, looking at the superficial physical evidence and concluding that the people who live there must be lazy, spendthrift, and unambitious. Once again, the actions that people with low incomes take to enable themselves to get by on what money they have are misinterpreted by the general public: cost-cutting strategies are interpreted as personal slovenliness. Closer analysis reveals that the cost-cutting strategies are essential means of dealing with the economic constraints and social needs characteristic of rural poverty.

The Junk Car Phenomenon

Many of the homes of rural poor people are flanked by junk cars strewn around the yard, a hallmark of a rural depressed area. The outside community often asks why a man would waste time and money on junk cars, why he would clutter up the landscape with old vehicles when his time and money might be spent in more profitable ways.

The first part of the explanation for this phenomenon is that rural poor people must have a way to get to town, but cannot afford to spend much money for cars. Consequently, the cars they drive may only be usable for a short time before they need repairs or give out entirely. Hence, it is helpful to have standby cars, cars that can be fixed, licensed, and put on the road as substitutes, cars that can provide a handy supply of replacement parts. By juggling cars and parts, a man can supply his family's transportation needs at a relatively low cost.

Second, as indicated earlier, the car business is a source of small amounts of cash; profits from $10 to $100 or more can be made if a man is skilled in repair work and has the time to invest in repairing and dealing. The cars in the yard are sometimes thought of and talked of as a bank account. Cars are liquid assets that can be sold or traded quite readily to raise cash or obtain goods.

Third, repairing cars provides a man with a means of using and exhibiting his skills. By avocation he may be an expert mechanic and may derive pride from his ability, although he might not want to be a professional mechanic, perhaps because he is not sufficiently sure of his competence to put himself in a situation requiring its daily validation. (Doing car repairs on his own, he can pick and choose, doing only those he feels confident to handle.) The junk car business allows him to use his skills and his time when he feels like it, not under obligation to a boss, and in a situation that involves more likelihood of success than failure. Car repairing is also a useful skill a father can teach his son, and may form a large part of their conversation and activity together. (Some women, also, are experts, but few engage in car repairing except when stranded along the road, which is a common occurrence.)

Fourth, the trading, buying, repairing, and selling of cars and parts all form an important aspect of the relationships among men in the neighborhood and on the job. It binds men together in a specialty activity, and offers them an opportunity to demonstrate competence to each other. Conversations frequently center on the merits of cars presently owned, formerly owned, or coveted, and on boasts of driving skill and special feats. Many of the men and boys obviously enjoy driving, and spend considerable time fixing up a car to run faster, noisier, more daringly. Reciprocal assistance in working on cars also forms positive ties among neighbors, and dealing in cars and parts is a major content of interaction between neighborhood men. (Interestingly, the fathers of some of these car-trading men were horse traders in their day, maintaining networks of individual acquaintances with whom they carried on an intermittent small-scale trade.)

However, the junk car business does have drawbacks. One problem is that it can consume too much of a man's nonwork time, and his wife or children may resent this as much as they resent the expenditure of money on car parts instead of other family needs. Also, a yard full of auto hulks may be dangerous, particularly for young children at play. Additionally, engines and other car parts, tools, rags, and grease sometimes take up space in the kitchen because there is no garage in which to work on repairs during winter. A wife may periodically nag her husband to haul away the cars he cannot sell, to clear his "junk" out of the kitchen, and he may eventually do so. But gradually, the yard and the kitchen fill up again, not because the man or his family likes it that way, but because this pattern of activity fulfills social and psychological needs and also provides a way to increase income and cut expenses, as well as supplying transportation.

The junk car phenomenon continues, then, because it serves a variety of needs of the residents. But the front-yard auto junkyards are offensive to passers-by and contribute to the public's stereotype of the rural poor. The visual offensiveness of the cars is interpreted by the outside community as a sign of the moral offensiveness of their owners.

Conclusions

Clinging on the Bottom Edge

On both sides of the economic ledger, the rural poor are locked into unsatisfactory positions: their employment income is low, with little prospect of increasing; their family needs consistently eat up the total income, making it unlikely that they can "save their way out of poverty." The poverty problem is entrenched and of long standing—there is an intergenerational history of limited income and self-defeating job experiences and there is a social and psychological legacy of a lifetime of economic deprivation. The resulting money management patterns and job histories lead, in turn, to a perpetuation of the money shortage. Families appear to make little observable economic or material "progress" over the years. And this lack of improvement, in turn, perpetuates the family's low social position and the neighborhood's bad reputation by confirming the stereotypes held by society at large. And so the cycle continues.

However, it is important to understand that these economic patterns exist because in some crucial ways they are positively functional and adaptive. The patterns continue even though the people understand that their economic activities and decisions have not lifted them out of poverty, but have merely enabled them to survive. Survival, in the sense of providing at least minimal food, shelter, and clothing, is obviously both necessary and a goal of the first order. Parents coming out of a period of crisis or multiple problems may be heard to say, with a sigh of relief and a touch of pride, "At least we kept food on the table and a roof over our heads." For families who have spent months or years living in old school buses, in abandoned one-room schoolhouses, in barns, and in tents, the continued provision of food and shelter is not something that can be taken for granted.

Beyond this level of bare existence, the spending patterns are positively adaptive in a second important respect: the maintenance of motivation. While the pattern of taking cash that had been saved toward a higher goal and spending it on a lower-priority item does not help in the long-run improvement of the family's economic and material position, it does have the important positive effect of providing tangible rewards in a system that otherwise seems heavily loaded with punishment. These rewards appear to be important to the preservation of mental health, often keeping a man from giving up entirely. They are also important to the preservation of a family's commitment to the broader economic and cultural system of American society. In a sense, these periodic small rewards are the mechanism by which a man who gains little from the economic system is able to continue to believe in the values of that system. The rewards serve as feedback that allows him to believe that hard, steady work is the way to achieve what he desires in life. They help reassure him that his children will be able to have a better life than he did, that hope is not foolish but both necessary and reasonable.

By these small rewards, rural poor families keep themselves within the mainstream of the American economic system, though clinging on its bottom edge. By the adaptive economic patterns described, most of the families have kept from dropping out in utter despair, severe mental illness, or paralyzing alcoholism. The economic patterns also have enabled most families to continue to subscribe to the socially accepted means for goal achievement. These points are important, for if either despair or deviance places an individual or family too far outside the dominant system, the chances of their ever rising to acceptable status in society are greatly reduced, and the chances for the children to do so are seriously jeopardized also.

By continuing to adhere to the dominant cultural values and norms, poor people remain in a position that allows them to take advantage of any opportunities that might come up as a result of improvements in the general social and economic structure. In a sense, they take a stance that allows them to "just get by" in their present situation, but does not close off any options for moving into a better position, should the system present the opportunity. In a sense, they are ready to take society up on an offer of a "good deal," should one ever come along, and if the risks of accepting it are not too great. In the meantime, each family does the best it can, balancing insufficient resources gained from hard work against never-ending demands, and trying to keep frustration and discouragement within tolerable limits. This economic balance is difficult to achieve and maintain, and society gives those who maintain it little credit for doing so. One woman pleaded for recognition of the effort.

> If people would only recognize that we are trying, that we are struggling with everything we've got. If they would encourage us when we're doing something to better ourselves, instead of faulting us for the way we have to live.

What if

Day in and day out, people in the rural poverty areas operate at or below the break-even point. Only once in a rare while do they get a small windfall to spend—a retroactive disability claim or an accident settlement—and this often goes to pay off back debts, to buy a slightly better car, or for clothes and household appliances long overdue.

Only in fantasy are people relieved of the ever-present constraints that limit their many economic decisions. On occasion an individual will let his imagination roam above the limitations of daily poverty living. Some people wonder aloud what they would do if they "won big" in the lottery or a commercial sweepstakes, or if that "rich uncle" left them a few thousand dollars. In most cases, though, the musings reveal the strains of a lifetime of money management on the brink. A big win would, at last, free them from the constant, crushing weight of debts, bills, and worry.[5] But the envisioned changes in material possessions and living situations are modest indeed. It is not a Cinderella dream, at least for adults, who clearly do not believe in fairy tales and who entertain no delusions of becoming princesses or princes living in palaces. A big, new house in the suburbs is not a part of the dream. If money suddenly became available, they would fix up the present house, or trade it for a slightly better one nearby. The women, particularly, say that they would go on living pretty much as they do, but with fewer discomforts and drudgeries. (One woman wished for an indoor automatic clothes washer with running hot water. She does the laundry now in an old wringer washer on the porch, with water carried from a cistern in the yard and heated on the kitchen stove, then poured into the machine outdoors.)

The limited nature of people's fantasies also reveals a fairly realistic appraisal of their lives. They realize that in their real-life situations, money is not their only problem, merely the most pressing and constant of many intertwined problems. They realize that instant money could not solve everything. But they know that it surely would help. Bogged down by worry, they muse aloud, and their words sum up well the economic picture in these rural pockets of poverty:

If we had all the money in the world, I ask myself, would we really be happy? No, I don't think so.

It's hard this way, with me not working. Every week we use up the money for just certain things. We pay one big bill, then we pay for groceries, then we just have a little left over for other things we need. But this week, I had to tell my family that we wouldn't have nothing but bread and potatoes, milk and stuff like that to eat 'cause we just don't have the money.

If we had *lots* of money? Well, I could get all the clothes the kids could wear on their backs, and I could have nice clothes too. And we could get lots of food. And we'd get a new car—newer than this one anyway. And we'd be out of debt. And we'd fix up the house.

As I say, I don't think having lots of money, being rich, would necessarily make us happy. But if we could just get $150 a week, though, we could sure use it. We could get along much better.

Marriage and the Family

Introduction

This chapter analyzes the structures and processes of marriage and family life in rural poverty enclaves. The analysis includes a description of the characteristic features and a delineation of the underlying goals and cultural values pertaining to marriage and family. The chapter seeks to identify the stresses that bear upon the family, the way these stresses affect marriages and families, and the way people absorb or deal with them. The analysis is based on long-term observations of many families, in Chestnut Valley and in other nearby rural depressed neighborhoods. Whenever quantitative profiles are used, however, they are restricted to the original twenty low-income families from the 1969 sample.

Characteristic Features

Three characteristics of family structure and process stand out. They are: the basic nuclear family model, the elasticity of the household, and the high incidence of marital disruption.

Basic Nuclear Family Model

A principal characteristic of the family structure is its conformity to the "standard" American pattern. In conceptual norms and in actuality, the standard nuclear family of a married couple and their young children clearly predominates. In 1969-70, eighteen of the twenty households contained a core married couple. In the remaining two households a single adult temporarily was living separately from a spouse.

In the twenty households, there were slightly more children (fifty) than adults (forty-five). There were children in fifteen households. (Three households had only grown, departed children; one household did not yet have children; and one household contained only an adult male.) In the fifteen households with children, the average number of children in the home was slightly over three, with a range from one to eight. The total number of children born to a family ranged up to ten; in the three-year period from 1970 to 1973, sixteen babies were born in the twenty households.

Elasticity of the Household

Although the predominant pattern is the nuclear family, the second characteristic is elasticity. Individuals, part-families, and entire nuclear families may be taken into a household temporarily. They may break away later, perhaps drift back, and then leave again, creating a shifting household structure. At any time, at least one-quarter of the families are expanded families, with some extra people in addition to the primary nuclear family. But the expansion does not create a permanent family form: families that are expanded at one time may be nuclear at other times, and vice-versa. In 1970, six of the twenty households were expanded. In 1972, there were five expanded households, but these were not all the same households. Only one expanded household remained that way for the two years; the other five had changed from expanded to simple, nuclear composition, while four previously nuclear families had expanded. Over time, then, the family structure is basically a nuclear unit, with temporary expansions to include extra people.

The most frequent form of expansion is the re-inclusion of a grown daughter with her children, if any. Three of the six expanded familes in 1969-70 were of this type, and remained this way for six months to more than two years. In some cases, more than one grown daughter with children were living in the parental home. Occasionally, expansion includes the daughter's husband or boyfriend, but this is usually a short-lived situation. Another common expansion pattern is the inclusion of a sibling, parent, or parents of a principal adult. In a few cases, a grown son and his wife and/or children become part of the parental household for a short time. Occasionally, an unrelated family or individual will be temporarily annexed.

Marital Disruption

A third characteristic of the family is the high incidence of marital disruption. Eighteen of the twenty households contained married couples in 1969-70, but two couples split up soon afterward, and all parties moved out of the neighborhood. One other marriage was in a state of informal separation (in separate domiciles in the neighborhood). In the succeeding five-year period, two more couples broke up. In addition to long-term separations and terminations, five more marriages underwent episodes of serious crisis and temporary separation during the research period.

Evidence of the long-term pattern of marital disruption is also found in those cases where a presently intact nuclear family includes children born of previous marriages. Additionally, the movement of individuals into and out of

Chestnut Valley is very often connected to or triggered by episodes of separation or divorce, or by the formation of a new union after dissolution of a prior one.

In addition to the high incidence of actual breakup, there is a much higher incidence of temporary but repeated and serious family disruption. Violent marital fighting, sudden departure of a spouse, mutual agreement to separate, and accusations or open acknowledgement of extramarital relationships are common in fact, ubiquitous in conversation, and pervasive in thought, fear, and suspicion.

Thus, whether one looks at the development of individual families over a period of time, or at situations in the total sample at one point, severe disruptions in marriage relationships appear to be frequent and characteristic. Although marriage and the nuclear family predominate as the modal type, marital breakup and altered family structure are characteristic also. What are the reasons for this paradox? What do people strive for and why? And why does the reality fall so short of the ideal?

Sentiments and Values Perpetuating Marriages

Family stability or instability is a complex phenomenon, and cannot be understood purely in terms of the statistical frequency of separations and breakups. If we merely count the number of broken and breaking-up families we get an exaggerated impression of instability, because we are using only one of several possible indices of family strength or weakness. Statistical counts of marriage dissolution neglect sentiment and values and tend to leave the erroneous or untested inference that the individuals do not place any emphasis on marital and family stability. In fact, although many of these marriages undergo serious disruption, most couples subsequently reunite, with a strong desire to smooth out the trouble and start over again. All three of the couples that broke up in 1969-70 were eventually reunited.

Many separation attempts—a husband or wife leaving the home, even going into court for initial protective or separation or custody procedures—are aborted because of the strong desire to try one more time to keep the marriage going. As one woman said, "I keep giving him one more chance, hoping that he'll straighten out." Many of the couples in the study had been married for decades, despite periods of intense stress, disruption, infidelity, and brutality that an outside observer might consider significantly damaging to one or both partners and to the children. All but a few of the disrupted marriages were subsequently reconciled. Those few couples who did finally and permanently divorce reached that point only after many attempts to repair their marriages, and the individuals soon established unions with other partners. The *longevity* of some marriages, despite serious and periodic disruptions, may be a more significant social fact here than the rate of breakup or disruption of marriages.[1]

Maintaining a stable, intact family is an ideal strongly held by both husbands and wives. While actual family life may periodically or frequently fall far short of being harmonious, the goal of an intact family is tenaciously held, and tremendous emotional effort is spent attempting to achieve it. There appear to be four chief factors that reinforce the goal of "family."

An Intact Family Is Important for Children

Many of the adults of Chestnut Valley whose lives today are most problem-ridden grew up in disrupted homes. Death of a parent, and periods spent in foster homes and institutions are common in the life histories of one or, in many cases, both parents.[2] As these adults reflect on their present difficulties and their probable causes, they invariably cite their childhood family situations.

> I really didn't have any upbringing. I just existed. And it was always a struggle. Before I was fifteen, I was out in the world alone, getting by however I could, always in trouble, constantly fighting.

> I had no family. I've always resented the fact that they didn't care enough about me to care for me.

> My husband always wanted a relationship with his children that he never had with his father.

> Both my husband and I want so badly for our kids to have the home and childhood that *we* never had.

The lack of a stable family during childhood is viewed as definitely contributory to adult life problems. Now, as parents, men and women fervently hope that their children will have a better life than they had. Providing a two-parent home is considered crucial. Parents believe that as long as a child grows up in his or her own family and, for the most part, receives love and care, periodic upheavals will not seriously harm the child. Parents assume that children are able to see beyond the short-lived fights and squabbles to the overriding fact that their parents love them and that they are doing the best they can to provide a secure home, better than the one in which they were raised.

Fear of Institutional Care for Children

Parents fear the consequences to their children if the family should break up. From their own childhood experiences, from those of friends and relatives, and from experiences with their own children, parents have a deep-seated fear of the possiblity of foster homes or institutional care for children. Divorce or separation might lead, eventually, to having the children put into such a foster-care situation, or even to having them "taken away" for good. Most parents, even those few who may appear to have a rather poor relationship with their children, are chilled by that possibility. Their fear of having the children removed, even temporarily, is partly based on negative feelings about the community and its institutions. Parents are convinced that keeping the family together at all costs is preferable to running the risk of having their children brought up by outside agencies, institutions, or individuals. They say, "no matter what it's like, the kids want to be in their own home."

Dependence of Parents on Their Children

Couples appear to perpetuate a marriage despite its stresses because, consciously or unconsciously, they are dependent upon their children. For many parents, the children are an extension of themselves, a means of self-fulfillment, and an important part of their self-image.

"Without children, there is no family," said one father.

"Where my children are, that is my home," said a mother.

"My children mean the world to me. They *are* my world."

Many women consider the role of mother to be far more important than that of wife, and generally far more satisfying and fulfilling. Some men are emotionally dependent on their children because they receive their main acceptance and admiration from their young children. In times of severe family upheaval, both parents may openly express their personal emotional need for their children. (This need is part of the explanation for the phenomenon of a mother's keeping a child home from school when the child is not ill.) Even estranged parents may recognize that they both have a right and need to continue seeing the children. A divorced woman categorized her relationship with her former husband this way: "We are no longer man and wife. But he is and always will be the father of my children, the grandfather of my grandchildren. So I can never completely cut him out of my life, no matter how much I hold against him for the way he treated me." And so it is hard to make a complete break, and the temptation to try once more postpones a decisive parting.

This dependence of the adults on the children keeps a troubled marriage going because each parent fears that in a separation he or she might be the one to lose the children, either by the simple act of the spouse's removing them, or by the processes of court action. Sometimes a husband attempts to keep a wife in line by instilling in her a fear that he could at any time have her declared an "unfit mother" and have the children taken from her. A similar threat is sometimes used by wives against husbands who do not provide support. Fear of losing the children has many times been mentioned explicitly as a reason for not leaving home. Even women who are brutally beaten believe that if they run away from home to escape domestic violence, they jeopardize their rights to the children. Thus, the ideal of preserving a two-parent home "for the sake of the children" also includes the unspoken need to preserve an intact home for the sake of the *parents.*

Dependence of Husband and Wife on Each Other

Adults also cling to a frequently disrupted and tension-filled marriage because of dependence on each other. This factor was apparent in several cases of long-term but unsatisfactory marriages and in marriages that only broke up after many years of recurrent fighting. Wives, especially, exhibit this dependence, particularly in cases where many years of married life have entailed virtual confinement to the home. In some cases, the wife has had little opportunity to operate as a responsible, independent individual in the wider world. In local phrasing, she has been kept "barefoot and pregnant." The only life she knows is keeping house, bearing and rearing children, soothing everyone's hurts. Even the meals she cooks may be prepared from food that she has not selected, because her husband is the one who drives, the one with the money, the one who gets the groceries. The decisions and interactions involving the big events and the little day-to-day activities may all be made by the husband: whether to buy that trailer or this car, whether to apply for food stamps, whether to take a child to the doctor. For a wife in this position, the contemplation of establishing a separate existence in a world she hardly knows brings tremendous fear and insecurity. This in turn makes her decide that it is better to stay put and take the inevitable blowups than to leave home and try to make it on her own. Her low self-esteem, her limited experience in the outside community, her fear of failure – all these underlie and are combined with emotional dependence on her husband, and give a woman strong reasons to remain with him. Rather than making a drastic change, she attempts to make the best of a bad situation.

In some cases, a wife stays with her husband mostly out of fear of him. On numerous occasions, an unhappy wife consciously decides against leaving home because she fully believes her husband's threats to harm her, the children, or himself if she should leave. Loaded shotguns are powerful deterrents to leaving home in the heat of marital squabbles.

Husbands, also, may keep a poor marriage going because of their dependence on their wives, a dependence more often based on emotional than practical needs. Although men seldom admit their dependence, it shows up when their women do leave them. In these situations, men exhibit a real state of emotional loss, appear helpless in coping with everyday life, and often go on a protracted alcoholic binge. A man whose wife has left him may claim that he can get along without her, and may boast that he can easily obtain sexual gratification with other women. But he may also go to great lengths to track her down and beg her to come home – which, in many cases, she does.

Mixed in with this dependence, there is usually an undeniable and strong bond of affection, and memories of better times together in the past. These, too, act to prolong even a seriously troubled marriage.

Sources of Family Stress

Despite the strong commitment to maintaining a marriage as central to a good home for the children and as emotionally important for the adults, rupture and temporary breakdown are commonplace. The reasons for marital upheaval include both long-term causes and immediate or triggering events.

The triggering event – the last straw – is usually perceived and emphasized by the individuals involved. In most cases, it is a small act by either husband or wife that is reported as having brought on the crisis. The wife may have purchased a relatively extravagant food item, or made an unauthorized purchase for the house. The husband may have refused to fetch the children from the neighbors; or perhaps he has procrastinated in repairing the heater, but is angered by his wife's oblique reference to how cold it is in the house. Sexual promiscuity – actual or imagined, recent or dredged up from years ago – is a frequent fight starter. Either husband or wife may have been seen in some questionable circumstance with someone of the opposite sex, and rumors fly quickly through the neighborhood.

These actions and events, however, are only potential triggering causes: whether or not they actually give rise to a marital fight depends on many factors in the state of the marriage and the individual's emotions. When the marriage has been fairly peaceful for a period, potential triggering events may be overlooked or ignored. However, if one or both individuals are feeling "down" emotionally, or are under the influence of alcohol, small triggering events may be particularly volatile.

Marital fights seem to go through several stages, usually starting with abusive verbal exchanges, goading, and name-calling. Accusations are exchanged concerning factual or fancied marital infidelities of the past or present, and there ensues a general berating and belittling designed to further undermine the fragile ego of the other person. Physical fighting often erupts, and may be brutal, with threats of even greater violence in the future. It is usually the wife who suffers the most physical damage, and furniture and household items are frequently broken. Children, too, may become involved, threatened but seldom physically harmed. They may take sides or merely scream at both parents from the sidelines. Often the row ends in a stormy departure by either husband or wife, and the action and tension subside.

Behind the triggering events that touch off such flare-ups lie long-run, semipermanent stresses on the family and its members. Couples apparently do not recognize or they underestimate these deeper sources of marital stress, dwelling only on the triggering events. But the underlying stresses are festering irritants, as each partner harbors a longstanding and complex list of grievances and accusations. They explain the fact that very minor events so easily erupt into major battles. At most times, a family is under pressure from several stress sources.

Chronic Economic Problems

As discussed in the previous chapters, rural poor families carry a perpetual burden of money shortage, back debts, unsatisfactory or insecure jobs, worry about where tomorrow's meals will come from, and undersatisfaction of felt needs. The financial squeeze is an ever-present source of tension in some households, and the necessity of coping with it, combined with the inevitability of worrying about it, causes an undercurrent of anxiety and tension.

The economic problem may be the triggering cause of any particular dispute, with many marital arguments arising over the expenditure of money: she spent it on a nonessential for the house; he spent it on booze; and so on. Money is also a cause of arguments between parents and children, and these, too, may trigger marital confrontations: a small child may throw a tantrum because his mother refuses to buy a treat to eat; a teenager may sulk for days because the father wouldn't allow her to buy new shoes. In such cases, the parent-child dispute may well end up as a marital fight when one parent takes the child's side in the argument. There are endless small confrontations over money, and criticisms of the way money is spent often enter into marital squabbles, even when they are irrelevant to the argument.

Even when not the cause of a particular dispute, however, the constancy of money problems causes a general tension and anxiety that erode family life. The economic situation is a seething substratum that is constantly present to fuel other problems in the household, to exacerbate interpersonal tensions, and to drain the strength of individuals.

Unresolved Emotional Problems of Adults

Various emotional problems, rooted in childhood, frequently appear as continuing sources of stress in later life. Most of the adults grew up in difficult situations, and many carry into marriage a residue of unresolved emotional conflicts. Because of factors in their early childhood – disrupted homes, deserting parents, abject poverty, foster homes, or homelessness – some adults may find difficulty later in life maintaining close interpersonal relationships. The psychological mechanisms that enabled them, as children, to weather the emotional stress of frequently disrupted family life may actually work against them when, as adults, they attempt to establish and maintain close interpersonal connections. Perhaps in childhood it was necessary for self-protection to limit close emotional ties and to withhold trust. But in adulthood, this insulating shield becomes an isolating wall. This effect was apparent in the case of the man whose childhood consisted of a series of "new mothers," each of whom subsequently left or died: he now reports difficulty in getting along well with his second wife, or any other woman, on a long-term basis.

Some marriages suffer from the fact that they began when the partners had not yet reached sufficient maturity to know what they really wanted or expected in a marriage, knowing only that they needed a refuge from personal and family problems in their parental home. But the emotional needs that give rise to an early escape from the parental home are not necessarily satisfied in the marriage. For example, a woman who married at seventeen, in part because of her need to throw off the controlling hand of her parents, finds that in marriage she is no more autonomous or free than she was in her parental home. The couple has recently been going through a difficult period of struggle for authority, with the wife eventually buckling under to her husband's will—but not without seething resentment that occasionally erupts into hostile rebellion. Likewise, a boy of sixteen has quickly found that establishing a household with his girlfriend and their baby has not magically turned him into a man, and that his problems of getting along with other people have not been solved, but have multiplied.

Built-in Tension Points

Tension may be structured into some families as a result of the family's previous history. For example, if the union is a second marriage for either or both partners, there may be problems connected with the former spouses, or with children of former unions. If the children in the family are from previous marriages or from extramarital relationships, these children may provide a built-in source of conflict between husband and wife. They may argue that "his" children or "her" children are getting inferior treatment, or special consideration, in the family. Accusations of favoritism toward one's own children and accusations of sexual advances toward stepchildren can be a continuing and bitter source of marital disharmony.

In-law problems may also cause strain. Relationships with his or her "people," particularly if they live in the same house or nearby, may provide built-in tension sources.

Presence of Extra Individuals in the Household

Stress in the marital relationship sometimes arises as a result of the characteristic flexibility and expandability of the household. Often the household expands to incorporate an elderly grandparent, disabled adult sibling, or a grown child or grandchildren. This temporary inclusion of others is seen as a fulfillment of one's obligation to help close relatives who have been unable to make their own way in life, an expression of lasting reciprocal bonds of mutual assistance. But it is viewed as neither the preferred nor the normal household situation. People openly state that such an expanded-family situation tends to cause tensions or provide fuel for existing difficulties. It drains family resources of food and money, often causes extra work, and reduces privacy.

The strains of having extra people living in the house show up particularly in the case of the re-inclusion of a grown daughter with her children, the most frequent form of expansion. The daughter may stay in the home because, without a husband, she needs the advantages of free or cheap room and board, she desires grandparental babysitting, and she seeks emotional and social support. In most cases, the daughter is in an anomalous position in the household, as role relationships, lines of authority, and division of labor are ambiguous.[3] Her father may assume a male authority role over both the daughter and her children, especially if the daughter has no man living with her. The young mother may come into conflict with her own mother with respect to the handling of and responsibility for her children. And in some cases, the lines of affect appear to be unclear, even to the children. A child in such a household may as likely go to grandmother as to mother for comfort, and in some cases may even address grandmother as "Mamma." In addition, the young mother may try to assume a disciplinary role toward her younger siblings in the household, as if they, too, were her children.

This lack of clarity in relationships between the basic family members and the annexed individuals is apt to create tensions that reverberate through the household, strains that are exacerbated by the temporary overcrowding of the home. The problem is even greater if only one member of the parental couple is parent to the daughter, while the other member is a more recent stepparent, officially or unofficially. Eventually, the strains may make the daughter move out, perhaps to a trailer or converted bus beside the house, or perhaps to join her husband or another man elsewhere. In some cases, the daughter may soon again need the refuge of a place to live and a family—and once more she will be taken into the home, with the difficulties and strains of the previous stay forgiven and forgotten. Occasionally, the length of stay may be protracted, and more than one daughter may be living at home at the same time. The strain on the central couple is usually apparent, and was described by one woman.

My husband and I need a life together, some privacy. We don't even have a chance to sit by ourselves and talk, or to sit in the living room and watch TV.

And we don't have the time we need to devote to the younger children because my grown girls and their babies are always around. It's so crowded here that my little one still has his bed in with us, and he has no place to play.

But even though parents would like their grown children to move into homes of their own, the parents continue to put up with the strain of an expanded household when necessary because, "she is our daughter, and we can't just turn her out." Marital harmony comes second.

Unsuccessful Role Fulfillment

Because of a host of factors in this multigenerational poverty situation, individual adults may be unable to perform their expected roles to the satisfaction of either themselves or their marriage partners.

The male role pattern appears to present considerable difficulty. The adult male is conceived of as head of household, sole sex partner of the wife, earner of the family's sustenance, provider for the family's secondary wants, and chief authority figure in the household, with the power to make decisions and the authority to carry them out and to use sanctions to secure compliance. In actuality, few men attain even an approximation of this ideal. Many of the male heads of households find that in the jobs they hold they cannot earn enough money to provide what the family needs and wants. And so a man's sense of his own worth may be diminished, in his own eyes and in those of family members. Many of the irritating situations of daily life—the "hungry Thursdays," the chill of the cement kitchen floor, the necessity of sharing shoes and a bed with a brother, the blurry picture on the old TV set—are somehow connected to the vague realization that the man is not successful as a provider for his wife and children. This low self-image is a clear contributor to marital problems.

For the wife, the role expectations are less impossible to achieve. In most cases she can provide her husband with sexual satisfaction and bear children. Mother and housekeeper, as well as mate, are roles she can perform with some degree of success. Whatever the margin of separation between her ideal role and her actual performance, that difference is not totally a reflection on her. For example, her performance as housekeeper may fall below role expectations held by her husband, her neighbors, or by the outside community, as well as by herself. However, the brunt of the blame for this shortcoming may not fall directly on her, but on factors beyond her control, such as inadequate facilities—lack of closets, of hot water, of a washing machine; insufficient money for cleaning supplies; and overcrowding in the house. The blame falls diffusely on her husband, on the job situation, on the fact that there are a lot of people in the household, and on the vague explanation of "that's just the way it is around here." Thus, her performance may not be questioned, her ego not threatened. Outside the home, also, a woman usually escapes the constant exposure to defeat and failure that her husband encounters. If she does take a job, it is an extra role, and she has some leeway to be unsuccessful or to quit without causing damage to her self-evaluation or to her husband's evaluation of her.

The greater attainability of women's role ideals, and the ability to direct blame for unsuccessful role performance away from the self, give rise to a frequently observed pattern in which a wife's ego strength and functioning level appear greater than those of her husband. Although many of the women encounter feelings of failure periodically, and occasionally quite strongly, on the whole the women are less perpetually and consistently assaulted by the sense of failure in fulfilling what they conceive of as their roles.

Although it might seem that this differential success in role fulfillment is a real plus for the women, the imbalance can also be seen as a contributing factor in the tension between husbands and wives. The differential possibility for fulfilling role expectations has been explicitly mentioned by several women, and is apparent in many of the instances of long-term marital strife.

Lack of Roles in the Outside Community

People lack access to secondary social roles in which they could gain a positive evaluation of themselves. This leaves both men and women highly vulnerable to ego damage if their performance in their primary roles (in employment and family) is inadequate. Since there are no other roles open that provide separate gauges of the individual's worth, too much personal evaluation depends on performance of basic husband and wife roles. A man's failure as family provider appears even more crushing than it would be if there were opportunities for him to be successful in other, outside roles. (Even success on a community baseball team or as a member of a volunteer fire department would help. But as we shall see in Chapter 10, the men of the rural depressed neighborhoods do not participate in such organizations.)

It was apparent during the course of observations that individual adults, both men and women, function better in their home and family roles when they are provided with some active nonfamily social role to fill. Success in filling even a temporary outside role apparently builds ego-strength and thus enhances performance in the primary roles. It also takes the mind off family problems. Several women, in the midst of a very demanding and stress-filled home life, have earnestly stated that they would like to be able to give some time to helping out in some worthy cause in the community, like a day-care center or a nursing home. While participation in such outside roles might not put more food on the table, the boost to the self-image produces a sense of well-being that results in smoother relationships in the home. (Some small-scale opportunities for this kind of participation were created during the process of fieldwork in Chestnut Valley, and each time it was clear that the women who participated felt a heightened sense of self-worth during and after the events, for they had given some of their own time, skills, energy, and even money for refreshments to help put on a successful activity for the children of the neighborhood.)

The interaction of primary and secondary roles is by no means a class-bound phenomenon. In the middle class, active community roles may compensate for or support weak marriages. But the people of the rural poverty enclaves do not have access to such substitute or compensatory roles—and one result is stress in marital relationships.

Discharged Aggression

Frequently, marital upheavals result from the fact that the family serves as the place where frustrations generated by experiences in the outside world are released. The many frustrations derived from experiences on the job, in the community, and at school cannot be expressed outwardly and directly, either because the source of frustration is diffuse and undefined, or because there is no avenue or mechanism for redress. Often the individual fears that direct expression of hostility against the perceived source of frustration would entail a large risk which he or she cannot afford to take. The consequences might involve losing a job, even worse treatment for the children at school, being dropped from welfare, being further looked down upon by the rest of the community. Some individuals fear that if they tried to express their disagreement directly to a boss or caseworker, their anger would boil up into furious, uncontrollable rage, making matters much worse. Instead of taking such a risk, frustrations experienced in the outside world are often held in (except when the individual is under the influence of alcohol), and are later vented in hostility toward the family. A marital blowup is much more likely when such pent-up frustrations are present. But many families appear to be accustomed to such venting, as one wife explained.

Right now my husband is doing the best he can. So we try not to get upset about his angry rages. If someone or something on the job upsets him, he takes it out at home on the family. Even the kids understand this and try to put up with his bad days. After all, its the same for the kids. If a child has a bad experience at school and he suppresses his feelings about it, he'll take them out on the family when he gets home.

This pattern of discharging aggression within the family is clearly not peculiar to the people of this study, or to people in poverty; certainly the bad-day-at-the-office syndrome is well known in the middle class. But the situation in rural poor families is more destructive of smooth family functioning because of several factors: (1) the frequency of frustration-producing experiences is higher; (2) the tolerance level for frustration may be lower, due to insecurity and low self-image; (3) the channels of redress are less accessible; (4) there are likely to be other sources of stress already at work in the family; (5) there may be a greater tendency to express anger in a violent manner rather than verbally; and (6) with the crowded conditions in the home, there may be no space or manner in which one individual can vent his pent-up frustration and anger without immediately impinging on all other members of the family. Thus, discharged aggression is a factor in marital difficulties.

In summary, these seven sources of stress, singly or in combination, press against the emotions and interpersonal relationships of a married couple and of a family. They provide a constant undercurrent of tension that erodes relationships as it erodes individuals. They provide a ready source of friction to touch off a marital row. In the face of these persistent irritants, the remarkable fact is that the marriages last as long as they do.

Processes in Marital and Family Adjustment

Despite these inescapable stresses and strains, people hold tenaciously to the ideal of marriage and an intact family life. Both young adults and older people expect that a marriage will have its stormy periods, but their hope is that their marriage can be better than that of their parents, that their marriage can withstand disruptions, can outlive the fights and separations. An analysis of the dynamics of family adjustment shows how the ideals are pursued, the hopes perpetuated, despite the strains.

Short Cycles of Fighting and Starting Over

It appears that the climactic blowups, caused by relatively trivial triggering events superimposed on deeper strains, serve to relieve a highly charged marital atmosphere. They force unvoiced problems and tensions out into the open, making each partner more aware of the depth of pent-up rage in the other. The blowups also reaffirm the commitment to the abstract ideals of marriage in terms of obligations, rights, and roles. Many of the battles concern accusations of marital infidelity and of failure to fulfill expected roles within the family. The strength of these accusations reveals to each spouse (as it also reveals to the social scientist observer) the esteem in which the marriage and family ideal is held by the individuals. The marital blowup thus serves several positive functions: it acts as a safety valve; it clears the air; and it reaffirms each partner's commitment to marriage and family life. It also sets the stage for "starting all over again," a theme that is quite common in accounts of family history.

One typical example of this pattern, a relatively common occurrence, is that of the wife who has her husband arrested and put in jail for beating her. To the bafflement of others, the wife goes down to the jail the very next morning to take her husband cigarettes and toilet articles. They appear to be on friendly terms. She refuses to press charges, and arranges to obtain his release.

The results of this episode are that the husband has had "the fear of the law put into him," and each partner has realized his or her dependence on the other. The stage is set for starting over again. A harmonious period in the marriage may ensue, perhaps with a pregnancy initiated at this time.

Thus, both the blowups and the re-formations actually serve to keep marriages going, as an ideal and as a practice. The social analyst must look at the many attempts to perpetuate a marriage, as well as at the forces that tear it apart. In this cyclic view of marital blowups and attempts to start over, it becomes clear that despite the high incidence of marital strife, a strong commitment to marriage and family life is indeed present.

The Long-run Cycle of Adjustment

In the developmental history of each family, these short cycles of breakdown and starting over are epicycles on a long-term cycle of adjustment. The long-run adjustment cycle is essentially a response to the varying degrees of stress engendered by poverty circumstances at different periods in the family's development, and there is a clear pattern, despite variations from one family to the next.

Before a marriage partnership begins, either member may be involved in premarital relationships, perhaps with a child born of the relationship. These involvements do not usually entail serious long-term commitment for the future, but may contain many of the secondary attributes of marriage. For example, the young man or woman may very easily slip into the role of unofficial son-in-law or daughter-in-law in the home of the partner's parents. In some cases this entails a very warm relationship between the young man or woman and the unofficial mother-in-law, who in some cases is clearly serving as a substitute mother, providing a relationship that may be almost as important to the young individual as the love and sex relationship with the partner.

In contrast to this tentative arrangement, a marriage relationship, whether or not it is marked by a wedding ceremony, entails a serious commitment and some feeling of intended permanence. A tentative relationship between two individuals may drift into a permanent marriage, including an official legal ceremony. In other cases, each member of the original tentative relationship finds a different partner for marriage. In either case, the new relationship is recognized as the real marriage.

A new couple starts out with high goals, with each expecting a good deal of the other. By the time the young couple has two or three babies and small children to care for, however, considerable marital strife may have developed as a result of several disappointment areas: the inability of each individual to meet his or her own expectations; the inability of each individual to live up to the expectations of the other; and disillusionment over the benefits of marriage itself. And all of these potential sources of stress are heightened and brought into action by the continuing and/or worsening struggle to make ends meet.

The years when the children are young may be dramatic, with many episodes of upheaval—although these are usually followed closely by attempts to start over, in hopes of keeping the family together "for the sake of the children."

By middle age, after twenty or more years of an often stormy marriage, and as the children are leaving home, the picture brightens. The income of the family may be higher, relative to expenses, and the irregular spending patterns of younger days may be more controlled, so that a greater portion of recurrent expenses can be met without strain. The husband and wife seem more willing to accept what they have. By this time, they perceive themselves as having learned "to make do with the things we have and live within the amount of money available." Thus, there are fewer arguments over "foolish spending," and fewer strains over inability to acquire desired goods. They also have learned to accept the faults or drawbacks of each other and "to know that the world isn't a bed of roses, and other people have had rough times also."

Several people have used analogy to describe the lifelong process of marital adjustment. One woman said that making a marriage work is a continuous balancing of both people's wishes, and she compared this to the process of making ends meet through continuous balancing of desires against dollars. The ability to strike this balance is seen as a sign of maturity, not as resignation. "We have accepted our life." Another woman summed up her observations on her own struggle and the balance she had achieved.

> When you're young, you have an idea. For instance, what kind of home you want. You keep striving towards that. But finally you come to the conclusion that you won't get there. Once you accept that, then you can accept your little shack as home. Then you try to make little improvements on it—paint, curtains, paneling. This will satisfy you, at least for the time being. It may not be the ideal home you had visioned, but it's better than what you started with. You have to compare what you have now with what you had in the beginning, not with the best you'd like to have ideally.

But this acceptance, and the peace it brings, usually comes only in mid-life, after years of marital stress, and after the crucial years of raising young children have passed.

The middle-aged period, however, may also give rise to new sources of stress that can create marital friction. Although the children have grown and left the house, they may themselves be going through the stressful phase of early adulthood, encountering problems with marital crises, babies, and financial burdens. During this period, the grown children and their problems may

become a preoccupation and a source of worry or dispute between the parental couple. Grown children may periodically return to the parental home,
with their own children in tow, coming back to the security of home after
having been beaten in their attempt to forge a life of their own in the outside
world. As a result of the parents' involvement, conflicts may arise to threaten
the newfound harmony of the parental household. Some men complain that
their wives give more time, attention—and money—to their grown-up
children than they did when the children were little, and more than they ever
did to their husbands. A few women have managed to remain aloof from the
problems and squabbles of their grown children, but most find their children's
dramas as compelling as the soap operas they watch on TV. And because
they are their own children and their own grandchildren, they feel obligated
to help in any way they can, even if it creates a strain in their marriages.

Eventually, as most of the grown children settle with their familes in independent, if nearby, residences, the older couple may again enjoy a more
stable relationship with fewer stresses and less interruption. Couples look forward to this achievement, to being by themselves, less burdened with the
problems of children and grandchildren, and free of the extra economic
demands. They anticipate this period as a reward for their years of work and
worry, and as it arrives, they may find new marital harmony.

However, this later-life situation is not usually idyllc. For one thing, the
lifetime of grinding worry, the cumulative effects of undernourishment and
limited health care, of many pregnancies in quick succession, of accidents, injuries, heavy smoking and/or heavy drinking combine to make many people
age rather rapidly. (Individuals in their mid-fifties are often peceived by outsiders as being nearly seventy.) Poor health in the later years and
deteriorative aging problems may provide yet another set of problems and
anxieties. Some people are partially incapacitated for many years. Financially,
many elderly people are worse off than ever, often subsisting on very meager
payments from Social Security (meager because the salary rate and years of
employment that determine their benefits were quite low); a pension of some
sort, such as a disability payment; or welfare if necessary. They cannot afford
to improve their houses, to modernize, or even to repair. For many, however,
there is the offsetting fact that nearby and all around them are their children
and their grandchildren, who keep them busy smoothing out problems,
soothing hurts, caring for babies, giving advice. An elderly individual whose
spouse has died may move in with his or her grown children, although others
prefer even an inadequate home of their own to dependence and chaos in
their children's homes. For a few individuals, loneliness is a painful part of old
age, but for most, the support of young family members all around keeps them
going.

This, then, is the long-range cycle of marriage and family, much simplified
and generalized, but characteristic.

Conclusions

Despite the eroding effects of long-term economic, social, and emotional stress, the family is of tremendous importance in impoverished rural areas. While certain trends in contemporary society have tended to weaken the American family and usurp some of its former functions, the situation appears to be somewhat different among the rural poor. Here, the family remains the major element in the lives of individuals—if only because there are no other social roles and groupings available to them.

Due to the collapse of the local rural community and the failure of the urban community to become a social substitute, the family in these rural depressed areas has been forced to take on extra functions. Because of the social marginality, the rural multigenerationally poor families must provide for their members most of the social and psychological functions that more affluent members of the community satisfy through a variety of secondary relationships and groups. By default, the family is the only group in which poverty-stricken rural people regularly participate on a sustained basis. It is the only social unit with which individuals identify. And, for better or worse, the individual's reputation is inextricably bound to his family's. In addition, the family is a cooperating economic unit, with continuing responsibilities to offer a home, food, and services to its members, even after they have left the nest. In a striking number of cases, the family provides a temporary or semipermanent home to its elderly, its disabled, and its mentally retarded.

The bonds among family members appear to have a high positive valence and considerable permanence, an ability to survive temporary rifts. The family is a fairly self-contained center of affect, activity, and social interaction, largely because there is no other available grouping, either on the neighborhood level or the community level (as will be seen in Chapters 9 and 10). But the family's broad functions also result from traditional cultural values: people believe that the family is and should be a strong, lasting unit. Adults believe that a stable home with both parents present is important for the long-term well-being of their children. And they conceive of family as a continuing entity, with life-long bonds of reciprocity and responsibility to its members. Thus, in sentiment and values, as well as in action, the family is the most significant social grouping.

However, the smooth functioning of the family is continually being threatened and undermined by the many stresses that impinge upon it as a unit and upon its component members as individuals. Family disruption results, despite the desire for family survival. Couples repeatedly try to patch up marriages that are fraught with tension and prone to periodic breakdowns.

As the family strives to surmount the stresses and to fulfill within itself the

functions that other people have long since delegated to the secondary and institutional community, it tends to become a separated segment, somewhat
detached from other families of the neighborhood (particularly when undergoing a rough period), and socially isolated from the people and institutions of
the larger community. There is one significant function that the family does
not serve. It does not act as a link between its members and the outside
world. Parents do not make connections for their children, nor do children
forge connections for their parents. The family does not effectively launch its
members into the wider community. Instead, the family is a refuge from the
wider world.

8
Patterns of Childhood

Introduction

Children are much in evidence in Chestnut Valley, especially in good weather, as small bunches of youngsters play beside the roads that run so close to the clusters of houses. Their old bicycles lean against the houses, their homemade go-carts, their dolls, balls, and torn rubber boots lie scattered on the ground. Inside the homes, the presence and importance of children is abundantly evident in the friendliness and noisy playfulness of children crowded into a small space, and in the frequency with which the topic of children figures in the actions and conversations of adults.

The presence of children is compelling in another way also. In almost every one of the intergenerationally poor families, the children are the promise of the future, the lifetime hope of their parents. And yet, it seems almost impossible to avoid the fact that these children are likely to become the victims of the bitter cycle of economic, social, and psychological problems that has crushed the hopes of one generation after another in these rural depressed areas. To anyone who works closely with the families caught in this cycle, it is hard to avoid the awareness that, despite occasional success stories and the many, many happy moments of warmth and fun, the long-term picture can be tragic. In a decade, we watch a child emerge from an innocent newborn to a sad, defeated youngster, conscious that he just can't seem to do anything right in school; from an eager kindergartner to an eighth-grade truant; from a lovely ambitious young girl to an anxious overtired mother who worries that her own babies seem to be growing up amidst the same kinds of problems and burdens that shaped her own childhood.

This chapter will focus on themes or patterns that characterize the sample of children who were observed from 1969 through 1979. The generalizations are based on unobtrusive observations made mostly in homes, but also in schools and other public places, and on a great deal of interaction and conversation with both children and their parents, particularly mothers, in a variety of settings and during many kinds of activities. For the observation of

125

children, the sample was expanded considerably beyond the original twenty low-income families in the 1969-70 base sample, to include children from several different rural poor neighborhoods. The inclusion of children from well over fifty families provided a greater range of settings for observations and more cases to substantiate the generalizations.

Some important points must be made at the outset. First, the children of the rural pockets of poverty do not form a single, uniform type. The children of any rural poverty neighborhood vary considerably among themselves. Social, psychological, and other factors of the individuals comprising each family, as well as particular situational factors confronting the family as a whole, contribute to the uniqueness of each child's primary environment. No two homes are exactly alike, and no single home environment corresponds exactly to the generalized, synthetic picture presented here. There is neither a typical Chestnut Valley pattern of bringing up children, nor a typical Chestnut Valley child. As in any other neighborhood, as in any other socioeconomic stratum, there are warm, supportive parents and cold, neglectful, or brutal parents; there are parents who are sometimes warm and sometimes cold; there are noisy, chaotic homes and quiet, orderly ones: homes where optimism prevails and homes full of unspoken anxieties. So, also, there are all sorts of children: there are boisterous children and shy ones, tall children and small ones, very clever ones and less bright ones, leaders and followers. There is no one type of child here.

Second, children from these rural neighborhoods are basically very much like any kids in any neighborhood in the United States today: they watch the same TV programs, they memorize the same commercials and wish for the same products; they go to the same kinds of schools, wear the same clothing styles, tell the same jokes; they have the same kinds of fun, get into the same kinds of mischief; and they exhibit the same range of endearing, humorous, thoughtful, and annoying behaviors. In other words, these are not "different" children, not a subculture apart from their contemporary American generation. These children are part of the mainstream of present-day American culture, and they need not and should not be labeled as belonging to a separate category.

Having made these two points, however, it can now be said that the children from these rural depressed neighborhoods do have some *different life experiences* than those encountered by the "typical" middle-class child. They grow up in the midst of problems that are more frequent in occurrence, more severe in degree, and more insoluble in nature than those of the "average" child of the same community and region. And despite the uniqueness of each individual's home environment, most of the children growing up in poverty in rural areas are affected by more or less similar stresses. The common denominators (operating in varying intensities at different times) are: (1) the continuing poverty in which the families are trapped, (2) the constant strain of worry and insecurity that accompanies poverty anywhere in American society, and (3) the deteriorative effect on individuals and on relationships of a continuing accumulation of self-defeating experiences. As a result of these prevailing forces operating on almost all of the families studied, there are certain patterns in the way children grow up in their homes, and certain patterns in the way children respond to and are affected by their home environments and the wider world. These patterns appear to produce somewhat similar long-run consequences in adult life, including restricted life trajectories and limited futures.

This chapter will delineate and analyze ten apparently significant patterns in the home environment and home experiences of children. Although some potential effects of these patterns on children's development will be suggested, psychological interpretations are outside the scope and competence of this ethnographic study. Some facets of the child's interaction in the world beyond the home will also be suggested, although a systematic examination of the role of such important community institutions as the elementary school could not be included in this study.

In addition to observing and analyzing situations and responses, it is important also to seek out people's conceptions, hopes, and aspirations regarding their children. And to the extent that a difference exists between the hopes and the realities, we must ask how people perceive and deal with the disparity. These questions will be addressed toward the end of the chapter.

Characteristics of Home Environments

Babies and Small Children are Cherished

Strong positive attitudes toward having a baby are revealed in connection with the normal occurrences of pregnancy and birth, and women exhibit concern over anyone's difficulty in becoming pregnant or fathering a child. Miscarriages are regarded as a real misfortune, and women tend to count and remember these occurrences in their life histories. Pregnancy is regarded as a state of being, and women often reckon time in terms of their series of pregnancies: "when I was pregnant for Peter." Abortion is strongly opposed as a means of family planning or birth control. Parents do not suggest or urge that their young unmarried daughters abort a pregnancy, nor is a family likely to agree to having such a baby adopted. "That baby will be our flesh and blood. If my daughter can't raise it, I will."

When a baby is expected, the whole family is filled with excitement and anticipation. This seems to be as true for the third or the seventh baby as for the first, as true for the birth of a grandchild as for a daughter or son. The strength of this pattern is indicated by the fact that the excitement is no less when a baby is born to an unmarried teenage daughter.

When it becomes known that a teenage daughter is pregnant (and is not married) the parents may at first be angry, disappointed, or even abusive toward the daughter. But as the baby's birth approaches, the parents not only accept the fact, but may look on it as possibly a good thing. Parents say, "it will help her to grow up," or, "it will give her something to live for, something to care for."(Likewise, in the case of a son whose girlfriend has become pregnant, parents feel, or hope, that becoming a father may make the boy grow up and take responsibility.) In the family of the young parent-to-be, all attention comes to focus on the future event, on the baby itself, not on its origin. As a young mother-to-be departed with her father for the hospital delivery room, her mother called out this last bit of advice. "Now, you just remember, when the pain gets bad, what I've told you before. Just think about what you're bringing into this world! Think about the reward! Then you won't feel the pain."

Upon its arrival home from the hospital, the new baby becomes an individual member of its mother's family, accepted on its own without regard to prior circumstances. It is given all the holding, cooing, and cuddling from its grandparents, parent, and young uncles and aunts that is given to any other baby in the household. As in the case of any new baby, various family members have managed to purchase at least some brand new bedding and layette items, a large supply of diapers (increasingly, disposable diapers), and in some cases a whole wardrobe. Family members may also have assembled used bedding and other appurtenances from relatives and friends. The pattern of preparation and excitement seems no different from that surrounding the arrival of any other baby into a household.

In most homes, any little baby is truly a center of attention for all members of the household. Most fathers, as well as older siblings, appear to derive considerable happiness from interacting with babies and small children, and openly demonstrate pride in a baby's development. Affection toward babies and young children is generally expressed freely and openly, but of course the frequency and intensity vary from household to household, from time to time. With infants, physical caressing, cooing voices, baby talk, friendly teasing, and endearing nicknames are all common.

Babies have a great deal of physical contact with family members. Generally, though not in all cases, babies are held much of the time, whether awake or asleep, by the mother, any other adult, or any capable child. They are handed along from arms to arms, lap to lap. Although one reason for this pattern may be a lack of playpens and baby chairs, even mothers who have some of this equipment seem to prefer holding their babies or asking some family member to do so. Special baby chairs and other furniture are status items, it appears – part of the image a mother, particularly a new mother, has about the things her baby should have. Even the bassinettes and cribs that are handed down through a series of babies may not be used a great deal, as an infant often sleeps in the mother's bed, an older baby often naps on the couch.

For most babies, there are also times when the mother and other family members are too busy or too burdened with anxiety and problems to give the infant more than minimal attention, and it may lie unattended for long periods. And there are mothers who have very little physical contact with their babies, initiating early the practice of propping the bottle rather than holding the baby for a feeding.[1] In such cases, physical contact and warmth depend on the other people in the household. But on the whole, most mothers place a very high priority on "keeping the baby fed and dry and cuddled," and will try to do as much of it themselves as possible.

As a boy child grows "too old for hugs and kisses" (at anywhere from one to three years) affectionate roughhousing becomes a common mode of interaction between fathers and toddlers. At a somewhat later time a mother begins to substitute frequent verbal statements of "I love you," though some mothers continue frequent caressing and lap-holding of both boys and girls well into school age. The verbal and physical demonstrations of affection are spontaneous and genuine. However, with toddlers and preschoolers, as with young school-age children, these expressions of affection may be offered most frequently when the mother is feeling unable to provide any other concrete benefits to the child, when a child is troubled or is in trouble, or when the mother has no control over the source of the child's pain. Perhaps she cannot remove the real problem, but at least she can make the child feel loved in the midst of a difficult situation. (Perhaps, also, the giving of more than usual physical affection reflects the mother's own stresses and needs.)

Love of young children may often be expressed through material objects (as was discussed in Chapter 6, in connection with economic decisions). Many parents would spend their only pennies buying the child some treat, although they may at other times clamp down on the children's begging and nagging for things. Presents on birthdays, Christmas, and other holiday times are viewed as very important, and parents may invest considerable money and ingenuity for months beforehand procuring the things that will make their children feel happy and well-loved at these special times. One mother rationalized her purchase of gifts for the children even though there would be little money for groceries. "I know they're a little old for believing in Santa Claus. But we have to have a little fairyland in their lives because the world is such a terrible place."

Parents also tend to express their love for their children in the form of hopes and aspirations for their future. One young father told how eager he was for his little son, age two, to become old enough so he could read to him about history. The father, himself a high school dropout, had found the subject of history fascinating, and he hoped the boy would too. He kept his old history books from school safely wrapped in a cloth and hidden away until the child was old enough.

Parents tend to be supportive of the childhood aspirations of their youngsters, rarely deflating their boasts of one day becoming a rich person, a famous race car driver, a teacher, a politician—even president of the United States. And many parents encourage and assist their children in the early years of school, urging them on, not letting them give up too easily, express-ing their hope that the child do well in school as the first step toward a more satisfying adult life. This, too, is regarded by parents as an expression of love and caring.

As adults talk about and enact their role as parents, they consciously link their belief in the importance of parental love and attention to their own recollections of having felt unloved by parents when they were young children. They are anxious not to cause the same doubts, pain, and deprived feelings in their children.

> The kids at school used to call me names because my father was drunk and my mother didn't care what I did. So I was always scrapping. I hated school. That's why, when my son was born, even though his father left, I vowed I would do everything I could to bring him up right, give him everything I could afford, and teach him how to behave.

Most parents, even those with large families, are sensitive to each child as a an individual. Their comments and their interactions with the family show that they seek out individual traits in children when they are very young, and appear perceptive to different styles and needs as the youngsters develop.

> All my kids are different. You have to treat them differently. Each one is an in-dividual.

The high valuation that parents place on proper care of children is also in-dicated by the fact that they severely criticize any person who exhibits carelessness and lack of concern about his or her children. In fact, the most caustic criticisms that a family makes about another family often have to do with the abdication of parental roles, and neglect or conscious abuse of the children.

> Why, we treat our animals better than they treat their kids!

The few cases of child neglect or possible child abuse that were observed dur-ing the research period were a subject of real concern to relatives and neighbors, most of whom stood ready to take the affected children into their homes. For although most parents had experienced times of great difficulty over their children, they generally have, as one man put it, "a soft spot in our hearts for kids, for anyone's kids, not just our own." One woman affirmed, "These kids! There are so many problems on account of them. But I wouldn't trade a one of them!"

The Child's Primary Environment May Include Several Adults

In many families, the infant or young child has a circle of adults who make up his world of interaction: grandparents, aunts and uncles, adult sisters and brothers, and other adults who are periodically and frequently around the house. Many of these are apt to help take care of and amuse him, and so the growing child recognizes a large number of other adults as being connected with his family and with himself.

The child is thus provided with several available parent-substitutes. If his parents at some time are unwilling or unable to care for him or tend to his needs, there are other adults, with whom he is already warmly familiar who can care for him. There are other adults to turn to, other models to follow. The close relationship between children and their older generation relatives has significant effects. Young children tend to approach nonrelated adults, even strangers, quite easily, and to expect response from them. Children who grow up in close association with grandparents, uncles, and aunts carry those relationships with them through adolescence and into adult life. In their turn, these new adults become active aunts, uncles, and grandparents to the next generations of children. The importance of other adults in a child's life shows up also in the fact that kinship terms are common in the speech patterns and stories told by young children. (Not only "Grandma Black," but "my sister's husband," or "my brother-in-law," or "Suzy, my little niece," are common expressions.)

The Home is Apt to be Crowded

Crowding in the home affects many young children, in terms of available space and density of people and activities. There is little space for young children to explore, and they are not encouraged to do so, partly because of the many dangerous or potentially harmful situations, such as a very hot space heater, an unflushable toilet, an open stairway without railings. In many homes, little or no space can be set aside just for children, except perhaps the beds they share. The young child has no place to be by himself, no place to retreat from the commotion of the rest of the household, no place to store his treasures.

In some cases, the crowding results in the child's appearing to be fatigued by overexcitement and overstimulation. Although a routine or schedule for the infant or small child may be attempted, it may be difficult to maintain because of the many distruptions and comings and goings of household members and extra people attached to the household. On the other hand, the child is seldom without people to watch and interact with and learn from, people to tend to his needs. He observes his family's life in close-up and all the time.

The Sibling Bond Is Emphasized

The sibling bond appears early, is encouraged, and usually remains strong throughout childhood and into adult life. The baby, toddler, or preschooler who has older siblings has considerable interaction with them. In many families, older sister and brother often provide a lap for the baby, feed a bottle, rescue a toddler from the brink of danger, remove valued or dangerous objects from a little one's grasp. Older siblings take considerable pride in the accomplishments of the baby, and teach him new tricks to perform, "walking" a six-month-old around the room, teaching a toddler to say words and repeat phrases. Older children eagerly show off the baby's new tricks, both to each other and to visitors, and they appear anxious when a baby is ill. In later childhood, older boys and girls tend, when possible, to include young siblings in their home play activities. By the time the "baby" approaches three or four years, the pride, fascination, interest, and playfulness that his older siblings have directed at him have usually diminished somewhat, perhaps because there is now a new baby. But a legacy of close sibling relationships seems to persist, a feeling of belonging together that outweighs the petty quarrels and day-to-day squabbles of childhood.

The sibling bond is reinforced by parents. They remind a child to "share those cookies with your sister," and "be sure your little brother stays off the road" (using the sibling term more often than the given name of the child). Both fathers and mothers expect older siblings to be concerned about younger ones. Fathers, especially, remind boys to watch out for their sisters, to help them if necessary. Parental praise reinforces the children's acts of sharing and caring, so that such behavior occurs spontaneously away from home as well. A school child will save in his pocket half a party cupcake to share later with a sibling on the school bus, or with a preschool brother or sister at home. Siblings stick up for each other in squabbles at school, and may win parental praise for doing so.

Parents explicitly verbalize their support of a strong sibling bond, and in cases of family upheavals parents attempt to avoid separating siblings. After a difficult period has subsided, a parent expresses pride in the fact that, "at least we were able to keep the kids together." Although childhood squabbling occurs as frequently here as in middle-class homes, the poverty-stricken families seem to have a stronger concept of siblings as a unit, of sibling ties that survive temporary rifts. Perhaps this is due to a realization of the actual instrumental importance of sibling solidarity. There are many occasions when siblings are thrown into mutual dependence – during family crises, for ex- ample – so the bond is frequently expressed in action and thereby reinforced.

As the children participate in the outside world, siblings appear to rely on each other to a considerable extent. In school, for example, the interactions between siblings from rural poor families seem to be more frequent and more supportive than interactions between siblings from middle-class families (who sometimes pay no attention to one another). This characteristically higher level of sibling interaction seems to reflect not only continuing parental rein- forcement, but particularly the need for protection. Mutual protection of sib- lings in school apparently arises as a result of the fact that many of the children experience difficulty in initiating and sustaining relationships with other, nonrelated children. This difficulty seems to result in part from children's early perceptions (by age seven or eight in some cases) that they are being avoided or rejected by others. Additionally, the difficulty results from the fact that their parents do not foster, either verbally or in action, social ties with other children, whereas children of more affluent homes receive encouragement and facilitation in developing an active social life and making new social contacts.

The close feelings among siblings appear to last long past childhood. Even in cases where adult siblings do not get along well – and this is by no means rare – there is a feeling of regret that circumstances, in-laws, or alcohol have separated them from each other. And even in these cases, when a crisis arises help will be sought and given among siblings. The basic and longstanding bond of protection and defense continues.

Parent-Child Bonds Persist
Despite Strain and Challenge

Children in the middle years appear to remain emotionally close to their parents. Usually the closer ties appear to be with the mother, for sons as well as daughters. During this period, child-parent relationships may be fluid, changing in intensity not only as a factor of the child's age, but also as a result of the circumstances or emotional ups and downs of the parent or the family as a whole. Such disruptive events as family upheaval, fights, and occasional brutality by a parent rarely cause permanent rupture of the parent-child bond, but they do seem to cause ambivalence of the child toward the parent, unpredictable fluctuation in the intensity of the relationship, and insecurity on the part of the child.

Some children sometimes exhibit exaggerated dependence on parents, cling- ing physically and emotionally to a parent, more often the mother. Perhaps this is a semiconscious device designed to force parents to restore normal relationships with the child, or with each other. Some children attempt to remain physically close to one or both parents as much as possible. One child, for example, frequently stayed home from school "because Mommy needs me," but it seemed plausible that the child was also staying home because she needed her mother. In some cases, the pattern of sticking close to a parent arises out of the child's fear that if he lets his parents out of his sight, they might leave home, or fight, or go off on a drunk.

Parents, particularly mothers, conceptualize their relationship to a child of elementary school age in terms of providing love, comfort, guidance, encouragement, and as much of the physical needs as can be afforded. Teaching the child right and wrong and teaching a child how to take care of his own needs as much as possible are considered to be a part of the parent-to-child relationship during this stage. But the preadolescent and early adolescent ages are considered to be far more complicated, and parents seem less clear about their role during this stage. Parents feel that teenagers have many more complex needs, needs that cannot be fulfilled by the simple infant-care techniques of feeding, clothing, and cuddling.

> The older ones—we try to protect them, to soothe their hurts, and to see that they get something to eat, that they're dressed clean and decent, and to hope they keep going to school, and keep out of trouble.

As they approach their mid-teen years, the children are making a stand for independence, and parent-child relationships are in a period of redefinition. Parents express concern about a teenager's behavior, and may become angry about flagrant defiance, perhaps punishing the child with restrictions on where and when he can go. But most parents feel that there is little they can do about their teenagers, either to prevent disapproved behavior or to promote desired behavior. They resign themselves to just hoping.

Although much of the friction between teenagers and their parents appears to be quite similar to the generalized version in contemporary American life, children from the rural poverty-stricken areas drift away from home earlier than their nonpoor peers. Some of them spend considerable time out of the home—perhaps loafing, eating, and sleeping in a relative's home, or in the home of a young friend or neighbor. In a number of cases where a young teenager attaches himself or herself temporarily to another family, one is struck by the ease and speed with which the teenager develops affectionate ties with the adults in the host household, and by the ready labeling of the host adults as "Ma" and "Pa."

The weakening of the tie between parents and their adolescent children is only a transitional phase, however. The two-way interdependence of parents (especially mothers) and children (both sons and daughters) continues throughout life, with both obligations and affective content. Grown children are frequently called on for assistance, and are expected to take in a parent in need of a temporary home, and to look out for their parents in old age. (Some do and some don't fulfill these expectations.) Perhaps the strongest expression of the lasting parent-child tie, however, is the continued obligation parents feel toward their children, always standing ready to provide an emergency home-haven. Parents know that they cannot guarantee their grown child a place of respect in society, or a good, well-paid job, or a big inheritance. But the one thing they can offer with some certainty is a temporary home: "You can always come back home." For the young teenager or young adult leaving home, this assurance provides a sense of security.

Discipline Is Primarily Considered Punishment and May Be Inconsistent

Parents conceive of discipline in terms of making a child do what he is told, which is primarily achieved by preventing him from misbehavior and punishing him for disobedience.

There is no typical pattern or general agreement as to what is the best way of preventing or handling misbehavior. Many parents relate their preferred pattern of punishment and control to their own childhood experiences. Some wives think their husbands are too harsh in punishing the children, and a few intercede on behalf of the children. But one woman felt the reverse. "My husband would never punish the kids till it got real bad. He never made them mind because his father was so strict with him when he was small. But I always felt he should have controlled them more."

In some homes, spanking and slapping of small children is rare, and reprimands are verbal and mild, whereas in other homes the situation is characterized by harsh physical punishments with no explanations. In some homes there is a constant tug-of-war between the wills of parent and child. In a few cases, yelled reprimands, verbal insults, slaps, shoves, and being sent to bed constitute a high proportion of the total mother-child interaction for a child of two or three years old.

Punishment patterns also vary from time to time within the same family. At times, the child's misbehavior goes unnoticed and unpunished, while at other times the same act is met with instant, harsh, physical punishment. The main factor that seems to determine the outcome is the situation and tension level in the household at the moment. It is the parent's momentary condition, rather than the degree of "naughtiness" of the child's action, that determines the severity of punishment. In some cases, in fact, it is hard to see the correlation between the child's behavior and the parent's response.

This inconsistency is exemplified by a scene that was typical in many—but not all—homes. A youngster is sitting on his mother's lap as the mother talks and drinks coffee with a visitor. She absent-mindedly strokes the child's hair, caresses his body. Suddenly, she thrusts him down, spanks his bottom, and yells at him, "You get back in that bed, you hear? Hurry up, or I'll swat you for real." He disappears for a while, but soon reappears asking for a drink of water. She satisfies his stated need, takes him up in her lap, caresses him for a while—then remembers again that she wants him in bed. So again she abruptly sends him off, this time with a solid spank and a stronger verbal threat. The pattern is repeated again when he comes out asking to have his sock put on.

From such experiences of inconsistent parental reactions, a child may have difficulty developing a clear idea of the goodness or naughtiness of his own actions, difficulty developing a fixed set of behavioral standards, and difficulty learning responsibility for his own actions. What he may learn instead is to keep a watchful eye on other people, rather than on himself. Certainly the rapid fluctuations and unexpected turns in his parents' actions toward him give an unevenness to his experience of discipline.

Another factor that works against children learning to regulate their own behavior at an early age is the fact that there are usually several older people around to administer restraints and punishments. Most children are kept out of danger and prevented from committing forbidden acts by some older person pulling them away, gently the first time, then subsequently yelling, spanking, and threatening. Younger children are controlled by an external hand and, as they grow older, they may frequently test for reactions to see what they can get away with. A child may also come to operate on the assumption that what he can get away with is all right, and he focuses on the punishment and punishers rather than on the act itself or his own potential for self-control.

The tendency for parents to rely on behavior control that is externally imposed and primarily physical rather than verbal may be functionally important in protecting young children from the many potentially harmful situations in the physical world that surrounds them: makeshift staircases and heating systems, car parts and kerosene in the kitchen. But some children come to depend on external intervention to protect them from harm; and when the child is not closely supervised, accidents happen. Consequently, mothers of school-age children feel that it is unsafe to leave their youngsters unwatched. They assume that the natural tendency of the child, especially a boy, is to get into trouble unless an adult stops him.

These patterns of inconsistent punishment and reliance on prevention by adults may have some negative consequences in the long run. They may underlie some of the behavior-compliance problems some children encounter in school. And the patterns seem to set up or exacerbate the later struggle for authority between parent and adolescent child. As parents sense their loss of control over teenage children, they may lay down stricter rules and intensify the severity of punishments. These tightened restraints, however, are often cited by the teenager as the reason he finally left home.

Still later in life, relationships with an employer or a spouse may be negatively affected by the individual's experiences of inconsistent parental control. For example, a young woman who perceives marriage as an escape from parental authority may find her husband even more restricting and punishing then her parents. For adult men, the lack of childhood experience in exercising one's own judgment and controlling oneself may be part of the reason why they seek out jobs where the decisions are made for them, where they are told each day what to do.

Home Life Requires Adjustment to
Unpredictable Relationships

Long before the child is able to understand conversation, the crises and upheavals of family life are obvious to him. Little attempt is made to shield young children from the turmoil. Several factors appear to underlie this lack of shielding: 1) the crowded living accommodations make it virtually impossible to hide tensions and fights from the children, (2) parents tend to underestimate how much of adult conversation and action a child can comprehend, (3) some parents underestimate the emotional and psychological impact of family crises on children, (4) parents assume that it's all part of family life anyway, and (5) a parent may consciously involve a child in his or her problems as an ally or a witness. In most cases, not only are the crises within the family fully obvious to the children, but also, little attempt is made to seek them out or to soothe their feelings afterward.

Many children learn from experience that crises come and crises go, and that the best thing is to try to forget the crisis once it has passed. But children also learn that they should expect more crises in the future. Although some children give an outward appearance of nonchalance about it, some appear haunted by this expectation. As one seven-year-old said, "Things are going really good now. But I know there's somethin' gonna happen soon. There's trouble on the way." Characteristically, the children whose lives have been fraught with family rupture attempt to stick close to the scene of the action, wanting to be at home if something happens. Some children are apt to stay home from school for this reason, or to suddenly back out of plans to go somewhere, like an overnight trip with a school group. Children may take an active role in trying to shape family affairs and prevent crises. A child may attempt to prevent the parent from leaving home by making a desperate demonstration of dependence—including overt affection, "babyish" behavior, or injury or illness. Since these and other preventive measures don't always work, however, children need to develop strategies for coping with the frequency of family upheaval and other home crises.

They develop a variety of techniques to insulate themselves from the hurt of family crises. Some children learn early not to take the words, threats, and actions of other people seriously. Perhaps they are assisted in this learning by the tendency of parents and grown siblings to tease them.

Some adults, in a playful setting with a toddler, will tease, make threats, ridicule, hit, or grab away a toy. When the child cries, the toy will be re- turned, the truth told, or a kiss given, to which the child responds enthusiastically. After a moment, a new round of teasing ensues, then reassurance, and so on. Some young children appear quite frustrated and ex- hausted by this rapid alternation of ridicule and comforting, punches and kisses. Their response is to run off to bed, perhaps sucking a thumb or a bot- tle, and drop off to sleep. In some cases, these same children exhibited very few overt signs of distress over family fights and crises, as if they had learned not to take people's actions too seriously.

Some children learn to cope with the unpredictability of interpersonal rela- tionships by attempting to remain on the sidelines emotionally. They reduce their emotional attachment to parents, rejecting parental affection even when it is offered. Some children have learned to deny their own needs for interper- sonal relationships, to withhold and withdraw from expressions of affection, because close relationships would make them more vulnerable. This pattern of denial of the need for interpersonal relationships seems to parallel directly the way a few children have learned to mute their awareness of physical needs.

One little girl was obviously undernourished, but even when food was of- fered in school, she refused it saying, "I'm not hungry." In fact, the child's main associations with food had been negative: her parents constantly argued about the amount of money spent on food, and her decayed teeth pained her when she chewed. In response, she had taught herself not to recognize her own hunger. Similarly, she apparently reacted to problems at home by be- coming somewhat withdrawn emotionally, rarely expressing affection or even enthusiasm. Interestingly, when this child played with her doll, most of the interaction involved force-feeding the doll, pushing food in its mouth, and bawling it out and spanking it for not eating.

Simultaneously with this emotional detachment process, some children develop new connections with some other person, usually a relative or other neighbor, and spend a good deal of time at that person's house. Young boys may spend most of their out-of-school hours hanging around with teenage boys and young adult men, as they work on cars, hunt or fish, ride around, drink beer, or just "fool around" in the neighborhood. Young girls may try to assume a "grown-up" role early, caring responsibly for younger siblings or nieces and nephews living in the home. They may spend their days in the home of an older sister, sister-in-law, or neighbor, investing their emotions more safely in a substitute family and in television soap operas.

Since interpersonal relationships in a child's family are frequently disrupted, it is functionally adaptive that children learn strategies for predicting, tolerating, or withdrawing from social rupture. But there may also be maladaptive aspects of these strategies. The insulative device of removing or withholding emotional commitment and the self-protective device of forming an expectation that relationships will be ruptured may both have a negative impact in the long run. Both may give rise to an observed adulthood problem of difficulty in developing and maintaining close relationships. The effect of this tendency on marriages was indicated in the previous chapter; the following chapter will trace its effect in producing unstable and volatile secondary relationships in the neighborhood. It is also likely that the necessity of adapting to frequent rupture of primary relationships within the childhood family underlies the observed pattern of rapid changes in intensity of relationships between individuals. A relationship may develop quickly between two people, may become quite intense in terms of frequent interaction and hanging around together, and then may suddenly be blown apart. Because people expect breakdown to occur in relationships, they do not cultivate skills for preventing social rupture, and they make little attempt to reduce or defuse growing interpersonal tension.

In many cases, however, the instability of interpersonal relationships in the home environment seems to have much less long-range psychological effect on the individual than might be expected. One force that seems to be quite effective in offsetting potential emotional damage is the constancy and/or warmth of maternal affection, especially during the earliest childhood years. Some mothers seem both consciously and unconsciously aware of the need to provide a fairly steady base of warmth and affection for their young children.

Children Grow Up in a Dramatic, Action-filled Environment

For many children, life is experienced and perceived as a succession of exciting happenings. Events past, present, and future make up their lives. Their experience of life is that it is dramatic, urgent, and filled with all-consuming events. Even when no crisis or major event is in process, there may rarely be a quiet moment in the day, with people constantly in and out of the house and, in some cases, a great deal of riding around in the car with father or mother.

Another aspect of the action-filled environment is that there may be little time for registering feelings and assessing qualities. Introspective pursuits may be given little opportunity or encouragement, perhaps partly because both parent and child are aware that brooding over troubles may be far more painful than putting them out of mind.

Because children grow up on action and excitement, to be without them may make a child ill at ease. It could be that this action-orientation is part of the reason some children express boredom when things are going calmly, and why some find it impossible, not just dull, to sit through hours of school every day. The action-packed environment may also be a factor in the high level of activeness that is rather loosely labeled as "hyperactivity" by school person-nel, pediatricians, and even parents.

In such an action-filled life, the child's perception of time may not be in units, sequences, and routines, but in terms of separate events. In actual ex-perience, there may not be a specific time allocated to a specific activity or, if there is, the patterning or routine may go unnoticed due to the more com-manding importance of little emergencies and helter-skelter commotion. Also, parents may not apply such labels as "dinner time" and "bed time," either because there is no specific hour at which these activities take place, or sim-ply because they phrase them in terms of "you go to bed now" rather than "it is time for bed." Sequences of events may be experienced, and even perceived, but not labeled or related to clocks and calendars. For example, even young children are well aware of the difference between the day before payday and the day after payday.

A child tends to express past time not by reference to calendar years or how old he was or what grade he was in, but by pegging it to impressive events and important people in his life: "the time the baby was in the hospital," "before Mommy had her accident," "after we were burned out," and "when my sister came home with baby Billy." Children also look to a fu-ture of events, more than an unfolding process or a sequence of uniform units.

It should be noted, however, that this action-orientation in children's home environments does not reflect a goal on the part of parents, or a sought-after lifestyle. In fact, adults often express a longing for a let-up from the rapid suc-cession of events, for peace and quiet without constant interruptions and things happening. Nonetheless, the life situation is such that action-filled time is both the experience and the expectation; it becomes, also, the framework of perception.

Opportunity to Develop Self-Confidence
May Be Limited.

If there is protracted marital strife in the home, the child may develop guilt feelings, thinking that he is the cause of the trouble, or that he ought to be able to protect his parents from each other. He may feel weak and powerless because he is unable to control the thing that matters most to him—his home security. (When children talk about family fights, very often they include their own actions just prior to the fight, indicating that they see themselves as somehow instrumental in starting the fracas.)

Additionally, the child's self-esteem is inevitably affected by his growing perception of his parents' lack of self-confidence. Some parents give the unmistakable impression that they are wounded creatures who have withdrawn from the world. The children catch these impressions long before they can put them into words, but as teenagers, some talk of their early memories of their mother's total avoidance of public places, their father's defensive attitude about various problems on the job or with "the authorities." Many children sense a connection between their parents' level of self-esteem and their drinking problems. Although some adolescent children have clearly stated that they want to do everything possible to avoid becoming a man or a woman broken down by failure, like their father or mother, in many cases the events, patterns, and examples of failure that constitute their early home environments have serious unconscious effects on the children's own self-images.

The inculcation of low self-esteem in children is certainly not something that parents of the rural poverty areas desire or intend. But it may be an unavoidable legacy of the parents' own sense of failure. A parent with low self-esteem may not be able to teach his child, either by example or by words, how to succeed in the world. All a parent can say to his child may be, "Remember, you're just as good as anybody else." Such a defensive statement, however, may foster rather than prevent the transmission of low self-image.

Most home settings allow in other ways for ego-building and positive development of children's self-images. Some mothers consciously attempt to provide opportunities for a child to demonstrate his skills to others and to himself, to feel good about himself. Mothers say it is important to provide a supportive climate of praise and recognition of individual accomplishment, and to overlook shortcomings. Consequently, many children appear to be quite creative in drawing, building, and problem-solving in their home environment, utilizing initiative and inventiveness to make up for the lack of art supplies, materials, and tools purchased specifically for children's use. But the self-esteem nurtured in good periods at home is not sufficient to carry over into other times and other situations. When a child leaves the supportive environment of home and enters the larger competitive setting of the school, he may request step-by-step directions from the teacher, and may need frequent help, approval, and encouragement to go ahead in a project. Children's lack of self-confidence outside the home environment is, figuratively, written all over their shirts. (In one case, it was even *literally* written on the shirt: a boy's tee-shirt slogan demanded, "Love me for what I am!")

The Timetable of Growing Up
Reflects Socioeconomic Factors

In considering the rates at which children grow up, some differences appear between rural poverty home environments and nonpoor home environments elsewhere in the community.[2]

It appears that the period of babyhood and dependence may be prolonged in poor families. Some mothers "baby" a child as long as possible, especially a last-born child or one who remains the youngest in the family for several years. The child may be referred to as "The Baby," and may continue to drink milk from a bottle until he reaches school age. Where this occurs, it appears to be a mother's way of shielding and protecting the child from what she perceives as a very difficult world. It may also be a mother's way of holding onto the mother-of-infant role in which she felt competent.

Children in the five-to-eight-year range sometimes appear to be younger than their nonpoor age-mates. Much of the reason for this is that they have less familiarity with aspects of the community and the world known to the more affluent child, and less familiarity with the kinds of knowledge expected and rewarded by schools. For example, the child of a rural pocket of poverty knows little about the community's museums and public libraries, and has rarely traveled outside his home region—he may never have seen a big city or another state, and may form inaccurate mental pictures to go with the words in his school books. However, he probably knows a great deal more than many of his classmates about how to clean a carburetor, how to apply for food stamps, how to deal with a caseworker, a drunk father, or an accident. (A ten-year-old, though his reading ability may be judged below grade level, may be the one who has to read to his parent the instructions on an application form or a legal notice from the county court.) Unfortunately, the skills and knowledge these children possess are not measured, recognized, or rewarded in school. And so the child of the rural poverty areas may be judged to be "immature," or "backward," compared to his more affluent peers.

The middle years of childhood, in contrast to the earlier years, may be shortened and rushed. Ten-year-olds may periodically be required to serve in child-care roles for younger siblings, even as substitute parents, running the home during a family crisis. By the time they enter their teen years, children from rural depressed neighborhoods often seem to be closer to adulthood in many respects than are their nonpoor age-mates. Although emotionally they may be no more mature than their more affluent counterparts, they have already begun to take on adult rules. Some of the rural children from poverty-stricken homes have already left home by fourteen, perhaps living with a grown married sister or brother. By fifteen or sixteen, when many effectively drop out of school, most of these "children" have had considerable experience of the "real world" as they will find it throughout their adult years: inability to find a job or dissatisfaction with the job they do get; the ins and outs of Medicaid, welfare, food stamps, unemployment insurance; perhaps being in trouble with the law; being sexually active and perhaps becoming a parent; perhaps being married. Thus, by the age of eighteen, the sons and daughters of the rural poverty areas are already launched into their adult world, while their former classmates of a higher socioeconomic level are deciding which college to attend to prepare themselves for the adulthood they will enter four or more years later. Although the parents may regret that their children did not finish high school, they are proud to see them assuming adult roles at an early age.

Parents' Perceptions of Their Children

Most of the children of these poverty-stricken rural homes have, or have had, at least one parent or grandparent who cares, who cares very deeply and tries to translate the caring into action that will help send the child on his way to a satisfactory adult life. But parents often feel that their caring goes unnoticed by the rest of the world.

> Society looks down on us because of where we live and because of our past. But they should give us credit for trying. They should know I'm trying to bring our children up with manners, with honesty. I don't condone them cussing in public. They should know that I try to dress the kids to the best of my ability. I always see that they leave home clean.

Aspirations

Parents want their children to behave and do well in school, and, if possible, to finish high school. They want a son to grow up to hold a steady job, one that is not as low in wages or prestige or security as their own—but not a white-collar job. They want a daughter to have a husband who is good to her, and they want her to be a good mother. Most parents believe that the responsibility for steering children toward such goals is their own, rather than the job of schools or other community institutions. At least some of the time, parents are confident of their ability to help bring about these results.

> If you teach your children right and wrong, if you bring them up knowing how to behave themselves and how to get along with other people, if they learn to take care of themselves and mind their manners, then if they're given a chance, they'll be able to show that they're just as good as anybody else.

Parents hope fervently that their children will fare better than they have. Many of their actions, purchases, and personal sacrifices are shaped by this goal.

> I always said that if I ever had any kids, I would give them what I didn't have when I was a kid. We really gave up ourselves because of the kids. If we only had a little bit of food in the house, they got it and we went without. I've seen the time we've had two crusts of bread in the house and the two boys got it. We went without. We've gone without clothes to give clothes to our kids.

Within this generalized hope for a better future for their children, parental aspirations may be somewhat unclear or inconsistent over time, or may differ between father and mother. In several families, the mother exhibits higher aspirations for the children than does the father, probably as a result of the greater sense of role fulfillment among women compared to their husbands. A mother may cling to her hopes longer, while the father expresses a preference for what he thinks of as more realistic expectations for the child. The child may be caught in the middle.

The mother is usually the parent who is most consciously, explicitly "molding" the children, attempting to give them some guidelines on how to get along in the world, shaping their motivations and expectations. Fathers more often teach specific skills, especially to sons, and when they do attempt to instill values and precepts, it is done with reference to concrete situations, by telling children that they should behave themselves, and stating that certain misdeeds will be punished. In some homes explicit verbal teaching and implicit teaching by example are both frequently evident. However, at other times, the same parents may be preoccupied or bogged down with work and worries, or sick, or hung over. At such times, children's behavior may go uninfluenced by the parents, or perhaps may be unexpectedly punished, often quite severely.

A poignant dilemma faces some parents, who consciously puzzle over what vision of the future, what level of expectation, they should try to inculcate in their children. A mother may dream high, but she knows reality. Just as she manages her own level of expectation, she tries to set a realistic level of expectation for her children, a level that is not frustratingly high but not too low. One mother put her conclusion into words.

> If you tell a child that he can't expect anything more in life than what he's got, when he grows up he will never have anything because he can't expect any more than that. But you can bring up a child to want something better, and to work to get it. You tell him, "If you want something badly enough, you have to go halfway — or more than halfway."

Doubts

Gradually, as the children mature, parents may perceive that circumstances within the family and outside it have given rise to behavior in a child that is working against his or her eventual success. Mothers express concern, even distress, over such behavior symptoms as slow progress in school, disciplinary problems in school, signs of emotional problems, loss of parental control over the child, and minor early encounters with police and juvenile courts. The nagging worry that one's children are headed for a life of problems and poverty comes out poignantly in parents' unanswered questions.

Will what happened to me happen to my kids?

Will my kids, when they get older, live the way I'm living today? Is this a cycle?

We don't want our children to grow up to be like us. We would like our children to have a better position than we had. But will we ever see that happen?

Parents may be unable to discern clearly the causative forces that have acted upon their children to bring about this threat of repeating the parental life history. But they tend to be very alert to the signals of failure in their children. Fathers, especially, may express anger and hostility when a child brings home a "bad" report card, directing the blame outward onto the school and its personnel for not treating the child right, as well as at the child, whom he may berate for "goofing off." Some parents may threaten the child with physical punishment if he doesn't straighten up, may require him to stay in the house after school, or may instill frightening images of what happens to the person who gets into trouble at school—he will end up a drunk like Uncle Harry, or in jail like the neighbor's boy. Other parents quietly accept the reports of poor performance or trouble in school, perhaps because they half expect it, perhaps because they feel that the fault lies partly in their own performance as parents.

Underlying most parents' reactions to children's problems in school, there is usually disappointment and fear, for a negative evaluation of a child means only one thing to the parents: failure. The hopes the parents had transferred from themselves to their children are threatened. The first inescapable evidence that the children, too, may be headed for failure in life strikes at the hearts of parents. Their memories of their own frustrating, underachieving school years are stirred, and their perception of their own failure as adults is heightened.

Acceptance

As time passes, the signals of failure may continue to appear: problems in school, truancy from school, troubles with the law, violent outbursts of temper at home, difficulty in interpersonal relationships. Even those parents who initially showed the highest interest, encouragement, and optimism concerning their children's future may gradually resign themselves to the likelihood that their child isn't going to make it out of the cycle after all.

> This kid is turning out to be just like his father.
>
> I guess that child just wasn't cut out for school.

If parental hopes have been dashed by their older children's inability to succeed, they may pin their hopes on the younger children as substitutes.

> If just one of my children would turn out all right, I'd shout it from the hilltops.

But unless family circumstances have greatly changed or the school environment is very different, one child's chances may be no better than another's, regardless of difference in potential. Some parents exhibit considerable anxiety about the fate of the younger children, and become easily upset over any signs of potential failure.

> Is there any way we can prevent the younger children from growing up with all the problems that their older brothers and sisters have?
>
> All the rest of my children have had problems: look at the difficulties they're in today. That's why I'm watching my little one so carefully. If she's given a hard time in school, I'll pull her right out of there, 'cause I'm not going to have that child ruined too.

An alternative response of parents is to lower their aspirations for the subsequent children, insulating themselves against the pain of more unmet hopes. And since parents perceive that they cannot significantly change the chances for success of a child once he or she has reached the adolescent years, they gradually adjust to accepting "what is." A woman talked with resignation about her sixteen-year-old daughter, whom she had just learned was pregnant.

> At this point, I can no longer take responsiblity for her. I am her mother, and I brought her up the best way I could. I tried to teach her right from wrong, just as I did with all the others. But she never listened. Always had to do it her way. Well, now it's her own life, and she'll find it's not easy. But I can't change that for her now.

Parents learn to be glad for small things, and to stand back and let their children make their own mistakes as they move out into the world, hoping that they'll "straighten out and grow up eventually." Meanwhile, the parents gradually become absorbed in the joys and the problems of having grand-children—new lives and new hopes.

For their part, children also come to limit their own expectations for themselves, to abandon the free, high-level dreams of childhood, to realize that the question of "What are you going to be when you grow up?" can no longer be answered with imagination and limitless aspiration.

Thus, the child and the parent jockey into a mutually shared view of the child's future. A compromise is reached between, on the one hand, the parents' displaced hopes and the child's dreams and, on the other hand, the growing realization that the cumulative experiences of reality are not adding up toward achieving the dreams.

A child of eight was discussing his future with his mother. He proclaimed that he would never live here in this neighborhood when he grew up. "I don't want anybody saying things about me. I'll show them. I can be just as good as they are." But the child's developing lack of confidence that he could actually be and do what he wanted in life began to affect his expressed life expecta-tions. Inability to succeed and perform in an approval-winning manner at school appears to have been an important contributory factor in limiting his dreams.

A year after he made the above statement, the boy's image of his future had shrunk considerably. He and his family were now talking about his future in terms of building a house adjacent to his parents, where he could live when he grew up.

Another boy had always been bright and successful in school, with a flair for learning. While he was small, both his parents encouraged and applauded his pronouncements about a big future. But before the boy reached high school, dreams and realities appeared more incongruent with each other, and the in-congruence could no longer be escaped by fantasy. The father appeared not to understand the studious bent in his son, berating him for his inability and lack of interest in performing "real work" at home, like repairing cars. In his early adolescence, the boy's identification with his father came to outweigh the dream he had shared with his mother—to finish high school, to go on to college and to bigger and better things. He also realized that to climb upward meant to climb outward, away from his family. Even though he felt that he *could* achieve these goals, he became less sure that he *should*. Con-sequently, the boy's school attendance dropped off, his work slipped, he lost interest, and then dropped out of school to become an unskilled teenage laborer.

Although many parents believe that education will help their children at-tain a better life, some of them find that schooling, in fact, seems to contribute no particular benefits. When their children are young, parents are optimistic about education.

> My son [four] is in the Head Start program now, and he's doing beautifully. Right there is where he is beginning to prepare for going to college. [A father with an incomplete elementary school education]

But as children grow older, a more limited vision and a more limited educa-tional goal is accepted.

> About the highest goal any of us here want for our children in education is to have them graduate from high school. But there's a lot of kids that won't get that far. For some, their parents don't really care whether they finish. For others, it will be all the parents can do just to keep the child in school until he's sixteen, just to keep the law off their backs. Only a few parents will see any of their children graduate. [A mother who almost finished high school]

Even those children who have been successful in their early years, and who have had a great deal of help and encouragement from dedicated teachers along the way, may gradually become aware that there are other factors in-volved in climbing the ladder of success, and that the dreams of childhood may be beyond reach. The realization slowly comes that who you are, who your parents are, and where you live are important determinants of what you will become. This realization may be crippling to the individual.

Conclusions

It seems clear that, in contrast to stereotypes, most parents in these rural poverty neighborhoods do, indeed, care greatly about their children. And they consciously try to bring them up with goals that will lead to a better future for the children. However, parents often find it impossible to translate their beliefs into effective behaviors, to channel their caring into concrete ac-tions that could help bring the dreams to fruition. The outside community sees only the actions, or the lack of actions, and interprets what it sees as being a result of the "fact" that rural poor parents do not care what happens to their children.

Most of the parents, in fact, have an overwhelming concern for the children's security, welfare, and future. But in so many cases, the realities of everyday life in poverty, the stresses of social marginality, and their own sense of failure render parents ineffective or even detrimental in terms of help-ing their children achieve the dream. Some parents realize and express ver-bally the negative effect that they have had upon their children's success chances, and harbor guilt feelings about this. Some parents have been hurt so much already that, out of a need for the protection of their already wounded egos, they more or less give up their sense of responsibility and commitment, leaving the child's future to chance, to the child himself, or "to God." At this point, their goal for the child becomes an amorphous one: "that she may be happy in her life, whatever shape it takes," or "that he may eventually straighten out." As the years go by, this limited goal is usually partially achieved, but the higher goal of rising above the poverty and problem-ridden existence of the parents has to be postponed for one more generation.

The patterns of childhood experiences and parental attitudes that have been described in this chapter represent adjustments or compromises between "what we would like, ideally" and "what we know life is like in reality." The patterns of raising children are derived from and adapted to the everyday realities of the home, the neighborhood, and the wider community. But the attitudes and skills the child develops to adjust to his home situation may not be congruous with those that are needed for success in the outside society. Some of the reactive adjustment patterns may be looked down on by the surrounding community; some may be poorly matched to the demands, routines, and expectations of the dominant society. And thus, some behavioral and attitudinal patterns may have negative consequences in rendering children less able to fit into and rise within the dominant community. But, for the most part, these patterns are necessary adjustments to or inescapable consequences of the constant stresses of a life of economic poverty and social marginality.

Neighbors and the Neighborhood

Introduction

The ultimate common denominator among the families of this study is that they all live in neighborhoods of low reputation in the larger urban-suburban community. The small clusters of tightly packed houses, the bedraggled remnants of once-active hamlets, the roadside settlements of trailers—all are characterized by the larger community as undesirable neighborhoods, "bad places to live," offensive to look at, and troublesome to deal with.

One public criticism frequently heard is that the people in the rural poor neighborhoods can't seem to get along with each other. Both fact and fable are cited to "prove" that these rural depressed areas are nothing more than combat zones, arenas of violence, thievery, and disorder. Cooperation among neighbors for any project or goal is deemed almost beyond hope. As a despairing community organizer once remarked, "They won't even *speak* to each other. How can you possibly get them to *work* together?" Most outsiders conclude that rural poor people either do not know or do not care about the way neighbors "ought to behave toward one another."

There does seem to be some grain of truth underlying the stereotype of violence among neighbors, for there is indeed considerable infighting, and it is common to find next-door neighbors not speaking to each other. But the prevalence of antisocial behavior has been exaggerated far beyond reality, and the exaggeration goes unchallenged. Entirely overlooked is evidence of opposite kinds of behavior, of positive social interaction.

The aim of this chapter is to examine the characteristics of social interaction, both positive and negative, in rural depressed neighborhoods. The chapter addresses the question of social disruption within the neighborhood and explores the factors that keep people in the neighborhood despite the squabbles and low reputation. Essentially, this chapter probes a paradoxical statement made by one rural resident.

The people here in this little valley can't get along together . . . but we can't get along without each other either.

Social Characteristics of Rural Poverty Neighborhoods

The Neighborhood Is a Social Field
Rather than a Social Unit

The rural neighborhood is actually a rather loose concept. Residents rarely talk in terms of a clearly bounded geographic entity with a roster of people who belong. This is partly because the geographical and social dimensions of neighborhood may not coincide. Some geographical localities, such as the former hamlet settlements, may contain families of a higher socioeconomic level, but these "better off" people are regarded as neighbors only in the geographical sense of proximity. The few residents of higher socioeconomic status essentially live in a different world from their poor coresidents: the experiences and patterns of their lives are entirely different, and they rarely interact.[1] To be a neighbor in the interactive and ideational sense, to become involved with others as a neighbor, is as much a socioeconomic phenomenon as a geographic one. Neighbors are nearby people who share a social stigma.

Rural low-income neighbors do not function as a social unit. Neighborhoods lack the formal structure of institutions and groups. However, a neighborhood is much more than a collection of physically proximate dwellings with a bad reputation. Disheveled and depressed as it may be, the rural neighborhood is a crucial social environment, the social field on which interfamily relationships are played out. No matter how vaguely defined geographically and how lacking in group characteristics, the neighborhood is very important in the thought, conversation, and action of those who live there.

Within this social field, interaction consists of a somewhat fluid and changing collection of separate, dyadic relationships between pairs of households or between individual members of individual households. There is a good deal of visiting back and forth, but each household or individual tends to visit with only one or two other households in any given period. A man and his wife may have quite separate visiting connections within the neighborhood, often with little overlap. Whole families seldom visit each other's homes or interact together at roadsides.

Men's visiting appears to follow lines of job cohorts, drinking friends, and relatives, and is particularly connected with the repairing and trading of cars and car parts, lending of tools, and occasional help in working on a car. Cars are also a main topic of conversation, although deer hunting, fishing, and brushes with the law are also topics of interest. Men who are self-employed or unemployed may be in and out of each other's homes during the day; men employed in urban factories see each other only on weekends and summer evenings outdoors. Occasionally two or three men will spend part of the evening together watching "rassling" on television in someone's home.

Women's visiting mostly occurs during the daytime. The networks of visiting relationships show a predominant and strong pattern of a young married woman visiting her mother or mother-in-law, or vice-versa. Sisters and sisters-in-law, if they live nearby, may also visit frequently or work together at household or gardening tasks, or at putting up food for the winter. Many visits involve dropping off children for babysitting, or going to town together. Although women do not purposely get together for watching television, the TV is apt to be on during visiting, and women exchange exclamations over the heroes and tragedies of soap operas. Women also discuss recent happenings in the family or the neighborhood, gossip about neighbors, and talk of the problems and progress of children, husbands, the garden, and interaction with community agencies.

Visiting between two nonrelated neighborhood women may sometimes become quite frequent, particularly if they both have young children as a common bond and activity, no matter how large an age span separates the women themselves. But the connection between women who are not related is less stable, and is likely to fade or to be ended abruptly by some altercation between the two husbands, or by quarrels between the children of the two families. Sometimes a husband puts a stop to his wife's visiting with a particular neighbor woman because he is suspicious that the friendship will lead his wife into trouble, perhaps into relationships with other men.

Some women, at some times, appear to be social magnets. Their kitchens are filled with a succession of other women who drop in—ostensibly to borrow or return a cup of sugar, some cigarettes, or a tool—but who stay on for coffee and companionship. Small children are often brought together in this manner. At the opposite pole, some women go through long periods of neither visiting nor being visited, interacting only minimally with neighbors. This may occur because the woman has withdrawn from social interaction after some painful episode: for example, she may be recovering from the disgrace of a public alcoholic binge. Or perhaps the woman does little visiting because she is rarely in the neighborhood during the day. She may be employed in the city; she may be spending most of her time with a daughter or mother elsewhere; or she may be one of the women who has access to a car and spends a great deal of time "just roamin' around the countryside."

Children are a source of both positive interaction and estrangement within the neighborhood. For the most part, children get along well, playing together in the roads, yards, and fields. And young children particularly create a basis for mothers to interact and visit. However, older children's squabbles and mischief-making may lead to friction between parents. Conversely, parental squabbles may give rise to verbal taunts and physical fighting among children.

On the whole, the neighborhood relationships are characterized by their fluidity. They are constantly undergoing changes, both in alliances and in intensity. At any given time, each individual has a collection of interactive rela-

tionships in the neighborhood. These relationships are always in flux—forming, breaking up, shifting, and reestablishing. There are no fixed positions, no
permanent groupings. The neighborhood is a social field, defined in terms of
proximity, poverty, and stigma. It is characterized by a shifting collection of
interactions among individuals and families.

There is Both Permanence and Turnover of Residents

At first glance, a striking characteristic of such rural neighborhoods is the
continuity of residents. The same family names have dotted the landscape
generation after generation: several names on the plat maps of the 1850s are
found on the mailboxes of the 1970s. Longtime residence in the area is common and valued. (In the original Chestnut Valley survey of thirty
households, one-third of the families claimed grandparents who had lived in
the same part of the township.)

However, this continuity of family names in the rural areas obscures the
fact that there is actually considerable residential mobility, mostly within the
neighborhood or within a network of several run-down rural neighborhoods
in the same region. The Chestnut Valley sample bears out this continuity-
mobility paradox. Starting in 1969, changes were recorded for the twenty
dwellings occupied by the low-income families in the original sample. From
1969 to 1974, only eight of the twenty dwellings were continuously occupied
by the same family, and there were actually twenty instances of families moving. Of those moves, six were moves within the neighborhood, six were
moves into the neighborhood, and the remaining eight were moves away from
the neighborhood. The moves within the neighborhood were often cases in
which part of an expanded family moved to a separate dwelling. The families
who moved in from elsewhere were mostly not strangers, for in half the cases
they had grown up in the neighborhood, had lived there previously, or had
siblings currently living there.

From the point of view of the individual household, the picture is one of a
considerable number of residential moves, but within a circumscribed area, a
kind of musical chairs among the available cheap houses. Several different patterns of geographical mobility occur, primarily related to factors of age and
socioeconomic status. The highest frequency of moves occurs among young
adult couples, but the range of their moves is the most limited geographically.
Many of the grown children of the poorer families spent at least some periods
of their early adult years living in the home neighborhoods, perhaps alter-
nately living in the husband's and the wife's parental neighborhoods. Their
moves tend to be dictated by such considerations as the availability of a more
suitable dwelling, the fact of having been "burned out" or "turned out" of a
previous home, the momentary state of relationships with relatives, and the
fluctuating state of the marital relationship itself. This pattern of mobility in

younger adult years tapers off to a somewhat more stable pattern in later years, when more established households remain for longer periods in one location, particularly if they own the home. From the point of view of the neighborhood as a whole, this means that a pattern of mobility of some residents is superimposed on a pattern of residential longevity of others. The additional factor of the circumscribed geographic scope of the moves explains the continuity that overshadows mobility.

Kinship Connections Knit
Neighborhood Families Together

A striking fact about many rural depressed neighborhoods is the dense and overlapping kinship connection or, as it's commonly described, "Nearly everybody here is related to everybody else." For example, out of the twenty low-income households in the 1969 Chestnut Valley sample, fourteen contained adults with a primary kinship tie (father, mother, brother, sister, son, daughter) connecting them to another household in the neighborhood. In eight of these cases, there were two or more ties of primary kinship among households. There are also numerous secondary kinship ties connecting the families of a single neighborhood, including marriage connections, first cousins ("own cousins"), aunts and uncles, and grandparents, as well as many more distant kin connections.

The density of localized kinship ties has been characteristic for generations. In the earlier rural community (for example, Chestnut Valley of the early 1900s through the 1920s) the high degree of interrelatedness among neighboring rural families resulted from geographical and transportational isolation. Today, however, the interrelatedness is due to isolation of a different sort: socioeconomic isolation expressed in selection of marriage partners and in residential location.

The social pool from which marriage partners are drawn is definitely restricted, and bounded by the limits of the parents' residential mobility and their social connections through jobs, kinship, and friends of friends. People from the poorer rural families tend almost exclusively to marry partners from the same socioeconomic level. Although a few households in the sample contain an adult, usually the wife, from a distant county or from out of state, most marriage partners come from the same or a nearby rural poverty neighborhood.

Residential location near parents or siblings has long been a pattern. Men and women who grew up in these rural neighborhoods tended to end up settling in the immediate or adjacent area, originally because of patterns of farm use and ownership, more recently because their limited economic resources have restricted them to neighborhoods of inexpensive housing. Additionally, the emotional and social dependence of young adults on their parents and

siblings tends to make couples settle near their relatives, reinforcing the kinship ties in a neighborhood. The kinship connections also are numerous
because relatively few unconnected people move into such a rural, depressed
neighborhood, partly due to its stigma. For these reasons, a rural, poor
neighborhood is apt to be made up of at least a nucleus of people who are
related to each other, with multiple crisscrossing ties of relationship, both
blood and marriage.[2]

The fact that many relatives live within or near the neighborhood and the
emphasis people place on lifelong sibling ties and parent-child ties produce a
situation in which much of the neighborhood interaction is between people
who are closely related. Visiting, assistance, financial help, and other interactions are all more common among relatives in the neighborhood than they are
between nonrelated people in the same neighborhood.

However, kinship does not necessarily preclude interfamily friction or
hostile relationships in the neighborhood. Squabbles between related families
appear to be as acrimonious and frequent as those between nonrelated
neighborhood families.

> He and his brother just can't get along. They hardly speak to each other.
> They've had some big fights.

But the reciprocal obligations continue despite any chilled relationships.

> Even though he and his brother don't get along, when something comes up in
> the family, like one of their kids getting hurt, or someone getting married or hav-
> ing a baby, then both families will be there. But except for those family occa-
> sions, they do best to keep away from each other.

In some neighborhoods, the population consists primarily of two or three
family lines, and the families may have a history of not getting along well.
One resident explained, "This neighborhood contains mostly two families, the
A's and the B's. By nature, the A's and B's never get along—like the McCoys
and the other ones. They're always running each other down." Even where a
neighborhood consists of two family lines, however, no clan grouping or permanent alliance actually develops among the people of each family line; no
permanent opposition develops between family lines. The absence of a protracted feud appears to be due to three factors: (1) in most cases, there are
crosscutting ties of marriages between the two kinship lines, reducing the
potential for group polarization; (2) individual families move around a lot
within and between neighborhoods, so that the actors in the neighborhood
drama are frequently changed; (3) there is as much potential for strained relationships within a family line as between different family lines.

Tension and Aggression Disrupt
Neighborhood Relationships

Suspicion, hostility, and antisocial acts appear frequently on the neighborhood scene. Most of the disruptive behavior is relatively minor, and frequently related to drunkenness. Scuffles and fights predominate, mischief is common – stealing from each other, and causing minor damage to house, yard, cars, or animals. In cases of severe, continuing, or unwarranted provocation, neighbors may call in the police or sheriff, but most incidents are handled by fights, by retaliation in kind, or by breaking off the relationship.

> The troubles we have with the neighbors are mainly over dogs and children and foolishness. But there have been big things, too. We even had papers drawn up through a lawyer against one neighbor once.
>
> There was a big fight between him and his neighbor on account of something that was said about his daughter.
>
> One of these days I'm going to call the law on them. I've warned them to stay off our property and leave our animals alone. The next time we find that something of ours is missing, or if this dog suddenly disappears, I'm calling the law.

More pervasive than the actual antisocial events, however, is the suspicion of wrongdoing. If an animal dies, or a tire goes flat, or "a turkey comes up missing from the freezer," one neighbor will be quick to suspect another, and may plan retaliation before seeking firm proof. Hardly a week goes by without talk of such suspicions.

Even more pervasive is the acrimony with which neighbors talk about each other. Sharp negative criticism and name-calling are common. But the criticism does not follow a linear pecking order: any family is potentially both critic and criticized. Parents may emphatically teach their children that the family next door is not fit to associate with. Meanwhile, the next-door family may be making similar caustic remarks about "them people." A mother warns her child, "Don't you talk that way. You sound just like the next-door neighbors. If you don't watch yourself, you'll end up just like them, too. It may be all right for them, living like pigs there, but in our family it won't do."

Because of these feelings, parents may prohibit their children from playing with certain other children. Although the children usually ignore such restrictions, a child may be ambivalent toward the children he plays with because they are so often cited by his parents as belonging to a family of worthless people. And children may readily hurl verbal insults at each other, based on the derogatory remarks made by their parents. Thus, relationships among neighborhood children can rather easily be punctured by fights and periods of coolness. The hostility often erupts in away-from-home settings – on the school playground, on the school bus, or in the high school.

Adults tend to accept the neighborhood suspicions and squabbles as inevitable. But on occasion, they also express dissatisfaction with the quality of social life in a place where "the neighbors are constantly downing each other." Usually the blame is placed on certain specific people who live in the neighborhood, but sometimes neighbors look at the situation more analytically. One woman reflected, "Parents are always running down the neighbors in front of their own children. It's constant backbiting and name-calling. No wonder the kids of the neighborhood can't get along and are always fighting. Their parents are to blame for it."

A few men indicated that part of the reason for the poor relationships among families was the lack of common neighborhood activities.

> If we only had a recreation center for the kids. A place where they could go and hang around, shoot baskets and stuff. I'd help with it, and I bet some of these other people around here would too. I think something like that would do us all some good. But will we ever see it happen?

Since there are no mechanisms that bring people into regular interaction, they tend most often to express and exhibit some degree of aloofness from neighbors. Even those relationships that become fairly close tend to be fragile: they may either terminate abruptly after an altercation or imagined slight, or they may gradually cool off. There also seems to be a purposeful distancing from neighbors. Several women saw social distance as necessary to coexistence with neighbors.

> If you keep your distance, you can get along with them. The friction arises when you have them around constantly.

> When they start getting too friendly and their kids start hanging around here too much, then something's bound to happen. It's best not to let things get too palsy-walsy.

A common pattern is a situation in which relationships between two families are normally cool, with only occasional interaction.

> I do go over there occasionally, just to let them know I'm still around and not too mad at them.

> My husband won't have anything to do with those people unless he has a car or car parts he wants to sell to them, or if he wants to buy or trade something from them.

Neighbors are Bound Together by
Common Problems and Mutual Assistance

Counterbalancing the acrimony, suspicion, and occasional outright hostility, an important characteristic of the neighborhood is a cohesive bond that
unites people. Neighbors share a sense of struggle and of rejection by the
larger community, and a commitment to helping each other cope with these
problems. Several people attempted to express this bond.

> I don't know what the bond is, but it's there. Even though we don't actually get
> along well, we're the same type of people. We're all having a struggle meeting
> payments. We're all having a struggle trying to bring up our children better than
> we were. So we understand each other, and we try to protect each other.
> Maybe we care about each other and help each other because we know that
> society couldn't care less about us.

> When you're down and out, you don't have anybody. You're rejected by the
> community. But you still have the neighbors to visit with. When it comes to
> down-and-outness, there's a real bond between us. We can depend on each
> other in that way.

This perception of being the same kind of people with the same kinds of problems and a shared "down-and-outness" is extremely important as a stabilizing
factor in the neighborhood, and acts to counterbalance the tendency toward
invidious comparison and pejorative criticism.

The bond among neighbors is frequently translated into action, especially
when a neighbor is in difficulty. Internal crisis or emergency, or difficulties
with the outside world elicit intraneighborhood assistance. There is a clear
feeling of protectiveness, of solidarity vis-à-vis the greater forces in life. Even
neighbors who may not get along well will rally to help each other. And each
action of assisting a neighbor tends, in turn, to reinforce people's awareness of
the lasting bonds between them. One woman summed this up very well,
using a recent neighborhood occurrence as an example.

> If you got into some sort of a mix-up with the law, everybody will pitch in and
> put in a few dollars so that a person can get out of jail. As long as you're not in
> trouble all the time, the neighbors will pitch in and help you get out of trouble if
> they can. Suppose a neighbor gets in trouble with the law. We may not think
> that what the person did was right, but we ask, "Why him?" Why can't they
> nab somebody else who has thousands of dollars? Why pick on this man who
> is just struggling? For him it is another setback. Now, maybe I don't like the
> way the guy lives, and my first reaction might be, "I'm glad he got caught;
> he deserves it." But that's just a surface feeling. We know that each one of us

is having our own struggles, and we don't like to see somebody else take a set-back.

Being a "good neighbor" is something everyone seems to value, and there is a clear consensus on the definition: one who gives assistance when needed, but otherwise does not interfere with another family's business.

> When somebody wants something, or wants to borrow a few dollars to hold him through until payday, he goes to a neighbor.

> Whenever anything happens, they'll help.

> A good neighbor is one who keeps to his own business. But when you need him he's there and helping.

People's realization that they are all vulnerable to mishap and emergency becomes a crucial factor in regulating neighborhood relationships. No family, no matter how separated or nonsocial, can take the risk of severing all its ties to neighbors, for it is likely to need help at times, and the kind of help that is needed comes mostly from neighbors. Although relationships among families are easily ruptured, most seek to maintain at least a potential for mutual assistance from a few other families. Thus, social rifts are patched up or overlooked; reconciliation or at least an aloof truce can occur after rather heated blowups; and new relationships are nurtured to substitute for old rela-tionships severed. Recognition of mutual interdependence keeps scuffles and fights from totally blowing the neighborhood apart.

However, because there is no institutionalized social structure, there may be little continuity or consistency in the relationships among neighbors. Be-tween one instance of mutual assistance and the next, there is a hiatus in the relationship. Interaction among neighbors tends to be situational, episodic, and disparate. Neither the shared ideal of good-neighborliness nor the perceived bonds between neighbors is strong enough to prevent the divisive occurrences, the social ruptures, that so often characterize the content of neighbor-to-neighbor relationships.

Sources of Strain in Neighborhood Relationships

Chronic Problems and Daily Frustrations
Undermine Relationships

A major reason for the instability, volatility, and negative content of neighborhood relationships lies in the difficult circumstances in which most neighborhood families live. Nearly all the residents are burdened by too many problems too much of the time. Crisis is frequent, tension is high, frustration common. Many people are so constantly worn down by money problems and attendant stresses that neither energy nor time remains for tending to the maintenance of harmonious neighborhood relationships.

The frustrations encountered in the outside world are often brought home instead of being channeled directly toward their sources, and are sometimes vented on one's neighbors, in much the same way as they are unleashed on the family. As a locus for discharging aggression, the neighborhood serves a needed function. But in the process of serving this purpose, the neighborhood is undermined by hostility and suspicion. As one man said, "Your neighbors, your wife, your kids – they're like your own personal shock absorbers. When you're going through rough times, they take all the knocks and bumps. But sometimes they get kind of worn out from taking all that."

Status Competition and Regulation
Give Rise to Hostile Acts

The lack of satisfactory social participation in the wider urban-based community leaves the neighborhood as the only accessible social field in which people can hope to gain recognition. Hence, the neighborhood is, by default, the audience to which nearly every resident plays. But there are no lasting positions, no clear-cut rankings, no formal roles. Position in the neighborhood is ephemeral and requires frequent revalidation. Within the neighborhood, there is keen awareness of who has what new status marker: a newer car, a color TV, a deer carcass hanging out front on the first day of deer season, a new porch or entryway added to the trailer.

> That is the way it is here – competition with the neighbors. If one adds onto his house, then pretty soon others do. If one gets a new car, then the other ones have to. Competition, competition, competition. That's all it is here.

This status seeking within the neighborhood often brings dissatisfaction and jealousy, which may be expressed in antisocial acts, such as destroying or defacing a neighbor's new mailbox, scratching his car, uprooting a bush just planted in the yard.

Minor vandalism against neighbors is not just an expression of jealousy, however. It is also one of the chief leveling mechanisms that keeps people from rising above the rest of the neighborhood. Other means of keeping a lid on upward mobility are gossip, gloating, and raising doubts.

> People are always spreading rumors about someone else. Probably they do it because their own back yard isn't too clean, so they don't want someone else's yard to look clean either.

> If a man sees a neighbor driving a newer car than his own, he may secretly be

glad when the neighbor wrecks his car. [And accusations may be made that somebody purposely tried to run him into the ditch in that car.]

If a woman lands a fairly high-status job (above factory or janitorial level), other women may pointedly ask her how she can feel comfortable working with "all those educated people." This casual suggestion may create or increase the woman's feelings of inadequacy to the point where she actually does fail in the job. And when she does so, neighbor women are quick to let her know that it's just what she deserves "for trying to be so much better than the rest of us."

These various efforts keep the neighborhood more or less uniform in its poverty and problem-ridden existence, and thus help maintain solidarity and ensure continued mutual assistance.

Other leveling mechanisms are aimed at keeping a neighbor's status from dropping too low. Residents are keenly aware that the neighborhood's reputation is a handicap to their children's future, and they resent those whose flagrant violations of community standards give the whole neighborhood a bad name. Gossip, criticism, avoidance, and even fights are used to bring into line a person who persistently gets into trouble with the law, one whose alcoholism leads to frequent fighting and vandalism, a parent who makes no apparent effort to keep kids out of trouble.

These various leveling mechanisms all serve positive functions. They preserve the neighborhood as a reference group, a field of potential social relationships, and a source of assistance – which is important to residents because they have no other social field available to them. But the same mechanisms also have negative consequences in that they lead to frequent hostility and continuous suspicion among neighbors.

A related factor undermining neighborhood relationships is that residents know that their neighborhood is scorned by the dominant community. They may even concur somewhat in the evaluation, and feel that by associating with their neighbors, they are themselves tainted. In measuring themselves against their neighbors, they may feel that they are only measuring differing degrees of failure. But the neighborhood is the only available field of social interaction and personal recognition they have. Caught in this bind, ambivalence toward neighbors is almost built-in. This ambivalence probably underlies a lot of the blow-hot–blow-cold nature of neighborhood relationships, and explains much of the paradoxical ways in which neighbors both play to and disavow the neighborhood audience.

Dependence on Neighbors Causes
Ambivalence Toward Them

The many emergency situations that arise in poverty living, combined with the ineffectiveness of assistance from the dominant community, force people into interdependence with their neighbors. The seeking and receiving of emergency assistance tends to strengthen the bonds between neighbors, but it may also have contradictory effects. Asking for help is an admission of weakness or inability to handle one's own problems. Furthermore, it gives the neighbor inside information on personal family matters. A family prefers to solve its own problems and keep private matters to itself. When a woman must use a neighbor's telephone to call the police to report her husband's abusiveness, she is admitting to the neighbors that she can't handle the situation alone, and she is giving them personal information that they may later use against her. Yet she has little choice but to use their phone. The realization of one's full dependence on neighbors in such situations can create ambivalence and resentment. It may also create anxieties that make the individual highly sensitive to any real or fancied rebuff or slight from those upon whom she or he is dependent, thus adding to intraneighborhood strain.

Why People Stay

The rural depressed neighborhood is both a necessary refuge and a comfortable trap. Most of the residents are fully aware of the stigma that their residential location places upon them.

> My wife's relatives won't come visit us because of where we live. This place has a pretty bad reputation, and they want to stay away from it.

> The welfare lady is trying to convince us to move away from here to a better environment.

In addition to being aware of the reputation, many residents, at various times, appear to concur in the judgment. To escape this enveloping stigma, and to escape problems with some of their neighbors, some people wish they could move away. A teenager said, "This is a lousy place to grow up in, and I can't wait to get out of here." Another said, "If people ask you where you're from, you try not to be too exact, 'cause if they know you're from this place, they think right away you must be no good."

But people generally do not move away. And if they do, they move to a neighborhood of similar reputation. Why do people remain in, or gravitate to, rural depressed neighborhoods with bad reputations? This question is frequently posed by the surrounding community, and is often answered in terms of common public stereotypes that cite personal weakness and lack of ambition.

> They just like to stick together. . . . They seem to seek out their own level. . . . They have no ambition for anything better.

The question of why people remain in such neighborhoods deserves closer attention. Residents usually answer in terms of the family's specific situation and connections. But long-term observation and probing of people's thoughts and decisions about whether or not to move, as well as study of the moves that people actually make, show that there are several common, recurrent factors holding people where they are.

Rural Preference

A strong preference for living in the country is commonly expressed. People assert that they "could never live in a city," even the small regional cities, which to them are big places.

> I grew up in the country, and I wouldn't live anyplace else.
>
> It's better for kids. Healthier. They can be outdoors and learn about life. There's less of a chance for a child to get into trouble. In the city, you hear a siren and you worry which of your kids it is. Out here, you know where your kids are, who they're with, and what they're up to.

Although some parents do not feel too confident about their children's activities in the country either, belief in the superiority of a rural upbringing is maintained because people blame children's problems on other factors, not on the rural environment.

Instances of people moving to nearby small and medium-sized cities seem only to confirm the contention that country living is better. Such was the experience of at least five families whose adjustment to city living was observed. In most cases, the urban transplants expressed a real dislike for living in the city and a desire to go back to the country if they could. They complained of noise, security fears, difficulty in supervision of children, lack of yards, trees, and hills, and of the impersonality of city life. These complaints, however, should be seen in the context of the fact that most of these moves to urban areas were induced by negative factors: a split between husband and wife; being burned out of a rural home; or being turned out by a landlord and unable to find another place in the country. The unhappiness over living in the city was therefore partially due to the unhappiness over the triggering events that caused the move; and the longing for the country probably reflected a longing for happier times of the past. Nonetheless, people believe and tell their former rural neighbors that the country is a better place to live than the city. Thus, the preference for rural living is perpetuated. Even young adults who move to an urban area upon setting up an independent household would rather live in the country if they could.

Family and Locality Ties

Kinship ties and ancestral roots in the rural neighborhood are also part of the reason people stay put. Although at times relationships with relatives may produce strains to and beyond the breaking point, the sense of a kinship bond and deep roots persists.

> We've thought about moving away from here, but this is the only place we know. This is where we've lived for so long. And this is where our people are. Anywhere else we'd be strangers. Here, we are at home.

> Several times we've had the trailer hitched up to the car, ready to leave this place, get away from all these problems with my in-laws. But we don't go. We can't. They're his people, the only people he has.

> This is where my grandparents were. We've always lived here. We wouldn't want to leave because we're part of this place.

Desire for Privacy

Another perceived advantage of a rural location is its geographical isolation. The distance from bureaucratic agencies and services, although a problem from the point of view of transportation, is perceived to be an advantage from the perspective of maintaining personal privacy. The location makes families less accessible to "snooping by the authorities." The rural location provides a comfortable separation.

Privacy from one's neighbors is also thought to be an advantage of living in the rural areas. Although in fact houses may be very close together and there is much awareness of the personal family life of neighbors, people can more or less hide in their houses, and can go for long periods without directly interacting with neighbors and family by simply going off into the woods. This opportunity is valued.

Economic Advantages

Economic considerations play the biggest part in determining residential location. Land, housing, and taxes in rural depressed neighborhoods are relatively cheap. The absence of zoning and housing codes in many rural townships is also of major significance – in such unregulated areas people have the freedom they need to keep their housing costs at minimal cash levels. Unfettered by municipal restriction, they can devise all sorts of cost-cutting strategies for keeping cash costs at an affordable level (see Chapter 6). Living in school buses, trailers, or jerry-built houses – and modifying or adding to them whenever and however possible – keeps housing costs quite low.

Other economic advantages of the rural depressed areas include the availability of game and some wild food crops on the hillsides (deer, game birds, rabbit, wild leeks, cowslips, berries, and fruits); free water in natural springs and hand-dug wells; free garbage disposal out back; free firewood nearby; and space in the yard for a vegetable garden, a potato patch, or old cars.

Although transportation costs may be somewhat higher because of the distance from jobs, services, and stores, the total cash cost of living appears to be substantially lower in the rural depressed neighborhoods. For people with very little available cash, unsteady income, and slim prospects for increasing or stabilizing income in the future, these considerations are very important. Anything else is unaffordable. It is not just the low total cost of living in the rural area, but also the economic flexibility that is important. Rural families feel they are able to make adjustments to meet changes in family circumstances.

The isolated rural setting may also be conducive to independence and ingenuity. Here people can attempt to live by the traditional rural ideal of "making-do on one's own" and remaining as independent as possible from government support. Residents also recognize that mutual assistance patterns among relatives and neighbors are an economic advantage that would not be available elsewhere. One woman summed up the economic considerations this way.

> Out here we're different [from people in the city]. We live differently. We learn to make do with what we've got. But we do it on our own. We have the space; we can add on to our house; or we can use our land to plant a vegetable garden to help us get by; or we can keep cars in the yard so my husband can fix them up to sell. It's up to us what we do and how we do it, but we manage to get by.

Social Compatability

Even if money were no limitation, however, other factors restrict people's residential choices to a loose network of run-down rural areas: insecurity about dealing with unknown social situations; the perception of the larger community's stereotypes; and the absence of social connections elsewhere.

The rural poor neighborhood offers a psychological comfortableness in that people know what to expect. In any very different kind of neighborhood, whether in the city, in a suburb, or in a rural village, they fear that they would not know what to expect of other people, nor what others would expect of them. Several women have expressed fear that they would not know the cues for behavior, and they imagine they would feel frightened and insecure.

> Even if I had a chance to live somewhere else, I wouldn't do it. Even if I were given $50,000 to buy a house, I can honestly say that I wouldn't move from here. And I don't think the neighbors would either. I couldn't live in some fancy neighborhood. I wouldn't be comfortable. I'd always have to be behaving in a put-on way. It wouldn't be me. No, I'll stay here.

The preference is to stay where the ground rules are known. For people who are poor, who lack self-confidence, and who occupy a marginal position in the larger community, this seems a reasonable preference.

Avoidance of Risks

Moving to a different place is perceived as risky: the house might turn out to have even greater drawbacks; the new neighbors might be even more quarrelsome; house payments might be unmanageable. One woman analyzed the reasons she and her husband had not pursued a possible chance to move out.

> If we want to improve ourselves, we would have to move away from this neighborhood because it is a bad place to live and a bad address. But if we moved to a better house in a better neighborhood, we would be under too much pressure. We would have a hard time learning how to get along with new neighbors, whereas here we may not get along [with neighbors] but we know what to expect of each other and how to act toward each other. And we would be under the pressure of making house payments, which might be very hard for us. We would not be able to have any luxuries at all, we would lose our serenity. So, even though we do want to better ourselves, we have come to a decision that it would be better for us to stay where we are and try to fix up this house and to do the best we can living here.

This reluctance to risk moving to a "better" location is similar to the men's reticence in seeking or accepting higher-level jobs (discussed in Chapter 5). In both cases, limited expectations and a rational assessment of future probabilities caused people to put up with the inadequacies of the present situation rather than take the risks involved in trying for a better situation.

When the families do move, it is usually to a similar place, and often such moves are made in haste, not planned or desired. Even when people talk about the vague possibility of moving in the future, their ideal seems to be a rural neighborhood, one that is not particularly "high-class" (like the suburbs), but one that is not weighed down by such a bad reputation. They envision, in other words, their own neighborhood or one like it, with somewhat better housing, fewer "undesirable" people, no stigma of being labeled "the worst place in the county."

> If only we didn't have the problem that everybody out there expects all people from this neighborhood to behave badly, to cheat and steal. No wonder some of us get discouraged and quit trying. If we didn't have *that* problem always facing us everywhere we go in the community, then it would be all right living here.

Conclusion

The neighborhood is where people live, where they feel they belong, and the source of their networks of social interaction and mutual assistance. Two salient factors underlie the social dynamics of the rural depressed neighborhood. First, rural poor people are dependent on their neighbors and neighborhood for social interaction and identity. Second, the relationships in the neighborhood are undermined by displaced aggression and ambivalence. Both of these factors result from the inadequate integration into the wider community (which will be explored in the next chapter). The run-down rural neighborhood is the only accessible secondary social environment, but at the same time, its social functioning is impaired. The prevalence of tension and suspicion and the frequent flare-up of hostility keep relationships in a constant state of flux, rupture, and realignment.

From the point of view of the neighborhood itself, the instability of relationships is unsettling, but not devastating. Since the neighborhood is not a social group or unit, but merely a social field from which dyadic relationships are formed, it can withstand rifts. Ruptures and realignments occur, but the neighborhood itself continues to exist as a localized pool of potential relationships.

From the point of view of the individual, however, the effects of these two intertwined factors may be more troublesome. Ambivalence and hostile behavior undoubtedly reduce the effectiveness of neighbor-to-neighbor bonds in fulfilling the psychosocial needs of the individual. Social relationships rupture easily; impermanence is expected. But the anticipation of rupture may, in fact, limit the quality and stability of social interaction that can be achieved. When people defensively restrict the depth of their commitment to relationships with neighbors, they may also be reducing the potential for deriving psychological support from these relationships.

The social marginality of rural poor families—attached to a larger community but unable to participate satisfyingly in it—is a two-edged sword. It restricts people to a very limited social world, and at the same time it undermines and weakens relationships within that limited social world.

10
Relationships with
the "Outside World"

Introduction

People in poor rural neighborhoods sometimes refer to the urban-based community to which they are attached as the "outside world." This chapter will explore the social and psychological dimensions of that designation, and describe the nature of rural residents' interaction with the larger community.

Whether the term "outside world" is actually used in speech or merely indicated in attitude, it is both a statement about the larger community and a statement about one's own identity. The concept is best understood as one part of a duality that exists in many people's thinking. The "outside world" is the "they" of a "we-they" duality; it is all that is not "us."

In this dualistic view, "we" or "us" is defined as "our neighbors, relatives, and friends who are struggling as we are" or, succinctly, "the people at the bottom." "We" is both a personal collection of people and a socioeconomic identification.

The "outside world" of the duality is defined residually as "everybody else" or "the rest of society." It encompasses all that lies outside the personal realm of "us" and "people like us." It refers to the entire urban-based community, its people and its institutions. The "outside world" refers also to people who are perceived as holding low opinions of "people like us." It is made up of "people who look down their noses at us," "people who think they're better than we are."

This polarity between "us" and the "outside world" does not appear to be class-consciousness in the revolutionary sense. In fact, when ideas of class struggle were expounded by young urban radicals in the late 1960s, they fell on deaf ears among rural poor people, who appeared to be totally opposed to notions of revolution and were not interested in uniting with other "poor, oppressed peoples" of the world, or even of the county. Their opposition quite clearly flowed from the fact that what they really wanted was to be accepted by the outside world, not to overthrow it. They wanted a slice of America's pie, they did not want the pie to be destroyed before they got to the table. Almost unanimously, the rural poor did not want to align themselves and their interests with urban poor people or with Black poor people in a "poor people's campaign." They wanted to be identified, treated, and accepted as *people*, not as *poor* people. To carry the banner of poor people was contrary to their long-term hopes. Additionally, urban and Black people, even though they may be poor, are definitely outside the recognized definition of "us." In fact, a fairly pervasive and strong racial prejudice exists against Blacks as a group.[1] Thus, poor people who are different or distant from "us" remained part of the "outside world," and class solidarity never developed.

The phrase "outside world" indicates the extent of the gap that separates people of the rural pockets of poverty from the large urban-based community, the community *to* which they are inextricably bound but *in* which they are marginal participants. It also indicates that the so-called isolation of rural poor people is more than a matter of geographical distance: it is a structural, social, and psychological separation.

Centralization Without Integration

Due to the major social trends of the last fifty years, Chestnut Valley and nearby rural areas have all been centralized into the larger urbanized community. Formal community functions such as education, employment, shopping, health care, government, police, and organized religious activities are now provided by (and only by) the urban-based community. But although the urban community has taken over these functions from the former rural community, it has not been an effective substitute for the people of lower socioeconomic levels in terms of the psychological and social functions of a community. The urban-based community provides neither adequate social participation nor a feeling of belonging and identity for the poorer rural people. They belong to it only in the physical and institutional sense.

Looking at the structure of the relationships from the community to the individual, it is apparent that the various separate institutions of the larger community are in no way unified vis-à-vis each individual rural family. Instead, the many disparate segments and institutions extend separate, parallel connections to each individual rural household. The individual does not experience a *community*, in the sense of a whole system, but a series of separate institutions—a factory, a school, a shopping center, a welfare agency. Identification with the urban-based conglomerate as a unit is thus almost precluded on structural grounds alone.

The connection in the other direction—from the individual to the community—is also fragmented rather than unified. Due to the collapse of the rural communities, there are no local subunits or intermediate-level building blocks to group together clusters of rural people and articulate them to the larger community. No connecting groups link the many separate rural families with the large, distant community. Consequently, each individual rural family relates separately to the central community.

The lack of a sustained social unit at the local level limits poor people's successful participation in the wider community in other ways too. For example, the lack of a local social unit means that there is little opportunity for them to learn and practice in a familiar, close-to-home setting the social roles and behavior required for playing successfully on the broader stage of the larger community.[2]

The lack of structural integration is particularly devastating because it is compounded by substantial attitudinal and psychological barriers, which will be discussed later in this chapter.

Spheres of Participation

For people of rural depressed areas, participation in the outside world is mostly confined to the inescapable spheres of employment, buying, education, formal services, and authorities. A brief run-down of each of these areas shows that participation is restricted, and is often characterized by unsuccessful experiences.

The Economic Sphere

In the economic realm (described in Chapters 5 and 6) people participate at the community's lowest levels, holding its least respected jobs, remaining in its lowest income brackets, and buying its cheapest goods at its least expensive outlets. To the extent they can, people operate outside official economic institutions: they avoid banks, they trade among themselves for goods, and they devise clever substitutes or supplements for cash income.

Education

For most adults in rural depressed areas, formal education was a limited, unhappy, and unsatisfactory experience. Adult memories of school, whether in the old one-room schoolhouses before 1950 or in the consolidated schools since then, are mostly not positive. Some adults stuck with it until graduation from high school; others dropped out in elementary school. The majority made it partway through secondary school—but did not necessarily obtain the skills commensurate with their last completed school year. A few people, particularly women, have resumed an interrupted formal education, taking high school equivalency exams or enrolling in vocational training programs in area adult education programs or community colleges.

Children today all attend distant, centralized, or consolidated schools. Theoretically, their inclusion in modern, high-quality school systems with heterogeneous populations should be advantageous. In fact, many of the potential benefits fail to reach the children of the rural poor families. For many children, the school becomes an environment of failure, a place of defeating experiences, a long series of blows to the sense of self-worth. Because of these psychologically negative aspects, many of the educational advantages and opportunities offered by a large, up-to-date school system are consistently and completely missed by certain children. (This topic will be further elaborated in the final chapters, as it is obviously full of implications for the continued intergenerational problem of rural poverty and marginality.)

Religion

Few families of the rural poverty areas participate regularly in organized church or church-related activities. Some people attend rural and small-town churches occasionally; some send their children to Sunday school and summer Bible school if transportation is provided; but most rarely enter a church. However, they resent the assumption that their lack of church attendance means that they are not religious people. In fact, many individuals hold fairly strong religious beliefs, generally similar to the somewhat fundamentalist emphasis common among the predominantly Protestant churchgoing residents of nearby nonpoor rural areas. But few adults feel comfortable in church. They feel that their reputation, as well as their clothing, sets them apart from other churchgoers.

Sometimes an individual or couple may begin regularly attending church, often as part of a general effort to "live better," to "start over in a new life"—perhaps following a major family crisis. They may express positive feelings about being able to act on their religious convictions, but they shy away from participation in the church's social organizations and clubs, and from any commitment to becoming a member of the church. If they sense pressure to attend regularly and to join, they are apt to stop going altogether.

Politics and Government

In the political sphere, also, beliefs and sentiments may be shared with a wider community, but not reflected in actual participation. A generally conservative political stance is combined with an inclination to see politics and elections as remote from their own problems. Convinced of the political impotence of the individual, especially "the little guy" or the poor person, very few people register or vote. Even though they say that in a democracy everyone has a right to be heard, they think their vote would make no difference. And they are skeptical about the efficacy of banding together in organized political action.

On the whole, interest in political matters and in state and national government is meager and trust is lacking. Typical also is the personalistic approach
to politics: a person may "like" some national political figure because he seems
to be a "nice guy." A man will "like" a particular state governor because under
his administration there was an improvement in salary or overtime benefits
for workers on the state highway crew. Several homes still display portraits of
John Kennedy, faded and curled at the edges, but conspicuous.

On the local level, attitudes toward politics generally involve more trust, as
well as, again, a personalistic approach. People tend to view the personnel of
township-level government not as local officials, but as local people. The
highway superintendent or town councilman may be someone who lives fairly
close by, someone who attended the same school, someone descended from a
respected farming family in the township. Even though this officeholder is
recognized as being in a higher socioeconomic level, his identity as a local person renders him a personal rather than a political figure.

Administration and Authority

People interact frequently with public authorities and administrators in the
county seat. They attend to numerous routine citizen matters, such as the
frequent licensing of cars, paying taxes, and so forth; and they encounter
regulatory and law enforcement institutions – sheriff, police, and county
court.

People rely on "the law," meaning the state troopers or county sheriffs, to
come out to the rural areas to break up fights, inspect malicious damage, investigate thefts, arrest neighborhood troublemakers, or to accompany
emergency cases to the hospital. On other occasions, however, "the law"
comes unasked and unwanted, trying to track down suspected lawbreakers
for deeds committed elsewhere in the county. People believe that these law
enforcement agents sometimes try to cause trouble, snooping around the
neighborhood. Neighbors attempt to protect each other from the law enforcement agencies, refusing to give information or warning each other of highway
police checkpoints where unregistered vehicles might be stopped.

Participation in court proceedings is also fairly frequent, and ranges over a
wide variety of types and severity of cases. Charges of vandalism, theft, and
assault, of harassment and of statutory rape, arise, but they are not frequent,
and seem most often to involve offenses against persons with whom the ac-
cused has some personal connection. Violations involving automobiles are
common: unregistered vehicles, uninspected vehicles, unlicensed operators,
speeding violations, and driving while intoxicated. Family court matters also
come up frequently: petitions for "an order of protection" against a spouse;
child support cases; legal problems involving custody of children; and court
hearings regarding "persons in need of supervision" cases, probation viola-

tions, and various offenses by juveniles. Most of these encounters are not particularly pleasant, and they reinforce people's desire to remain aloof from the urban community.

Problems in Interaction with Service Agencies

People of rural depressed areas interact with many of the community's human services. Their interactions with service-providing agencies, offices, and institutions form a large part of their relationship with the outside world. Conversely, rural poor people make up a large proportion of the intended beneficiaries or target population and client caseload of many community services. From the viewpoint of the client, the agencies are categorized by the functions they serve. There are providers of money (department of social services for welfare, Medicaid, food stamps); goods (Salvation Army, churches, and other outlets for free food and free used clothing); services (antipoverty agencies, nutrition-education programs, child health clinics); job skills (government programs in various agencies and educational institutions); and counseling (family service agencies, alcoholism programs, mental health clinics).

For a variety of reasons, however, an agency and a rural poor person in need of its service may not come into contact with each other. Rural poor people frequently lack adequate information on available and appropriate services, or the lack of a telephone or a car prevents a person from getting service from an urban-based agency. But there are other, more deep-seated, reasons – having to do with attitudes and perceptions rather than simply information or physical access. Sometimes people simply do not recognize that they have a problem or they deny its existence. Even if the problem is recognized, a person may believe that it is just part of life and cannot really be resolved, so there is no point in going to an agency about it.[3] In other cases, the reluctance to intitiate contact with an agency may be primarily due to fear and a sense of unease about the first encounter. "Will I wear the right clothes, do the right things, say what you're supposed to say?"[4] This fear reflects the basic lack of self-confidence vis-à-vis the "outside world."

Poor people may also resist making connections because they view service agencies as potentially meddlesome, interfering with the individual's ability and right to decide on his own how to handle problems, set priorities, make compromises, and devise substitutes. A related and commonly held perception is that many agencies employ threats – of cutting off financial support, of reporting disapproved behavior to other agencies, or of removing children from their parents. Another deterrent to seeking assistance from community resources is the general preference for standing on one's own – a reluctance to turn to others, especially outsiders, for help. Seeking institutional or agency help is believed to be an admission of personal failure. Going to a mental

health clinic "proves" that one is "sick in the head." Shame and guilt about being in such circumstances often prevent people from turning to an outside
agency for help.

Despite these deterrents, however, many service connections are made.
But even the connections that occur may often be unsatisfactory from the
point of view of either the provider or the consumer of such services, or of
both. Despite considerable effort and good intentions on both sides, relationships may remain negative in tone or minimal in effect. There may be problems in developing a relationship that is deep enough or sustained long
enough to achieve a beneficial outcome. Analysis of a variety of individual
cases of unsatisfactory or unsatisfying relationships reveals some common
underlying factors.

One cause of problems in the agency-client relationship may be the disparity of views concerning the kind of relationship that *should* exist between
them. Clients enter the relationships with assumptions, expectations, constraints, and needs that may differ from those of the service provider. The
rural poor client who is reluctant to seek outside help tries to make the situation more acceptable to himself by defining the caseworker-client relationship
in a personalistic manner. The client may place emphasis on the relationship
between himself and the professional worker as an individual, not as an inter-
changeable member of the agency staff. A client who feels comfortable with a
particular agency worker may feel that the worker in some sense belongs to
him, and may be particularly upset by being switched to another caseworker
within the same agency: he may refuse to talk with a substitute, and may terminate the relationship with the agency. The client may also feel, perhaps unconsciously, that whenever he needs help the worker should be available to
him, rather than being available only during business hours and by appointment. Conversely, when the client feels his need for service is not particularly
pressing, he may simply not bother to keep his scheduled appointment.

The personalistic approach to agencies and institutions also works in
another way. If a client has had an unpleasant experience with one individual
in an agency, he may judge the entire agency negatively, and thus not return
to it. On the other hand, if there has been positive experience with one individual in the agency (even the receptionist or secretary), the client may feel
more comfortable about interacting with the agency: he has found a way to
personalize his relationship with what he would otherwise perceive as an impersonal institution. This personalistic approach to relationships with institutions may be a heritage of the small face-to-face rural community. It also
reflects people's insecurity about their self-worth, their awareness that the
"outside world" as a whole looks down on them, and the real need they have
for personal relationships.

Another problem in the interaction between rural poor people and urban
service institutions is that of premature termination. After the first several

visits, a client may suddenly (and usually without notification) terminate what seemed to be a satisfactory relationship with an agency. This cutoff may reflect different expectations of client and agency. In many cases, the individual seeks assistance only as a last resort. He therefore needs and expects quick relief, assuming that if the practitioner is really any good, the results will come quickly and dramatically. A client may feel that remedies offered by a professional or agency are too long-range to have any effect on the immediate crisis. Or the client may be seeking help for a very specific problem—the straw that broke the camel's back—not the whole tangle of underlying problems. The client may not see the feasibility or necessity of addressing anything deeper than the immediate precipitating event, and may resist the professional propensity to probe beyond the immediate complaint. Sometimes the client finds the professional advice, prescription, or counseling process totally unrealistic and impractical, given the realities of the situation at home. (For example, the mother of three active preschoolers whose doctor instructed her to stay in bed all week, or the distraught woman who was advised by a social worker that she was excessively wrought up and should try not to think about or believe her husband's threats.)

When a rural client perceives that the hoped-for assistance is not forthcoming, he may, in frustration, break off contact. Although neither the client nor the service worker is at fault, each tends to blame the other, when what really happened is that the relationship was hampered from the start by differences in the expectations and perceptions of the two parties.

Another cause of premature termination is that the situation that propelled the client to seek assistance in the first place may change suddenly and drastically. An unexpected alteration in the client's home situation may make continued interaction inappropriate or impossible. A client who was reluctant to seek help in the first place may be particularly quick to terminate the relationship if his or her situation or needs change.

- One woman finally agreed to get help to patch up a difficult marriage. She abruptly stopped seeing the counselor when her husband left home, for she felt her problem was over.
- Another woman several times seeks counseling to plan for a separation from her husband. Plans proceed, and her confidence grows that she can make it on her own. But suddenly the husband either beats and threatens her and she drops the idea of leaving, or he promises to reform and she agrees to give him one more chance. In either case, she sees counseling as no longer relevant, and so she does not go to her next appointment.
- Yet another undergoes all the necessary laboratory tests preparatory to having long-overdue surgery. At the last minute, she cancels the

operation because her husband has gone out on a drunk, her mother-in-law is sick, and there is no one else to care for the children.

Premature termination becomes a self-fulfilling prophecy. Because the relationship is severed before recognizable benefits can occur, the client is confirmed in his belief that social service agencies are of little help. At the same time, agency personnel are confirmed in their belief that some clients do not really want help or do not want to invest any effort in the helping process. Although there have been numerous successful interactions, and a great investment of time, effort, and money in providing effective services, these problems in the interface between rural poor people and the human service network may limit the relationships and perpetuate lukewarm or negative attitudes.

Lack of Participation in Voluntary Groups

The rural poor play little part in the panorama of voluntary organizations of the larger community. The men do not belong to local township fire companies (which draw on a higher socioeconomic level for membership, and function as social clubs). Men who belong to unions tend not to participate in the related social affairs. Although they may associate with co-workers off the job, it is done informally – trading or repairing cars, drinking, or fishing together, not in group activities like bowling leagues or baseball teams. Families who own snowmobiles do not participate in the clubs, organized activities, and expensive outfitting common at higher socioeconomic levels. A few men and women do belong to and attend meetings of Alcoholics Anonymous.

Women rarely belong to or attend groups connected with school or church, or any other formal groups, such as Cooperative Extension's homemaker units. Only a few women have ever been involved in bowling leagues, in networks of Tupperware parties, or other quasi-social events. Although they may maintain active home visiting relationships outside the neighborhood, these predominantly involve relatives or other families in similar poverty areas, and are not organized group activities.

A comparison of formal social interactions of poor and nonpoor families of the same rural region reveals a vast difference in both frequency and type of activities. Even when lower-income people do participate in voluntary groups and activities, they are usually quite different from those of the more prestigious mainstream groups, and participation is apt to be sporadic and short-lived. The difference can be seen in the activities of two rural women, one from a low-income family and the other from a more affluent home.

The more affluent woman served as hostess in her home for three members of a Bible study group, the tiny remnant of the once important ladies aid society of the local church. In contrast, the woman from the low-income family, on the same day, traveled a half-hour by car to attend a Bible study session organized by an agency outreach worker with whom she had become friendly. On another day in the same week, the first woman drove to a neighboring community to attend a large monthly meeting of the local home demonstration unit. The group was made up mainly of elderly and middle-aged women whose husbands or fathers had once been the more prosperous farmers in the township. On the same day, in the evening, the second woman was attending an Alcoholics Anonymous meeting in the urban center.

Children also tend to be minimal participants in voluntary activities. Parents of preschoolers do not generally put their children in organized play groups, formal day-care centers, or private nursery schools. Again, the personalistic emphasis shows: Grandma, a grown sister, or a neighbor is much preferred over an impersonal institution for young children's care. Children of elementary school age tend to be less involved in clubs and activities than their nonpoor classmates. Although lack of money and after-school transportation are often factors, the deeper reasons lie in patterns of social acceptance and self-image. Also, parents do not foster or facilitate their children's participation in clubs, sports, and activities outside school. As children get older, the participation gap widens significantly, so that unless they are encouraged and pushed, poor children in high school participate in few nonmandatory sports or social activities. These are not the boys and girls for whom the opportunity to be on an athletic team provides incentive to stay in school.

Deterrents to Social Participation

Limited social participation in the "outside world" is primarily related to status differences, perceptions of the community, and perceptions of self. Most people of rural depressed areas feel uncomfortable at mixed-status events, and try to avoid them. They may feel, rightly or wrongly, that their presence is not really desired. They feel that they have little to gain from such social participation, for it only confirms their low status in their own eyes and in the eyes of the "outside world".

They [the higher-status people] have no use for us except to be the bottom.

The PTA wants us to come [to meetings] only so they can have someone to gossip about afterwards.

A real deterrent to participating in socially mixed groups in the larger community is the fear of unknown situations where social cues might be misread and responded to inappropriately. This anxiety probably further increases the

potential for making a mistake and incurring embarassment. A related problem is that of inadequate or inappropriate props. With only a limited inventory of clothing, accessories, and other props, the poor person cannot project
a desired image to a status-conscious audience. One woman cited an example
that conveys beautifully the importance of possessing appropriate props and
knowing appropriate behavior, and the insecurity that arises in their absence.

> The PTA dish-to-pass supper really puts pressure on families like us. You have
> to bring silverware. Well, that might be hard for some. And not one of us in this
> neighborhood would know the proper way so far as what to do and what to say.
> How do you act at a buffet? Do you take a little bit of everything so you won't
> hurt anybody's feelings? But if you do that, will they think you're being greedy?
> And what about the food you have to bring to it? I know I'm a fabulous cook for
> my own family, but could it be considered good enough for other people? If I
> brought something, people might know who cooked the dish, from which family,
> and they might not eat it. If my food wasn't eaten, I'd really feel bad. No, the
> dish-to-pass supper scares me, and nobody could persuade me to go. I'd rather be
> home.

Rather than subject themselves to such difficult situations, poor people
simply avoid mixed-status social participation, usually saying they're too
tired, or they don't have transportation or a babysitter. When an individual
does attend a mixed-status activity, he or she is apt to take a brother, a sister-
in-law, or a child for support.

A variety of other factors also inhibits participation in group activities.
There is typically a wait-and-see attitude: until one has some assurance that
an activity or an organized group will be beneficial and successful, people
hesitate to join. As one man told a community organizer, "Show us you can
do something, then maybe we'll get together on it."[5] People perceive no advantage to investing time, social commitment, and emotional resources in an
activity if it has only a marginal chance of some payoff.

Another important factor limiting participation is the unpredictability of
the future. Participation in voluntary activities and organizations requires a
greater predictability of future time, events, and confidence levels than most
rural poor families have. People feel they cannot make commitments for future
dates because of the real possibility that "something might come up" that
would be sufficiently pressing to preclude their attending a scheduled event.
(The "something" that comes up could be anything from having been beaten
black and blue in a fight with a husband or neighbor, to having sick children
with no one to care for them, perhaps a breakdown of the family car, or a sum-
mons to appear in court or at the welfare office.) There is also the fact that a
person cannot predict how he or she will feel, psychologically as well as
physically, on any given day in the future. One cannot be sure that one will

have the necessary confidence when the time comes. And, in fact, anxiety about the upcoming event may reduce confidence to the point where participation, promised a week ago, seems beyond one's capabilities when the date actually arrives.

Furthermore, people are reluctant to create situations in which others have certain expectations of them; they are afraid they won't live up to those expectations. By not committing oneself ahead of time, a person does not incur expectations. When the event actually takes place, the individual may spontaneously decide to attend and participate. Appearing unexpectedly and at the last minute, he is less likely to be a disappointment to others and to himself. (But to community workers, the frustrating fact is that the person often does *not* show up, whether expected or not.)

A particularly significant limitation on the frequency and satisfaction of social participation in the outside world arises from the negative stereotypes that the dominant community holds about rural poor people. Socioeconomic differences and socioeconomic stereotypes can have the same force in a community of fewer than 100,000 people that racial differences and racist stereotypes do in a large urban environment. In the smaller community, individuals are readily identified with the low reputation of their neighborhood, family, and relatives. The individual from a family or locality that is stigmatized as "poor white trash" finds that the community has formed its impression and expectations of him before he has a chance to do anything on his own. The stereotypes not only follow him wherever he goes in the community, they precede him in all his actions within it. A child inherits a reputation, finds it waiting for him when he enters school, his first major contact with the outside world. In a relatively small community, it is difficult to outdistance the stereotype.

One mother felt this stigma keenly.

> My husband's brother's name has been in the paper all the time for this or that crime. Finally, he got put in prison, and that, too, was reported in the paper. Well, my kids are getting teased all the time about their uncle. These kids have really had to pay for it because they have the same last name as their uncle. But *they* didn't do all those crimes. *They* didn't get put in jail. It's not fair for them to have to take all that.

People's perception of their ambiguous, marginal position in the larger community is poignantly revealed in fleeting moments of reflection, and shows amazingly acute sociological awareness.

> The people of the community have their own code and mode. Anybody who does things differently is some kind of animal, not human, according to them.

> Low income people have a fear. It's not because of their income. It's because of

the way the community treats them. They could have a million dollars, but the community would still treat them the same. So they'd have the same fear.

I'm not looking for status. I don't want to be one of them. I'm *not* one of them. I belong here with the people on this road. What I'm looking for is my self-respect and my respect from the community.

We're from the low-income group. Do I expect too much from the high-income people to treat me just like anybody else?

What I want is to be treated equal, to be treated as an individual.

These comments and many others like them were spoken with deep personal feeling, often with bitterness, at times with despair. These perceptions and feelings are at the root of the limited participation in the voluntary groups and activities of the wider community.

Conclusion

The real bind on the people of rural poverty neighborhoods is that they cannot successfully participate in the "outside world" and they feel scorned by it, *but*, at the same time, they do not have the option of withdrawing from and ignoring it. They are inextricably included in the larger community for schooling, work, buying, settling official matters, and seeking help. They are tied to it also by the fact that they share its cultural values, aspirations, and norms. They want to possess the goods that its members consider desirable. They want their children to succeed and gain acceptance according to the rules and patterns of the dominant society. They want to be part of the community in action and in perception.

But since they seldom experience satisfaction in their interactions with the larger community, rural poor people attempt to protect themselves by minimizing participation and avoiding humiliating situations. They see no benefit in increasing their level of interaction. And so, to the extent they can, they maintain their distance.

This aloofness, so clearly expressed in the duality of "us" and the "outside world," is an understandable adjustment to the social and attitudinal barriers that limit successful participation in the broader community. At the same time, there is a longing for something more in the way of a social community, a desire for a community with which one could identify and in which one could operate freely and confidently.

Aloofness from the wider community is not a cultural preference, then, but merely a way of coping with a difficult social situation, a response to a fairly accurate perception of social realities.

Part 4

Conclusion: Causes and Cures

Why Poverty and
Marginality Continue

Introduction

This chapter will synthesize the economic, social, cultural, and psychological aspects that run through the study. The synthesis revolves around one basic question: Why is the problem of rural poverty so tenacious? Ten causes of the persistence of rural poverty, generation after generation, will be discussed. First, however, some general statements should be made.

1. These ten causes are not separate entities; rather, they are inter-woven, interacting, and tangled together in the flux of real life.
2. The sequence or progression of the causes is, in itself, significant, and the effects of the causes are cumulative. Each derives from the previous ones in the progression; each cause shapes and helps to cause the successive ones.
3. Some of the causative factors listed are not unique, either to the geographic location or to the economic stratum of poverty. What *is* unique is the peculiar concatenation of the interwoven causes, which makes the problem of rural poverty so intractable
4. The ten causes are of two different types. The first five causes listed are *primary causes*. The second five are *derivative causes*, resulting from the primary causes.

Primary Causes

The primary causes of rural poverty are factors embedded in the economic and social structure of American society. They are forces that operate systematically, if not purposefully, to create and perpetuate poverty in some sectors of the population.

1. The Continuing Impact of History

The antecedents of today's rural poverty and marginality are the historical forces of earlier times. But history does not stop; its effects do not cease. Different degrees of success in adapting to sweeping economic changes of an earlier period continue to leave their mark. In the first decades of this century, some individuals were unable to adapt and maneuver from a position of economic strength. They and their children and grandchildren have not yet been able to make up the difference, while the rest of the community has run on ahead.[1] Restricted resources continue to prevent some people from making the adjustments that would enable them or their children to catch up. On the lifelong economic ledger, the balance brought forward for the next generation has often been a debt instead of a nest egg.

In terms of adjustment to social changes, past inadequacies have been carried forward into the present. During the transition from rural hamlet to urban-centered community, some families were slower to forge new ties and new identities in the growing urban-based community. It was a source of concern to rural sociologists studying the regions of New York where farming had declined that some rural families were consistently underrepresented in the granges and churches, the extension units, school groups, social clubs, and community activities.[2] Generally, these were the same families who participated least in new technological and consumer trends such as autos, tractors, and telephones; the people who lived on marginal farms along unpaved roads. Today, descendants of these marginal families still live on parcels carved out of overgrown hill farms, and many still have not become socially integrated.

In the modern complex community, as opposed to the small rural community, there are few social institutions that effectively incorporate poor and nonpoor people in regular interaction. Poverty has thus become a socially isolating condition, and a stigma.

The impact of history, therefore, is that poverty continues to be handed down to succeeding generations, but now with an overlay of social isolation as well. This heritage sits on the shoulders of each generation, slowing them down in their effort to gain a successful entry into the modern social and economic community.

2. The Crippling Economic Situation

Poverty severely affects both day-to-day living and long-run well-being. By any measure, most of the people described in this study are impoverished in terms of the chronic insufficiency of their financial resources to meet their needs.[3] In most families, there is an almost constant shortage of money and buying power. In a condition of perpetual deficit financing, trade-offs are necessary, and certain needs and desires must often go unmet. People plan, save, stretch, substitute, and go without. Adaptive techniques of financial juggling enable them to cope with their poverty, to survive, to derive some pleasure from life, and to raise their children. But the coping strategies that enable people to accomplish this much cannot lift them out of poverty. They remain on the economic margin, hovering around the arbitrary official poverty line, hovering along a vague boundary between just getting by and not making it.

Rarely a day goes by without the consequences of their poverty being painfully obvious to a family: the worried breadwinner is laid off; the housewife wears her tattered rummage-sale coat for another winter; the car insurance bill can't be paid; work on the half-completed front entry stopped when cash and time had to be diverted to car repairs; the hospital is sending threatening notices about the back bill; the kitchen cupboards are nearly empty, and the month's allotment of food stamps is already gone; a child stays home from school for lack of winter boots.

Difficult and painful as these day-in, day-out money problems may be, however, chronic poverty is even more serious in its long-run effects. For example, when cash is limited or unsteady, expenditures for food are low and erratic. Nutritional intake is jeopardized and children may suffer long-range deficiencies in growth, development, and general health. These deficiencies in turn may limit potential lifelong earning power.[4] Similarly, perpetual money problems may also cause deep emotional discouragement, diminished self-confidence, and psychological exhaustion that may, in turn, restrict people's ability to operate at their full potential. One woman spoke of this effect with deep feeling: "When things get so bad that you're discouraged every time you turn around, it seems to take away your ambition. It sometimes seems as if there is no point even trying, because you just can't get anywhere."

Another long-range effect of continued poverty is the inability to win community acceptance. For the most part in modern American society, people are judged on the basis of externally observable factors such as occupation, place of residence, and possession of status-invested consumer goods. The people of the rural pockets of poverty rank low on the first two criteria. And with limited and insecure incomes, they have difficulty acquiring the coveted status symbols, and are therefore unable to project a successful image in the community.[5]

The economic stranglehold of poverty operates like a timed-release capsule. Some of the effects are felt immediately and every day—inadequate resources to satisfy material needs and the constant grinding-down effect of worry and struggle are the essence of daily life. But the economic handicap is also released gradually and continuously over years and generations. Adults may become bogged down and disheartened to the point that their ability to operate in the world of work is substantially diminished. Children who grow up in the emotional and interpersonal tension spawned and exacerbated by economic poverty are more likely later to fall into the stranglehold of an insecure, insufficient economic status. The economic constraints of poverty are self-perpetuating.

3. Inadequacies of the Social Structure

An important conclusion of both the historical study and the contemporary observations is that in the poverty-stricken rural areas there are neither viable local-level social groupings nor satisfactory structural bridges linking people with the new larger community. This social-structural hiatus is intimately connected with and constantly reinforcing the poverty of the rural areas. Four negative effects of the inadequate social structure can be cited here.[6]

First, rural people have no local opportunities for prelearning and practicing secondary social roles. Consequently, they may find relating and interacting with the distant, larger community difficult.

Second, social relationships in the primary group setting are weakened or jeopardized. An overload is thrown onto the family, because it attempts to provide social and psychological supports that otherwise would come from participation in a secondary social environment. And, as the stresses from unsuccessful interaction in the larger community have no appropriate outlet there, they are often discharged within the family and the neighborhood, disrupting primary social relationships.

Third, people have difficulty defining themselves. Lacking a satisfactory identity on the community level, they can only define themselves in terms of their neighborhood and family. But because the neighborhood is denigrated and the family often disrupted, the individual may not be able to derive much strength from either identity.

Finally, attitudinal separation is perpetuated, reinforced by negative stereotypes widely held by the dominant community. In a vicious circle, the attitudinal separation, in turn, makes it harder to build the needed social bridges.[7]

Through these four processes, the inadequacies of the social structure are self-perpetuating. And the structural inadequacies also perpetuate poverty, as they restrict and reduce people's ability to function effectively in the world of work.

4. Barriers to Upward Mobility

A strong desire for upward mobility is evident in much of the observed behavior – particularly in thinking and decision making. People aspire to a better future, with more security and fewer problems: "to improve our situation," "to make a better life for ourselves and our children."

The crushing fact, however, is that there is very little upward mobility. It is true that some individuals have "made it" out of this poverty situation; and some of today's young adults and children will eventually "make it" after an initially difficult period. But there are few instances of significant upward mobility, and those who do move upward usually have moved out of the area first, thus further reducing the availability of local role models of successful movement out of poverty and marginality. Most adults know they are caught in a rut, making only intermittent and limited headway toward a better social or economic position. Women, in particular, are keenly aware of this, and willing to talk about it.

> Sometimes it seems as if we just aren't getting anywhere. Things happen faster than we can handle them, and we never catch up, let alone get ahead. It's so discouraging. We struggle so hard, but nothing seems to come of it.

Given the economic structure, upward mobility appears nearly impossible for some people. Their limited economic resources are barely adequate to maintain their present low position, and far too meager to propel them upward. Few can gain access to appreciably greater resources than they now command. The lack of economic mobility is attributable to a variety of complex factors. Some are of a broad societal nature: the general structure of employment and wages, and relatively high unemployment rates; the faltering economy of the northeastern region and rising unemployment in nearby urban centers; decreasing local control over industry, leading to plant closings, automation, and an increasing demand for technical or managerial skills.

It is important to note also that certain factors that restrict upward mobility for some groups of Americans living in poverty are not relevant in this particular case. In this example of a rural enclave of poverty in northern Appalachia neither race nor ethnicity, for example, is a pertinent factor. Nor are rural poor people kept at the bottom because they hold different or deviant cultural values: these people share and attempt to live by most mainstream societal values. They believe in the importance of working for a living, and they work hard to obtain widely coveted material items and to achieve other socially approved goals, hoping all the while that they will eventually see their children move up from the bottom into full participation in society and a greater share of its rewards. But believing in these societal values and attempting to live by them is not, in itself, enough to bring about the desired improvement in status.

In the realm of consumption patterns, for example, rural poor people, particularly of the younger generations, are well tuned in to media messages and consumption drives. The currently popular, heavily advertised items (CB radios, snowmobiles, children's toys seen on TV) may be regarded almost as necessities, and their absence leads to feelings of deprivation just as surely as does the absence of food. If a person spends his limited cash to procure these status items, however, he not only suffers hunger pangs from skimping on necessities, he also incurs criticism for careless spending and pleasure-seeking. If, on the other hand, a person spends his money only on necessities, he lacks the socially recognized material items that stake his claim to status. Either way he cannot win status and public approval through consumer goods. For people caught in this bind—people who cannot afford both necessities and status items—one basis of upward mobility, conspicuous consumption, is unavailable.

Nonetheless, people continue to believe in the possibility of upward mobility—someday—at least for their children. The mobility they hope for is really rather modest: a reduction of the painful consequences of their low social and economic position, release from stigma and denigration, and an opportunity for their children to make a decent, less burdened life for themselves.

People believe that education may provide a means for their children to succeed. But public education has not been as effective in lifting intergenerationally poor people out of poverty as it once was in setting penniless immigrants of the late nineteenth century on the road to full participation in the expanding American economy. In educational institutions themselves, there are barriers that reduce the mobility-effectiveness of education.[8] Among these barriers are the negative stereotypes held by the larger community.

5. The Corrosive Stereotypes

Throughout the preceding chapters, we have noted the stereotyped images that American society as a whole has about poverty and poor people. These stereotypes operate on the local level, clearly shaping the way in which the dominant community perceives the people of the depressed rural neighborhoods. Against the background of pervasive stigma in the community, the attempts of struggling individuals, their small successes and achievements, go unrecognized.

> If a kid comes from the town and his name is Jones or Samson or Dominick, then everything's fine. He can behave as he pleases. But if he comes from out here in Chestnut Valley, and especially if his name is X or Y or Z, then they're watching every move he makes. They accuse him of being the cause of every fight in school. They watch him in the store, 'cause they think he's sure to be a thief. They teach their kids to make nasty remarks about his raggedy clothes. They're convinced, before he even does a thing, that he's bad. So he hasn't got a chance.

Some people cry out for individual recognition, rather than group stereotyping.

Why isn't society willing to allow that we could be a little different from the others around here? If I'm in a store and the cashier sees my signature on the bill, he says, "Oh, you're one of the Pratts from Chestnut Valley?" I tell him, "Oh, it's only a distant relationship."

Those who are blanketed by these stereotypes despair of ever being able to convince the outside world that they do not deserve the negative judgment. They feel that every action they take is interpreted through the lens of stigma. They know that the stereotypes precede them and their children in their every foray into the outside world. The stereotypes are already there, preventing a man from getting a desired job, influencing a teacher's perception of a child's aptitude.[9]

The most devastating effect of the stereotypes, however, is the degree to which they may be internalized by their referents. Some people who have grown up in the stigmatized neighborhoods, or who carry surnames of stigmatized families, appear to have partially accepted the stereotypes as fact, to have internalized the judgments and turned the condemnation inward. Partial acceptance of the stereotypes compounds the problem of low self-image. Often the damage is done early in life, during the child's first encounters in the larger world, and affects all his subsequent interactions with it. To the extent that the stereotypes are internalized, they also undermine relationships in the family and the neighborhood, and contribute to the high level of ambivalence, suspicion, and hostility.

The stereotypes also can be self-fulfilling prophecies, and people's behavior comes to approximate the very stigma they resent.

If you tell a guy long enough that he's nothing but a drunk, he'll prove to you that he's nothing but a drunk. To survive and have society accept him, he has to be a drunk, because that's what they expect.

There are certain times when my confidence leaves me. In my low times, you can really knock me and tell me I'm no damn good, and I'll go along with the idea. In fact, I'll go out and prove to you that I'm no damn good.

Some individuals consciously try to protect themselves from the corrosive effects of stereotypes.

Society looks at our failures and our mistakes and says, "You'd expect that from them anyway." But those same people, do they ever see the good things we do? Are they willing to admit that we are trying? No. They've already made up their minds that we're lazy or good for nothing. There's no way we can convince them differently. But we have to watch out that we don't let them convince *us*.

Children as well as adults cry out, "I'll show them that I'm just as good as they are." But it is usually a cry of desperation, not affirmation.

Derivative Causes

The derivative causes that perpetuate rural poverty are quite different from the primary causes. I call them derivative, or secondary, because they are results of the five primary causes, results of the destructive effects of poverty on people's lives. Once created, these effects become self-perpetuating, and thus they are also causes of the ongoing cycle of intergenerational poverty. The derivative causes both result from and perpetuate poverty.

6. *Constant Pressure of Too Many*
Problems at the Same Time

Many families have a high potential for crisis, which is both a result of and a cause of continuing poverty. The perpetual shortage of money; the inadequacy or unreliability of housing, household appurtenances, cars, and other material goods; continuing health problems at both subclinical and acute levels; the insecurity of jobs; volatile relationships with neighbors; the children's poor performance in school or in the outside world; tensions in the family—all these problems and many more may be present at any one time, forming a pool of potential crises.

Given this potential, the frequency and severity of actual crises is high. Poor families are apt to live in a structure (be it a shack or an old trailer) that is fire-prone. The chance of being burned out is greater and the effects likely to be more disastrous than they would be for more affluent people.[10] Similarly, among women who eat an inadequate diet (as do many of the women studied), the chance of incurring health problems is increased. And, in a chain of causality, a malnourished pregnant woman may deliver before full term, thereby creating a long-range potential for problems in the child. As in so many aspects of life, the actual crises and problems are prevalent simply because the potential for them is high.

With so many potential sources of trouble, there is no way to predict when or where a new and acute problem will arise. There is only the sure knowledge, from the experiences of a lifetime, that crisis is always a likelihood.

> All the little crises that arise. There's not enough money, or you can't pay the bills, or you can't afford enough food. What little happiness that comes, you're ready to grab it and scream it out to the world. But on the other hand, when things do go well, you try not to get too excited about it 'cause you know that before the day is out, something bad will come along.

One result of the confusing and rapidly changing panorama of problems is emotional exhaustion and/or behavioral paralysis. The overwhelmed person is rendered nearly incapable of initiating action: Where to start? What to do?

Faced with several urgent problems, all pressing simultaneously for solution, the family may try to juggle them, just as it juggles financial resources. Temporary patches are applied to one problem in the hope that its resolution can be postponed briefly while attention is focused on more pressing problems. But most families do not have the opportunity or the luxury to cope with problems one by one, for the problems are all jumbled together. They can't pick out a single issue, work on it, get it solved and out of the way, and then go on to the next problem. Few problems are ever settled so completely that they need no further attention. They merely become lesser irritants in the pool of potential crises.

Problems accumulate, rather than being resolved. One reason for this is that individuals who have grown up in problem-ridden families generally lack successful experience in problem-solving, and therefore have little confidence in their ability to solve problems and little faith that other individuals or agencies could help solve them either. This attitude has two long-range effects: problems continue to fester and feelings of helplessness may be increased. The constant pressure of too many problems becomes, in itself, a contributing factor in the continuation of the poverty-marginality cycle.

7. Difficulty of Balancing Aspirations and Achievements

An inescapable fact of everyday reality in the poverty-stricken areas is the disparity between aspirations and achievements. People are constantly faced with this disparity, and they are aware of its power to erode emotional strength. Consequently, they have developed strategies by which they attempt to keep aspirations and achievements in balance.

Poor people consciously and unconsciously regulate their aspirations and their commitment to them. Just as they cannot afford to take financial risks with their limited dollars, so also they cannot afford to take psychological risks with their limited resources of confidence and self-respect. And so they regulate the psychological resources they commit to a specific, distant goal, often telling themselves that it doesn't really matter if they achieve it. They evaluate the potential of a situation, withholding commitment of psychological resources, money, and effort until they can be reasonably sure the goal is achievable. Some people quite consciously attempt to keep their aspirations in line with achievement levels by restricting their aspirations.

You have to learn not to place your hopes too far above where you actually are . . . because if you fall from high-up hopes, you may never get over it.

Our eyes are set a little above what we have now, but not as high as what we would like ideally. We aim for something a little better than what we have, but not that much better. Then, if we can't achieve our hopes, it's not a great disappointment. You have to learn to try for a happy medium.

People attempt to reduce anxiety about unachieved goals by stressing the value of the things they already possess, rather than those they lack.

> You learn to come to terms with what you have, learn to accept it. Even though you want to get better, you know you can't. So you work with what you have. And you learn not to be jealous of your neighbor if he gets a new car, and not to make your husband feel bad because he can't get a new car too. Or maybe you are jealous, but you go out and polish up your old car.

> We try to teach our children that it isn't all that important to have brand new clothes all the time and the latest fashions. As long as they look clean and neat, they should not feel badly about their clothes.

People also substitute nonmaterial goals, values, and qualities for unachievable material goals.

> We don't have all the material things, like a complete bathroom or a bedroom for each person. But in this family we have something which all the money in the world couldn't buy: love.

In the eyes of outsiders, goal substitution, goal reduction, and restriction of psychological commitment may be interpreted as "lack of motivation," "apathy," or "improper values." But the strategies seem to be positively func-tional in that they preserve mental health by maintaining a tolerable balance between aspirations and achievements. The necessity for such maneuvering is pointed up by those cases where individuals have not modified or substituted for high goals, despite repeated proof of their elusiveness. These are the most tragic life histories, individuals who suffer tremendous emotional ups and downs and a great sense of failure. It could thus be argued that aspirations that are too high compared to achievement levels may actually work to perpetuate poverty by causing psychological damage to adults and consequent strain in the home environments of children. By contrast, those individuals who have reduced their goals to a level where some are easily at-tainable appear often to lead more stable emotional and family lives.

Another common pattern for handling the disparity between aspirations and achievements is to modify behavior in such a way that a sought-after goal becomes irrelevant or out of the question. There are many examples. A child who is frustrated in school by his inability to succeed academically may gravitate to the role of class clown or troublemaker. A teenage girl may become pregnant and drop out of school, or an older woman may bear another child—both may be avoiding setting and striving for other goals. An adoles-cent boy with some scholastic promise sabotages his eduation by getting kicked out of school. An adult relapses into drinking after a long dry period. In each of these situations the individual has put himself or herself in a position where attainment of a certain goal, or the performance of a certain role, is no longer appropriate or expected, and he or she is thereby released from the frustrations of pursuing it.[11] (Here again, it should be noted that such mechanisms are by no means the unique province of the rural poor. They occur in all segments of our society. They are discussed here because of their frequency in a life situation in which one of the ever-present problems is the difficulty of accepting and managing the gap between goals and achievement.)

When the various mechanisms for fending off the disappointment of unmet goals are not effective, the result is deep, prolonged frustration. This may lead to outbursts of physical violence and destructiveness, in the home, in the neighborhood, or in the outside community. Prolonged frustration may also lead to resignation, to temporarily giving up. People worry that they are "cracking up," and some periodically sign themselves into state mental hospitals when their burdens become intolerable. Some people talk of suicide, and some attempt to blot out their troubles with heavy drinking. They lose hope, and fear they can no longer continue the struggle.

> There's a limit to how much my husband can stand before he gives up altogether. It seems like we just begin to see our way clear towards getting some little thing accomplished, like maybe we have almost enough money set aside to put in a septic tank. Then something big comes along, like our car gives out, or he gets laid off, or one of the kids has some kind of trouble. Then we have to scrap our plans again. He was so disgusted the other night I was afraid he was going to crack up. He just can't take it any more. There's got to be some let-up for him. We have to get some results from all our struggling. There must be some good to come of it all.

Walking this difficult tightrope, making slow and halting progress toward hoped-for rewards at the other end, requires delicate psychological, behavioral, and aspirational balancing, and constant readjustment. People cling to the standard societal goals and norms, however, and strive toward a better future, because they recognize the danger of resignation.

> If we gave up our hopes, we might as well die.

They also cling to their hopes because of their children. Having projected their own unmet aspirations onto their children, their greatest desire is that their children have a better life than they have had. Parents know that if they give up caring and trying, the likelihood of their children's "making it" will be seriously jeopardized. In their children they perceive the best chance for the fulfillment of dreams they once had for themselves. They continue to struggle so that their children may some day achieve those dreams.

Meanwhile, the gap between aspirations and achievements, however it is balanced and managed, continues to be an active cause in perpetuating poverty and marginality because of the damage it does to emotional well-being, family relationships, and general life functioning.

8. The Failure Syndrome

Closely related as an ongoing cause of intergenerational rural poverty is the cycle of failure. Repeated experiences of failure, almost unavoidable for many people, lead to low self-esteem and lack of confidence. This, in turn, leads to limited expectations for oneself that are apt to cause further failures and reinforce the low self-image. The cycle continues, in all spheres of life: on the job, in school, in dealings with community agencies and institutions, in social relationships, and in marriage and family relationships.[12]

Observable behavior and verbalized sentiments reveal the ways people attempt to protect what shreds of self-confidence they still possess. They try to regulate their experiences and situations so that the risk of incurring failure is kept as low as possible, partly through assessing situations and hedging on commitments.

> Everything we do is a big stepping stone—if we succeed. But it's hard for us to take disappointments. We've built up such a lot of resentments from all our disappointments. So, we always try to size up a situation and figure out what's in it that could be good for us, and what's in it that could hurt us.

They exercise caution in setting up expectations for themselves, and expectations purposely may be set low. A typical example is the man whose wife has left him. He vows that he will go out and get some other woman to fulfill his sexual needs. But he aims very low, talking of substitute women whom, at other times, he has labeled tramps. With them, he can be sure of success in reaffirming his power over women. These low aspirations, however, reveal both the depth of the wound to his self-esteem, and the urgency of his need for protection from further ego damage. Caution in setting up expectations may also involve setting goals that are short-term rather than long-term.

> We learn to live one day at a time. We try to get through today as best we can, and not worry about tomorrow until it comes.

The efficacy of this short-term strategy would appear to be validated by the fact that it is the foremost tenet of Alcoholics Anonymous. But when people apply the same strategy to coping with poverty, the nonpoor conclude that they are "present-oriented" and "unable to think past today." Consequently, although dealing with one day at a time may preserve the poor person's mental health, it may also reinforce stereotypes and add to an internalized negative self-evaluation.

The individual also attempts to reduce the likelihood of failure by manipulating others' expectations of him. He limits his participation in community institutions and organized activity so that participation will not be expected of him. Even in elementary school a child may perform at a level that allows him to stay in the slow reading group, although he might actually be able to do better. Promotion to a higher-level group would increase the risk of failure. Men turn down promotions to more responsible jobs for essentially the same reason.[13]

In many ways, then, people minimize the risks of potential failure. But knowing that not all failure can be avoided, they also build in cushions to soften the impact when it does occur. When people are trying something new, they often keep the old tried-and-true pattern alongside the new, just in case the new doesn't work out. A family will hold on to its former shack, just in case payments on the trailer they're buying cannot be kept up. Parents will assure grown chidren that they can always return home if they can't make it on their own.

The impact of failure is also dealt with, and muted somewhat, by beliefs about the causes of failure. Specific failures are often blamed on forces beyond one's control, thus removing the blame. Some explain events in religious terms: "God has His own purposes" and "His own plan," and "He intends us to profit from our tribulations." (This can explain anything from mental retardation to a teenage girl's pregnancy.) Others cite "bad luck" or a series of "bad breaks." (This might explain a fire, loss of a job, or an accident in a "new" car.) But the lifelong pattern of consistent, repeated disappointments is harder to accept and explain. Long-term failure is usually explained by reference to a deprived childhood, lack of education, other people's interference (all causes external to the self), and by a vague belief that some people are simply more prone to have trouble than others. Hardly ever does anyone say that his or her problems are the fault of the American economic structure; few see themselves as casualties of "the system." Individual operators in the system—the boss, the welfare worker, the judge, or a neighbor—may be blamed, but not the system itself.

People perceive events and difficulties as "happening" to them, rather than as the direct result of the individual's vulnerable situation or his actions. For example, a "burn out" (serious house fire) is not usually connected to the family's living in a highly flammable house heated by an unreliable kerosene stove—it's just another event in an unexplainable series of things that happen.

All the bad things that have happened to us have happened on holidays. When we got burned out it was my birthday. When my first husband died, it was on Christmas. My accident happened on Thanksgiving, and my brother's accident happened on my birthday.

Despite the strategies for testing situations, for managing expectation, for hedging against disappointment, and for externalizing the causes of failure, many people are frequently exposed to personal feelings of failure. Because they must participate in a community in which they do not have the economic resources, social skills, or personal confidence to compete successfully, many individuals live with a fairly high and unremitting sense of failure. Although men seldom mention this feeling, except sometimes when they're drunk, women talk quite freely of their own and their husband's sense of failure.

> My husband is so discouraged. Sometimes he feels as if he's fighting the whole world. And when he gets discouraged this way, he just can't seem to do any-thing right. And that makes him all the more discouraged. He's really down now, and it has me worried.

While it is not true that everyone in Chestnut Valley experiences failure every day and wallows in a pervasive sense of failure, for many people there is a cumulative lifetime experience of failure that generates future failure, because it erodes self-confidence and because it strains family relationships, affecting the children as well. Parents with low self-confidence are unable to instill high levels of confidence in their children. This is the failure syndrome, a vital factor in the perpetuation of rural poverty.

9. Psychosocial Deficits from Early Childhood

The experiences of childhood, first in the homes of a rural poverty-stricken neighborhood and later in the "outside world," have long-range effects on an individual's psychological adjustment and the quality of his social interaction, and thus on the continuing cycle of poverty.[14]

Adults trying to sort out and explain their problems most often refer to their childhoods, to factors of social and emotional deprivation as well as poverty. However, neither the material deprivation nor the social marginality in which they were raised has been eliminated in the intervening years. The same socioeconomic conditions that existed a generation ago and caused the problems now experienced by adults still exist today, and may predispose today's children to suffering the same problems as their parents. This cycle continues *despite* the parents' hopes and their efforts to provide a different and better life for their children.

Any emotional difficulties that parents carry over from their own childhoods will form part of the environment in which they bring up their own children. Unresolved emotional and social problems of one or both parents, *exacerbated by the strain of living in poverty,* may jeopardize the children's home environment and interfere with their psychosocial develop-ment. For example, if family life is often disrupted by fighting and one or both parents periodically leaves, the child may conclude that people are not to be

trusted, and that close attachments are dangerous. To avoid further emotional pain and social loss, a child in this situation may restrict his emotional
involvement with others, acting as if they are not important to him. As the
child matures, he may exhibit difficulty in establishing and maintaining interpersonal relationships, both within his home and in the "outside world."
This effect perpetuates marginality and poverty.

Whatever psychosocial difficulties the child experienced in his earliest
years are often reinforced and worsened by his experiences in the outside
world, primarily in school. Since schools generally reflect the stereotypes and
social separations that exist in the society as a whole, a child from a rural,
depressed neighborhood is usually labeled upon entry into a heterogeneous
school system, and repeatedly made to understand that he, along with his
siblings and his cousins, is on the bottom. His weaknesses are brought out, his
strengths overlooked, and he fails to develop a sense of mastery and control.
For some children, the emotional and social damage incurred in the elementary school years may be an even greater loss than the academic under-
achievement.

In each generation the same poverty and struggle, the same inadequacies of
social participation and support, the same interpersonal unpredictability and
self-doubt—all these form the atmosphere in which crucial childhood experiences take place. The psychological effect on children may be long-lasting,
affecting the environment that they will create when they, in their turn, raise
the next generation of children.

10. The Closing-in of Horizons

The final factor perpetuating rural poverty is a cumulative result of all the
other factors woven together. As an individual experiences years of the
failure, frustration, struggle, and disappointment that are inherent in poverty
and marginality, his horizons close in and he or she becomes locked into a
world of limited hopes and bounded environments.

Some people respond to the narrowed horizons with bitterness, resignation,
and/or alcohol, but most adults eventually accept their situation. Withdrawing into this restricted world, they feel at home in it, despite its physical
discomforts.

> I used to have dreams. But gradually I learned to accept what I have and try to
> improve it by degrees.

> Some people here have been disappointed because they haven't been able to ac-
> cept the things they couldn't accomplish. Others gradually come to terms with
> what they have.

> Look at my neighbor. Once she learned to accept the fact that her husband
> would always be that way, and that they would always be just getting by, then

she was able to settle down and get some pleasure out of the things she did have.

Horizons become limited also because of fear of the unknown and the anxiety people have about trying new things or subjecting themselves to unfamiliar situations—unnecessary ego risks. Given the inadequate social connections between the fringe and rural areas and the larger community, individuals cannot be assured of success in community participation, and there are no ways to prelearn appropriate roles nor opportunities to forge an identity with outside groups and situations. As a result, individuals who feel marginal to the larger community usually limit their participation in it as much as possible. Their range of identification and interaction remains almost totally restricted to family and neighborhood—while the dominant pattern in American society is moving in the opposite direction.

Likewise, in his choice of role models, the child who once identified with firemen, schoolteachers, nurses, doctors, even presidents, may grow up to identify only with persons in the home environment, because he perceives that it is unrealistic to pattern himself after the models presented to him in the "outside world."

This closing-in of horizons is both a curse and a salvation to young adults. The knowledge that they can always retreat to the safety of home, accepting the limited horizons of the rural, depressed neighborhood, probably has the negative effect of reducing the effort some of them put into making it in the outside world. On the other hand, unless and until the outside world becomes more accessible, the home neighborhood—as both a physical and a socioeconomic niche—is an essential haven for the preservation of the self. Thus, horizons close, and limits may come to feel welcome, rather than constraining.

Conclusion

The causes of poverty in rural America and the factors that perpetuate it are complex. There are no simple villains or scapegoats. There is no single cause. Rural poverty involves a cluster of problems that are the result of a whole set of interacting causes.

The ten causal factors I've discussed, viewed as overlapping and interacting phenomena, provide an explanation for the fact that rural poverty and marginality have persisted with such tenacity generation after generation. The adverse legacy of history (primary cause 1) continues to leave its imprint because it is reinforced by other factors (primary causes 2, 3, 4, and 5). These five primary causes bring about the derivative causes (numbers 6, 7, 8, 9, and 10). And each of the ten causes is also self-perpetuating. Hence, poverty and marginality continue on and on in an intergenerational cycle.

The ten factors analyzed here are *ongoing* causes: they operate now and *will continue* to operate, shaping children's lives and futures—unless significant changes are made.

Changes can be made. Knowledge gained from studying Chestnut Valley could serve as a basis for designing changes and implementing programs that could help unspring the trap in which the people of many marginal rural areas have been caught for so long.

Suggestions for the Future

Introduction

When the burden of poverty and its related problems becomes particularly heavy, Mary Crane sometimes daydreams.

> If only there was a magic button we could press to make all the problems go away. Then we could start all over again with no old problems hanging over us. And we'd be able to keep on top of things.

American society as a whole often seems to wish for a "magic button," a swift and sure means of eliminating poverty. Perhaps the War on Poverty was America's magic button, but although we pressed it for nearly a decade, poverty did not disappear. We are beginning to realize that there are no magical solutions.

Poverty will not vanish of its own accord, either in the nation or in one little valley. The problem of poverty in rural areas is *self-perpetuating, not self-curing.* Ignored, it will become ever more intractable, as its causes interact and reinforce each other. Only a conscious and purposeful attempt to eliminate the multiple causes that perpetuate poverty will break the cycle that traps people generation after generation.

This chapter will explore possible approaches for breaking into the cycle of cause and effect. For each of the ten ongoing causes of rural poverty, identified in the previous chapter, some general suggestions are offered, then one particular aspect is singled out for specific remedies and proposals. Here again, it should be stressed that the division of the list of ten causes into two groups — primary causes and derivative causes — is not merely a framework for organizing discussion, but represents a significant dichotomy in reality. The five primary causes of rural poverty lie essentially outside the run-down rural neighborhoods; they are embedded in the larger society, facets of society's structures and processes. Hence, removal of the primary causes of rural poverty will require changes in the society itself. The derivative causes, on the other hand, have arisen in response to the difficult situations created by the primary causes. This fact has two significant implications: (1) attention must be directed first and foremost to the primary causes and (2) if the primary causes are removed, the derivative causes will almost automatically diminish. Thus, addressing the primary causes will pay double benefits.

The suggestions offered in this chapter are not intended as a blueprint for all of rural America, or all poverty, for the data cannot be generalized that broadly. Besides, it is important to realize that the solution to poverty is really many different solutions, each tailored to the particularities of a specific poverty situation, a specific set of needs. The suggestions put forth for this particular case apply only to situations having roughly the same general configurations and needs. The suggestions offered in this chapter are also limited in that they do not go beyond or contradict the substantiating data of this study. For example, the chapter does not advocate either major economic revolution or sweeping societal reorganization, for such suggestions would run counter to expressed goals and preferences. Rural poor people want an improved opportunity within the existing system; they want to partake of the American Dream as it is defined in the late twentieth century.

The suggested remedies do involve some changes and new directions on the national, regional, state, and local levels. But all of the suggestions are realistic within the framework of present societal capabilities. Many of them are based on observed situations and programs implemented in various communities. If implemented on a more general scale, these suggestions could result in a better future for the people of Chestnut Valley and for people in similar situations elsewhere.

Dealing with the Primary Causes of Rural Poverty

1. Shaping the Impact of History

In searching for historical factors underlying rural poverty, we saw that the people of these upland areas were gradually squeezed out by economic and social changes that swept over rural America during the past century.

Now, in the late twentieth century, significant changes are taking place, and the consequences for marginal rural people look just as serious. National patterns affecting the local situation include: (1) increasing concentration of agriculture only in the most technologically efficient regions, (2) the declining industrial economy of the Northeast, (3) reduction of low-skill entry-level jobs as industry contracts and automates, (4) continuing centralization of community functions, and concentration of programs and services in more densely populated areas, and (5) new land-use patterns related to suburbanization. These new trends are modern parallels of the historical changes that brought about the problem of entrenched rural poverty in the first place. All of these new forces may have serious implications for the future, not only in Chestnut Valley, but elsewhere throughout the region. These forces should be monitored for their potential impact on the people of rural areas. If a possibly negative impact is recognized early enough, it could be averted or controlled so that further socioeconomic displacement could be avoided. At the very least, the negative impact of such trends could be cushioned.

CUSHIONING THE NEGATIVE IMPACT OF SUBURBANIZATION ON HOUSING.[1] As suburbanizing pressures push outward from urban centers, the housing situa-tion for rural low-income residents gets worse. The price of rural land and housing rises markedly; taxes increase dramatically; and the supply of inex-pensive rural housing shrinks. People of limited financial resources can no longer obtain old tumbledown farmhouses, abandoned one-room school-houses, and vacant house sites, for these are quickly bought up by more af-fluent exurbanite renovators, investors, and back-to-the-land enthusiasts. Poor people already living in the area cannot compete in this market, and their sons and daughters may be squeezed out because they are left with few options for meeting their own increasing housing needs: they can make over and expand their homes; they can build modest houses on land owned by relatives; or, increasingly, they can turn to the house trailer as the only affordable form of housing.

However, as suburbanization proceeds, not only is there escalation of hous-ing prices, but also elevation of housing standards. As population density in-creases, housing and sanitary codes are tightened. As new residents settle in, they seek to protect their investment and their image of the rural environ-ment. "Junk ordinances" are enacted and enforced, building permits are re-quired for construction, and zoning laws regulate density and type of housing. Trailers may be restricted to mobile home parks. Municipal pressure is brought against the jerry-built shack, the converted school bus, the cluster of dwellings sharing a single lot and a single septic facility, and against the perpetual process of piecemeal building and modifying of homes.

The net result of these new patterns of rural land use and regulation is that poorer people cannot afford to stay in their home area because their makeshift housing is gradually squeezed out, and they can no longer find or devise the cheap housing they require (described in Chapter 6). Consequently, poorer rural people, especially younger couples, are forced to move farther away from the urban growth center. They move into more peripheral townships or counties, where there is less land pressure and therefore less cost and restric-tion on housing. They stay there until, once again, the pressures of expanding suburbanization catch up with them, and they are forced to flee to another as-yet-unwanted rural area.

This rural "musical chairs" pattern has serious drawbacks as a solution for coping with these new trends. First, important sustaining ties to family, relatives, heritage, and a place are weakened or broken. Second, imper-manence may become a way of life, with a pattern of running away from situations, of searching always for a safe haven elsewhere. Third, and perhaps most important, the connections to a community (its people, its sense of coherence, its schools, churches, and voluntary groups, its doctors and counseling services) become even weaker than they were. Adults move from one community to another without ever plugging in well to the facilities and services they need, without establishing social ties. And the communities to which they move tend to be nonaffluent communities, with insufficient tax base to support a high level of human services. The children of mobile low-income families move in and out of different schools, never getting settled enough to make significant progress. This transience is superimposed on the already difficult problems children from low-income rural families meet in their school experiences, and its detrimental effect has often been remarked upon by school administrators in the area. The market-generated residential mobility could thus have long-term negative effects on a whole generation of rural people.

To deal with the housing pressures now faced by rural poor people, I would suggest a three-pronged approach.

• *Monitor the supply of inexpensive rural housing available for people of limited economic resources, and consider the impact that market forces and proposed municipal regulations might have on this housing supply.* For example, although public sentiment may object to old trailers and shacks as ugly blots on the landscape, ruling out such facilities in rural areas would surely have a detrimental impact on people for whom this housing represents a necessary compromise. Ordinances forcing trailers into mobile home parks significantly raise the housing cost, because most trailer parks charge a fairly high space rental and some do not permit old and modified trailers.

As a general policy, perhaps the concept of protecting rural environments should be more broad-mindedly defined. Is it really a violation of the rural spirit to have a tight roadside cluster of houses and trailers if there is a wooded hillside behind them? Is it necessary for suburban municipalities to set housing-density limits that rule out such de facto "cluster housing?" Can a rural residential area be protected against commercial development without being turned into a highly restrictive and high-priced suburb? Raising such questions will help ensure that new population influx is not inadvertently allowed to squeeze out inexpensive forms of rural housing.

• *Help low-income rural people bring their housing up to a level of greater health, safety, and comfort—a level that more closely approximates community standards.* Since major improvements, such as septic and water systems, cost much more than many rural families can pay, and normal bank loans are far too expensive, government programs for home improvement assistance are clearly needed. But most of these people do not qualify for the low-interest home improvement loans available from the Farmers' Home Administration, as they require far greater economic stability and a higher income than many of the people of Chestnut Valley have. The loan programs have little flexibility in the standards by which they judge loan applicants and their proposed projects: women heads of families have difficulty qualifying; trailers and substandard homes do not usually qualify at all; and land titles must be clear. Obviously, loan programs should be more closely tailored to reflect the specific needs and situations of the people who most need help in improving their homes.[2]

Even if home improvement loans were made more accessible, however, they would not appeal to all rural poor people, since they run counter to traditional strategies for getting by financially, strategies that stress minimization of cash outlay and avoidance of fixed or long-term cash obligations (see Chapter 6). Therefore, in some cases outright grants may be necessary. Several federal programs (Farmers' Home Administration, Housing and Urban Development) are beginning to move in this direction—albeit in very small steps and with difficulty obtaining needed funding levels.[3] Perhaps some assistance might also come from other government sources, such as programs that help small municipalities fund sewer and water improvement programs. Such funds might possibly be used to underwrite the design, development, and installation of septic systems appropriate for clusters of three to six households in rural areas.

• *Help rural people compete in the changing rural housing market by increasing their buying power.* This would imply a more general economic improvement, which will be discussed in the next section of this chapter. Specific to buying power in housing, though, one encouraging development along this line is the extension to rural areas of the federal "Section 8" HUD housing program that subsidizes rent, in which the family pays only one-fourth of its income toward the rent and the government pays the shortfall to make up fair market rent for the landlord. The program may be particularly helpful for young adults, young families, and people with a low but steady source of income, whether from welfare or employment. But the program is not appropriate for those residents who do not have the security of a steady income, those who find it more economical to own than to rent, and those who are currently paying less than the government's benchmark of 25 percent of income for housing. More appropriate housing assistance would concentrate on raising income levels and strengthening income stability so that people could handle their housing needs on their own.

Focusing attention on the need to monitor and improve the *rural* housing situation, however, does not imply that urban housing units are not also needed. Urban housing, affordable and decent, should be available as an option for those rural people who would prefer to move into the cities, as well as for urban people. But it is clear from this study that a move to urban housing, though it may bring improved physical conditions, also has significant drawbacks as a solution for rural people's housing needs. Not only does it weaken important ties to people and places, it also undermines independence and individual initiative. Furthermore, urban housing is apt to be more expensive, both to the individual and to the public, than rural housing. Even when urban housing rents are publicly subsidized on a sliding scale, the occupant may pay far more in cash rent than he would for rural housing. Urban rents, even when subsidized, may be more than a family can afford, thus forcing people to seek public assistance. Thus, the real cost of supporting rural people in urban housing may be far greater than the cost of providing grants for improvement of rural housing.

The general point is that rural people who are poor should have several options for meeting their housing needs, and some of those options should be designed to enable them to remain where they can live inexpensively and maintain important socioemotional supports – and still obtain better housing than they now have.

2. Changing the Economic Situation

It is clear that the people of the rural depressed areas must have more money available to them for meeting their needs and alleviating the constant stress of insufficient and insecure income. However, this study shows that the answer lies neither in "handouts" nor in "incentives to work." Most rural poor people are already basically committed to working for a living, and most of them attempt to live by that commitment. The thrust of change must come in assuring the adequacy of employment: more available jobs, more appropriate jobs, greater employment security, better wages and benefits, and increased opportunity for personal satisfaction on the job.

One useful approach would be to identify crucial points in an individual's life or in the family's development cycle when holding an adequate job would bring most benefits for the individual and the household, and to provide assistance and support at that time to make sure the individual is able to find and keep a job. One such intervention point would be during the late teen/early adult years; another would be at the stage in family development when a woman can realistically consider going (back) to work. At both these turning points, those individuals who have been able to enter the work force successfully have significantly improved their financial, personal, and family stability. Those who have been frustrated by inability to obtain secure jobs appropriate to their needs and abilities at this crucial time tend to become mired in worsening financial and personal problems. These turning points are too important in the lives of individuals and families to leave the individual's employment to chance and the uncontrolled job market. Focused assistance to help people enter the world of work satisfactorily at these important times would have long-range impact.

Coupled with such expanded employment opportunities, however, it seems that a federal guaranteed minimum income, or a negative income tax, would also be needed. This would assure sufficient economic security for all households, including those with no members able to work regularly and those in which the ratio of wage earners to dependents is too low to support its members adequately from employment earnings alone. A combination of employment improvements and some form of guaranteed minimum income is in line with much current thinking on the eradication of poverty in the nation as a whole.[4]

IMPROVING THE ECONOMIC SITUATION FOR WOMEN. This in-depth case study leads to a conviction that the cause of women's economic difficulty is *not* that they are lazy and unwilling to work, or happy to depend on welfare. Some of the women have been fairly steady workers, and others have taken jobs periodically. But their economic status should be strengthened.

Government coercion for women to take jobs (as in the Work Incentive pro-gram, WIN) is, however, not an appropriate strategy. The application of eco-nomic sanctions—such as cutting off food stamps or AFDC benefits for women who do not register for employment when their youngest child is more than six years old—is not a solution at all, and may be counterproduc-tive.[5] For one thing, this may be unrealistically early for some women to take on the triple role of wage earner, homemaker, and mother. The benefits of a mother's remaining at home, even after all her children have reached school age, may outweigh the relatively low wages she would earn in the kind of job she might get. Second, there may be complicating problems in her home life that make it nearly impossible for a woman to take an outside job, and that may predispose her to lack of success in both the paid job and the home job should she try to do both. For example, she may already be overtaxed by health problems, emotional exhaustion, low self-esteem, marital problems, ex-tra household members, insecurity about the future, problems adequately supervising children when they're not in school, and the demands of doing a lot of housework with inadequate facilities. (Although AFDC and food stamp work regulations include exemptions for medical problems, the diffuse condition of generally poor physical and mental health may be difficult to diagnose and document for exemption.)

Instead of attaching an arbitrary across-the-board work requirement to assistance programs, it would seem much more effective to concentrate on making improvements in the employment situation. This would involve a combination of improving the employment opportunities for women and enhancing their employability. Particularly helpful would be: (1) increased op- portunities to work on a periodic, part-time, and flexible-time basis when a woman's situation warrants and can sustain it; (2) improved education, voca- tional counseling, and job experience for teenage girls and young women out of school; (3) expanded work reentry opportunities for women of middle age, with appropriate counseling, training, and placement assistance; and (4) development or expansion of a system of wage increments for people who per- form well but for various reasons need or prefer to remain on the common laborer level.

Observations of working women in both the young-adult and the mid-life years indicate that women generally benefit in personal as well as financial terms from employment if the jobs are appropriate for them and if other fac- tors in their personal and home life do not interfere. The status or glamour or career-ladder concept of the job may not be the most important factor to a woman from a low-income rural background. Janitorial work in institutions and assembly-line work in factories have been quite acceptable to some women, and are often preferred by middle-age women, for whom the pride of holding a job and earning an income seems to outweigh the career or status aspects of their jobs. Other women desire more people-oriented work, as nurse's aides and hairdressers, for example. The range of jobs available should be as varied as the women and their needs. Individualized assistance in preparing for and finding appropriate work would be far more effective than coercion to take whatever job is available.

Other economic changes for women should be made outside the regular employment sphere, for even women who are not employed participate in the household economy. Women usually take care of the lengthy paperwork and numerous official appointments necessary to supplement the family's income through food stamps, welfare, and so forth. As consumers, women go to rum- mage sales and low-price outlets to save money on living costs. These income- earning or expense-saving activities should be given recognition and credit, for women are using their time and energy to make a direct contribution to the household economy. Restriction of cash outflow is as important a con- tribution to family economics as increasing cash income.

Women should also receive realistic payment for the care-giving services they provide for extra children, physically or mentally disabled relatives, and elderly people whom they keep in their homes. If they were paid for this work, rather than just receiving an allocation of money from public assistance benefits for the home-cared individual, women would also be building up their financial position for the future through Social Security.

It is important to point out that these suggestions for improving women's economic situation should not be carried out in a vacuum. Corresponding im-

provements in the employment situation for men must also be made, especially since one of the deterrents to women's successful employment is their
husband's jealousy over money-earning roles. In fact, any improvement in the
income-earning situation of men would almost automatically have the extra
benefit of enabling women to participate more successfully in the world of
work.

3. Correcting the Inadequacies of Social Structure

This study has indicated two important social contributors to the problem
of entrenched rural poverty: the collapse of the rural community and the incomplete integration of rural poor people into the larger urban community.

The question arises whether viable small communities could be re-created
in each of these rural depressed localities. The realistic answer would seem to
be "no." Societal changes have gone too far to make this a feasible solution.
Special interests and activities, rather than locality groupings, now form the
basis of social interaction. While it may be that some community institutions
may be stirred back to life by energetic local people or newcomers, only in
rural areas with a fairly large population and more affluence would significant
resurgence of the community be likely to occur. And only with concentrated
effort and attention would the poverty-stricken "native" residents be caught
up in this essentially exurbanite, educated, affluent movement.

RESISTING FURTHER CENTRALIZATION. Pressures toward further centralization of services, education, and organizations should be resisted at this time.
The negative consequences of earlier centralization, as in the school consolidation movement of the post–World War II era, have not yet completely
disappeared. Before initiating another round of centralization, more positive
steps must be taken to treat the casualties of the last round. State funding
schemes should not penalize school districts that resist official plans for merg-
ing into larger, conglomerate districts.

Another centralization drive that should not be blindly accepted is the
propensity of states and counties to consolidate youth recreation services
under county-wide umbrella organizations. This represents one more lost
function for the rural township or village (which may be left with little more
than snowplowing and dog licensing functions to fulfill – and even these are
increasingly being taken out of their hands).

Centralization of recreation, as of education, may throw poorer rural people
into a situation in which they feel like outsiders and participate only minimally, if at all. Good local programs, with local input in planning and managing, would attract more people from poorer families. Local programs would
serve as a training ground from which youngsters could move out into the
wider world of urban-based youth activities, and in which their parents could
get a taste of success in planning, organizing, and participating at the local

level. There should be more, rather than less, support for small-community programs.

In other municipal functions, such as child care and health, for example, state and federal money has often favored large municipalities and consolidated programs. Federal revenue-sharing funds have to some degree counteracted this tendency, giving townships some decision-making power and program control. The federal government also is beginning to recognize the needs of rural areas, and may be taking steps to help rural areas and small towns get their fair share of federal grants and programs.[6]

BUILDING SOCIAL BRIDGES. New avenues could be built to facilitate successful and satisfying participation by rural low-income people in the social activities and groups of the larger community. This improved social linkage would also contribute to smoother relationships within the neighborhood and family.

One point made clear by this study is that rural poor people do not want to participate as "the poor," as members of "poor people's groups," as "low-income parents," and so forth. Rather, they need and want to participate as *people* – as individuals, as parents, as children – *regardless of income level*. To the fullest extent possible, the community's institutionalized activities should avoid treating low-income participants as members of a separate socioeconomic class – as "the disadvantaged" or as the people from a particular locale – for the stigma of poverty and "bad" neighborhoods is already too strong. Increased public labeling is definitely not beneficial.

A potential, though often overlooked, social bridge to the dominant community is that of volunteer service. Several women have, in fact, expressed a desire to contribute their time to the community, perhaps caring for people who are old, ill, or disabled. But there are no readily available avenues for such participatory contributions. Perhaps if transportation and other incidental costs could be subsidized (on the same basis as the federally sponsored Retired Senior Volunteer Program, which offsets the expenses incurred by senior citizens doing volunteer work), women who are not employed could contribute needed human services to their communities. In so doing, the volunteers would also learn employable skills, make satisfying new connections with the dominant community, and improve their own self-images. A woman whose family life is chaotic and whose children are difficult to handle may make an excellent care-giver outside her own home, and her competent performance may actually improve her functioning at home.

4. Locating and Removing Barriers to Upward Mobility

Several barriers to upward mobility have been identified in this study: (1) lack of economic resources sufficient to provide for both necessities and status goods, (2) absence of social entry points for participating and gaining acceptance in the wider community, (3) pervasive negative stereotypes, (4) the fact that the problems associated with lifelong poverty create such strains that failure and limited achievements come to be accepted as inevitable, and (5) the inability of public education to compensate for socioeconomic handicaps. Since the first four barriers to upward mobility pertain also to the other ongoing causes of rural poverty, suggestions for dealing with them appear under various other headings in this chapter. Here we will concentrate on the educational barrier.

INCREASING THE EFFECTIVENESS OF PUBLIC EDUCATION. As a society, Americans believe in education as the path to economic and social success; and that belief is reinforced by statistics showing direct correlation between income level and amount of education. This view is shared by many poverty-stricken adults of Chestnut Valley, who are well aware of the drawbacks of their own limited educations. For themselves, however, they feel it is too late in life to use education as a tool to surmount their poverty. Thus, they may underutilize available education programs for adults, including basic literacy programs and community colleges. Adult education programs may also be underused because they are not sufficiently flexible in terms of locations, hours, curriculum, bureaucratic requirements, and expectations. Too few programs reach people where they are (geographically, educationally, or financially). For some of the younger adults observed during this study, however, the community colleges have been a very effective bridge into stable and satisfying employment, a significant factor in upward mobility. But not very many have followed this route.

In local belief and practice, it is the education of young children that is stressed as part of the deferred dream of escaping from poverty. And it is here that education falls short. Although the elementary and secondary schools of the region surrounding Chestnut Valley are of high caliber, serving the majority of their students adequately, the children from the rural poor homes consistently do not benefit from their years in school. Many teachers and administrators recognize the problem and are concerned. An administrator in one rural district commented, "We know those kids. They're maybe 10 percent of our school population. We think we know what they need. We try – I honestly think we do our darndest – to be effective with them. But I've got to admit that in many cases – too many – we miss our mark. We do not succeed with these kids." Despite good school systems, despite the touted advantages of a heterogeneous pupil population, despite honest desire to serve low-income rural children better, some children systematically fail to thrive in school. Many children fail to benefit enough from their schooling to succeed in their postschool endeavors.

Several needed changes or redirections of emphasis can be suggested that might increase the effectiveness of education in preparing children from rural poverty backgrounds for successful participation in the wider world.

• *Explode a societal myth.* As a start, the myth that education is *the* key to escaping poverty should be questioned. Since insufficient education is but *one* facet of poverty, better education and more of it would only attack the poverty problem on one front. To say that lack of education causes poverty or that more years spent in school would overcome poverty is to oversimplify the problem of poverty and to misrepresent education. Despite recent educational innovations (such as Head Start), schools have failed, and will continue to fail to lift people out of poverty because it is simply too much to expect schools to be societal panaceas, magic carpets out of poverty.

• *Bury an old argument.* It is time to put aside pointless arguments over who is to blame for the documented fact that children from lower socioeconomic levels are found disproportionately in the lower achievement levels in schools.[7] The frustrated, defensive attitude many educators take comes out in their statements that the children have no worthwhile role models at home, that their homes have no books, and that the "damage" to the children is already done before they come to school, "so it's not our fault that we can't do anything with them." Parents, for their part, say the schools "don't want to be bothered with kids from this neighborhood" and "don't really give our kids a chance." "They don't really educate our kids, don't teach them, just pass them on from grade to grade."

This old argument continues, in words, in attitudes, and in preconceptions; and it influences actions on both sides. As long as the argument is continued, time, commitment, and effort are diverted from the real job at hand – improving schooling for youngsters from lower socioeconomic backgrounds.

• *Build a new relationship.* Schools sometimes reflect the public stereotype that poor people do not care about their children and their children's education. The parents from these rural areas do indeed care. But their caring is not recognized because of several factors: (1) parents may not express their caring in ways that the school understands or expects – such as making sure their children attend school every day and coming in for conferences with teachers; (2) parents may care so very much that they are deeply hurt by any hint of a child's difficulty in school and may consequently withdraw from contact or become hostile toward the school; (3) parents may have unrealistic hopes, expectations, and fears about schools, education, and their children; and (4) parents may be bogged down by too many other problems and crises to pay much attention to the everyday details, notices, and requests that children bring home from school.

Schools could work to build new avenues for parents to express their caring by becoming involved in the enterprise of educating their own youngsters. Perhaps the recent trend emphasizing professionalism in the teaching of young children could be reversed. A parent with limited formal education is particularly vulnerable to the underlying message that parents are inadequate to the task of helping children learn. It would seem possible, instead, for schools to help parents develop skills and confidence so that they could assume a more active role in their children's education. At the very least, such an attempt would improve communication and understanding between parents and schools, would set them up as partners rather than adversaries in the education of children. Especially in the case of young parents whose children are just beginning their school careers, such efforts could have significant effects.

Fundamental to any such efforts, schools should simply adopt the assumption that, unless it is proven otherwise, parents from the rural poverty areas *do* care. Beyond that, schools could try a variety of innovative methods to bridge the school-home gap. Successful methods include: a home-school coordinator or aide to serve as a go-between and facilitator of communication; school-community activities to get children out into the community; and special programs at the school that draw parents in for comfortable, nonthreatening, and informal interaction. (Programs and activities at the school are more easily attended by low-income parents if they can bring their children, including babies, and perhaps other relatives as well.)

• *Study the schools.* A school is far more than the sum of its academic programs; it is a gestalt that includes a myriad of social systems, interactional patterns, unplanned activities, and microenvironments. A school could conduct a thorough study of itself as a total institution to see how the children from rural poor families fit into it. The study would encompass not just teaching methods, but every type of academic, para-academic and non-academic situation, every nook and cranny of the school facility, every minute of the school day. It would include a study of the informal social hierarchy and social attitudes that children bring with them, and how these are played out in the school environment.

The study of a school should provide extremely useful insights into what really happens, what doesn't happen, and why both parents and school, as well as children, are often disappointed with the results of schooling. It would point up the particularly supportive and successful microenvironments where children from low-income backgrounds function well and develop confidence. These could be expanded and duplicated elsewhere. The study could identify situations that seem to be most damaging to self-confidence, and raise some questions about points where the school and its children do not mesh well. For example, such a study might shed light on how to handle the problems created by the disparity between a child's home-life pace, which is constantly alive with unpredictable activity, and his school environment, which puts a premium on routine and control.

• *Avoid negative attitudes toward children.* Negative attitudes and assumptions about children from poverty-stricken homes may sometimes slip in despite the best of intentions. These attitudes come out in many little ways: the administrator who believed Sally should not be furnished with free lunch because "it's about time Sally's parents took some responsibility for her"; the frustrated elementary teacher who followed a child out into the hallway after class and shouted above the din, "Richard, *why* do you always have to be like your cousin Joe?"; the teacher who explained to me, "I don't expect to get any place with this child. I had her oldest brother in my class years ago, and I couldn't do a thing with him."

The common thread running through these incidents is that school personnel (probably unwittingly) are judging the child for things over which he has no control, punishing him for the shortcomings (real or imagined) of his parents. The child is blamed for who his parents are, where they live, how they live. He is stigmatized on the basis of what the school thinks his older siblings have done or not done, by the reputations of his cousins.

Schools must become conscious of such judgments to stop them. Otherwise these insidious attitudes toward children can undermine and undo the benefits of even the most conscientious teachers and the most effective teaching methods, for children read these negative messages more clearly and deeply than they read any benign messages.

However, this suggestion does not mean that schools should remove all responsibility and expectations from the children of rural poverty-stricken families. The child should, indeed, be held responsible for his actions, to the extent appropriate to his age and experience, and to the extent that his actions are within his control. The school must set its expectations for the child on the basis of the child, not his relatives; then express approval when the child achieves and let the child know when he has fallen below expectations. Beyond this, schools could actively foster self-accountability through providing cumulative and graduated experiences, coupled with encouraging support. This might accomplish a great deal toward enabling the child to feel that he can deal successfully with the larger world, that he has some mastery and control.

These five suggestions, taken together, are intended to show that schools could be more effective than they are in fostering not only academic skills but also a sense of confidence and competence, which is so crucial to the actualization of children's potentials. Although schools cannot be expected to cure rural poverty, they could do more to prepare children from poverty-stricken backgrounds to deal effectively with the wider world.

5. Combating Corrosive Stereotypes

The people of Chestnut Valley are well aware of the stereotypes and how deeply they corrode. They even have ideas of what it might be like if those stereotypes didn't come between themselves and the community.

The people along this road don't live this way because they want to. They didn't even ask to be born. But if people would treat them like human beings, encourage them when they're doing something good, then maybe they'd try even harder. If they're fixin' up a room, praise them; or if they're out mowing the grass, tell them, "Gee, your lawn looks nice." It would make such a difference to hear that kind of encouragement for our efforts, instead of always criticism for what we don't do.

Can communities, indeed, a whole society, drop their stereotyped thinking? Can they learn to see the good in others rather than judging only in terms of negative preconceptions? The change will not be accomplished by pious sermons in church, by celebration of brotherhood week in school, or by appeals to the collective conscience in newspaper editorials—though such reminders do have their usefulness.

The long-range hope is that the stereotype problem would quite naturally diminish if poverty itself were eliminated through significant changes in the employment picture and general economic situation of rural families. With greater economic stability, there would be less basis for invidious comparison. Superimposed on economic improvement, social bridges between rural areas and the urban-based community would reduce the separateness that fosters stereotypes. New social interaction patterns can be created and developed, and attitudinal changes will follow. However, extra care must be taken, particularly in settings involving heterogeneous mixtures of young children and teenagers, lest situations arise that would either reinforce stereotypes in people's minds or permit discriminatory behavior based on stereotypes. Merely putting children together is not enough; situations must be creatively designed to foster healthy interaction.

FOSTERING BETTER UNDERSTANDING. Careful observation and analysis can supply new perspectives that may eliminate the need to rely on prior judgments. As new bases for understanding people's actions are provided, old errors of misinterpretation and stereotype can be overcome. Three points stand out concerning the use of increased knowledge to combat stereotypes.

• *Look at contexts of behavior.* Looking at economic patterns, for example, it is obvious that poor people have a smaller pie to distribute (less total available money) and they don't know how large tomorrow's pie will be, or next year's pie. Consequently, they may cut their pie differently. For example, the poor people of Chestnut Valley often spend considerably less than one-quarter of their income on housing costs, and do everything possible to avoid the kind of continuing fixed-cash outlay for housing that middle-income people regularly incur. As a result of economizing on housing costs, they sometimes are able to spend a greater percentage of income on leisure and recreation than might be the case for middle-income people, though of course the figure in absolute dollars would still be much lower. The higher percentage allocated to recreation does not mean that the poor are wasting money on leisure, or that they value recreation more than housing; it suggests that, in order to maintain healthy lives and keep some happiness in their homes, the money they are able to save on housing may be assigned to the satisfaction of pleasure needs. Because of their unsatisfying jobs, ever-present worries, inadequate social ties to the community, overcrowded housing, and low self-esteem, rural poor people may have a greater need than others to spend money to bring relief and happiness into their lives.

When a poor family purchases a motorcycle or snowmobile, a fancier-than-necessary car, a color TV, a CB radio set, or a trip to the stock car races, they are emulating the contemporary American pattern of leisure, oriented toward buying heavily advertised fad items. Even poor people feel a need to indulge their desire to be "with it"; and they can sometimes do so because they have reduced expenditures elsewhere. Furthermore, the expenses on leisure-recreation in Chestnut Valley seem to fit well within the general themes of economic decision making, and effectively reinforce people's commitment to earning money. Hence, such expenditures are healthy and sensible patterns—*given the context* in which they are made.

It is the understanding of context that renders spending patterns intelligible, no matter what the economic level of the spender. The spending patterns of poor people in the rural areas are, for the most part, as rational in the poverty context as middle-class spending patterns are in middle-class contexts. But the patterns of one group cannot be judged in terms of the context of another group; one group should not be denigrated because it does not apportion its money according to the designs that other categories of people in other situations find appropriate.

• *Do not confuse quantitative statements about actions with cultural values.* In much of the social science literature, in program design, and in public thinking, there is a tendency to equate statistical norms (frequencies of actions) with cultural norms (learned, shared values). The equation is not merely erroneous, it inhibits understanding and perpetuates stereotypes, as can be seen in the interpretation of marital conflict (Chapter 7). The actual incidence of marital upheaval is indeed high, but the cultural value, the goal for which people strive, was found to be marital persistence, not marital disruption. Marital instability is the result of an assortment of social, economic, and emotional stresses correlated with poverty; it is not the result of insufficient commitment to the ideals of marriage and family life. In the stereotyped view, people's actions are a direct reflection of their preferences, and thus it is assumed that "those people don't value marriage and family living." This confusion between statistical frequency and cultural preference has been fostered by social scientists, particularly by the "culture of poverty" framework, which

has become firmly embedded in the public mind and in the thinking of government planners. It clearly perpetuates false stereotypes and misperceptions.[8]

• *Design stereotype-free programs.* The understanding of contexts and the
decoupling of statistical norms from cultural norms would help combat not
only the blatant public stereotypes, but also the subtle preconceptions that
creep into programs aimed at "eliminating poverty" by changing poor people,
and teaching them "how to live right." Government programs dealing with
poverty are sometimes built on the assumptions that people are poor because
they don't want to work, they don't know how to save, and they have no
concern for the future. Consequently, the programs often stress dangling incentives in front of people, teaching them skills, and changing their priorities.
But if the underlying assumptions about poverty and poor people are wrong,
the programs not only will be ineffective, but they will be wrong. As earlier
chapters demonstrated, people do not need incentives to work as much as
they need good jobs at which to work. Focusing attention on work incentive
programs will only perpetuate the stereotypes.

Handling the Derivative Causes of Rural Poverty

Thus far, we have discussed suggestions for reducing the five primary self-
perpetuating causes in the cycle of rural povery and marginality. Before going
on to the other five causes, it should be stressed again that these are
derivatives of the first five. Hence, if causes one through five were reduced,
perhaps along the lines indicated, causes six through ten would almost
automatically be ameliorated. Attempts to overcome rural poverty should
concentrate on the five primary causes. Cures and preventions cannot start
with the derivative causes.

Nevertheless, some attention should be turned toward the derivative
causes. Since these secondary causes have been operating over generations,
they and their negative effects are not likely to disappear instantly when the
underlying primary causes of poverty are attacked. In the common metaphor,
while Band-Aids should not be substituted for treatment of the underlying
cause of an infection, it may be necessary to continue to apply them while the
infection is being treated and the wound is healing.

6. Reducing the Pressure of Too Many Problems

Clearly, the overburden of problems would be lightened if the primary
causes of continuing poverty were removed. Improving and stabilizing the
economic position, primarily through adequate and flexible employment
possibilities and suitable programs for interim income backup, would end the
day-in, day-out worry over "keeping a roof over our heads and food on the

table." This, in turn, would significantly lower the level of stress that in-sidiously saps energy, reduces effective functioning, exacerbates other prob-lems, and often flares up into anger and violence in the family or neighborhood. Likewise, improving social connections would reduce the number and pressure of "too many problems all at once." If avenues could be created for successful interaction and roles in the secondary community, primary interpersonal relationships would be less threatened by overloading and by the pattern of displaced hostility.

However, even significant improvements in the five primary ongoing causes would not quickly or completely wipe out all the related problems that burden families; it would only gradually reduce their number, their complex-ity, and their incessant pressure. The physical, mental, and social wounds already inflicted by past burdens of problems might continue to fester. People may need extra social, medical, and counseling services for a long time to come. Hence, human services for rural poor people must be given adequate recognition and funding.

DELIVERING HUMAN SERVICES EFFECTIVELY. Attention should be devoted to improving the quality, nature, and accessibility of human services as they are rendered to people in the process of emerging from poverty. Two points can be stressed.

• *Examine the interface between service provider and client.* An understand-ing of the different expectations held by service providers and by rural poor people would facilitate a better match between services and needs. It appears that the most effective and utilized services are those that offer a personal ap-proach, multipurpose workers, and an ability to respond rapidly and flexibly to urgent needs and sudden changes. Some of the problems in service delivery include: the need to break away from concentration of services in centralized city offices, by taking services out to small communities and to homes; the need to create personal toeholds in the bureaucratic facade; and the need to minimize personnel turnover in agencies, so that clients who expect and need personal ties with an individual worker are not, instead, offered only a profes-sional relationship with the agency as a unit.

• *Consider the long-range as well as the immediate benefits of services to clients.* When social, medical, counseling, and other services are provided, not only are people's particular problems addressed, but at the same time they also gain experience in solving problems. Positive attitudes—even the very at-titude that problems *can* be solved—are certainly fostered by experiencing success in solving problems. Skills for dealing with problems are also developed during the process of successful problem-solving. This secondary aspect should be given more consideration, for it has long-run implications. The skills needed to recognize and define one's problems, to locate appropriate community resources, and to utilize them effectively should be taught and reinforced as an integral part of the process of helping people with their specific problems.

7. Altering the Balance Between Aspirations and Achievements

As previous chapters have shown, the poverty that grips generations of people in these marginal rural areas is not due to lack of aspirations. In fact, given the tenacity and complexity of the rural poverty problem, limited aspirations are a realistic response to people's actual and projected situations. Thus, it seems that the popular belief that raising people's aspirations will lift them out of poverty is inapplicable here. More than that, it is also a cruel hoax. High goals, if consistently unattainable, do not lift anyone out of poverty; they may instead destroy the person. And if the damage to that individual's functioning is recurrent or severe, it may limit the chances that his or her children, in their turn, will achieve those higher goals. It is not the aspiration level, but the achievement side of the balance, that must be addressed.

CREATING OPPORTUNITIES FOR ACHIEVEMENT. Opportunities and situations must be created, through reduction in the primary causes of rural poverty, for the achievement of goals.

The economic sphere, primarily jobs, is where opportunities for higher achievement are most needed. But the uncontrolled job market does not usually provide these opportunities. New hiring patterns will have to be encouraged, private-sector involvement solicited, and public-sector jobs created as needed. Again, it may help to target particularly crucial turning points in the lifecycle when the availability of new opportunities for achievement would have the greatest positive effect and would most readily be accepted.

Whenever possible, there should be opportunities for people to try new situations under conditions of limited ego-risk. As poor people hedge against personal failure and are particularly reluctant to take on risks to their self-esteem, new opportunities must be offered with a built-in risk protection. Whether in the realm of better jobs, home improvements, or completed educations, planners should be aware of the risks that potential participants may perceive, and should build in controls or cushions for any unavoidable ego risks. For example, a job training program might guarantee that if a person's new skill has no local market, or the new job proves to be unsatisfactory for the person, or he for it, he will be eligible for another paid training program. When the risks to a person's sense of worth are regulated, he or she is more apt to push on toward higher goals, rather than substituting easier-to-reach goals. The same principle applies to education, whether for young children, teenagers, or adults: risks to the ego should be minimized to make a high-aspiration program acceptable to a person of limited confidence.

8. Overcoming the Failure Syndrome

The self-perpetuating sense of failure cannot be overcome merely by telling people to stop thinking of themselves as failures. But reduction of the primary causes of poverty would almost certainly provide many more experiences of success that, in turn, would help reduce the failure syndrome. For example, if men's earnings on the job were high enough to meet more adequately the needs of their families, they would probably exhibit a considerably greater sense of self-worth, for they would be more adequately performing the provider role that they regard as important.

However, change will be slow. An adult who has lived through decades of failure may continue to be burdened by its psychological effects even after his or her economic situation has been improved, social connections strengthened, and the community's stereotypes muted. Moreover, the failure syndrome of parents may already have been transferred to their children before beneficial changes are made in the family's situation. Hence, we cannot expect a sudden bursting forth of self-confidence: it must be carefully built up and nourished.

PREVENTING INADEQUACY FEELINGS IN CHILDREN. One particular point might be stressed here. According to Erikson's stage theory, the development of a sense of inferiority is most likely to occur between the ages of six and eleven.[9] These are crucial years, when a youngster is changing from a homebound child to an operator in a much wider world. During this time, the experiences both at home and in elementary school can either contribute to or ward off a sense of inferiority. If the parents have low self-esteem, it is unlikely that they can instill confidence, individual initiative, and independence in their children, no matter how much they may wish to do so. Therefore, it is particularly important that the schools and other institutions of the community help. But too often the schools also fail to foster a sense of competence and mastery in these youngsters, thus adding to the sense of inferiority and contributing to the failure syndromes.

Three points seem particularly important if schools are to help break this intergenerational transmission of a sense of failure. First, whatever confidence and security the child does derive from his home surroundings should be recognized and valued, rather than called into question by negative aspersions cast upon his parents, his neighbors, and himself. Second, young children, in schools and in other community institutions, need as much exposure to success as possible. Their microenvironments should be examined and carefully monitored. Situations in which the child is apt to fail should be reshaped or eliminated. Third, children of all ages need to acquire a wide range of skills and tools to build their confidence in dealing with the larger world. Elementary schools have a particular challenge because they work with children at the crucial stage when they are most vulnerable to developing a sense of inferiority, and they are the first potential bridge between family and the rest of the world. By rewarding individual initiative, schools can help children develop moderate risk-taking attitudes and assume independence and learn self-direction.

9. Avoiding Psychosocial Deficits

Here again, the problem will be greatly reduced once the basic continuing causes of poverty and marginality are addressed. But since the healthy development of children cannot wait for such reforms, there must be direct attempts to address this self-perpetuating cause. Erikson's theories of the stages of development sound a warning note here too.

Young children need situations in which to develop basic trust, environments that encourage autonomy, experiences that foster initiative. Because the foundations for these characteristics are laid in the period up to age six, the quality of the child's early home environment is crucial. A holistic approach is needed, to assist the child by strengthening and supporting his home environment, rather than serving the child only in away-from-home settings such as day-care, preschool, and foster care. The supports must be given to the whole household – to all of its members – rather than just focused on the child.

The potential for the home-environment-centered approach is indicated in evaluations of the Head Start program that point out the importance of the out-of-classroom components of the program.[10] A number of program benefits are usually extended to the families of Head Start children. Visits by the social worker and nurse bring to the child's home environment specific services, social contacts, information and assistance that connect the family to other community services. In some communities, mobile programs take educational activities out to the younger siblings of Head Start children; these seem to be effective and well received. Head Start parent groups, regarded as an integral part of the program, not only involve parents in their children's education, but also foster social contacts for the parents. Through Head Start, the child thus becomes a connection between his parents and the wider world, a connection of particular benefit for families who are marginal to their communities. The classroom component of the program is reinforced and enhanced by these supportive services directed to the home environment.

PROVIDING MULTIFACETED SUPPORT FOR FAMILIES WITH YOUNG CHILDREN. A multifaceted attempt to stabilize children's primary environments during the crucial early years at home would break the vicious circle whereby economic,

personal, and marital problems so common in the early years of a poverty-
stricken household create psychosocial deficits in the children that may, in
turn, predispose them to poverty and problems when they become adults.
Breaking this cycle is very much a matter of timing, for the family is apt to be
under greatest stress just when the children are most vulnerable to incurring
long-term psychosocial damage; most likely to develop self-doubt, guilt, and
dependence. Conversely, supportive intervention at this time would pay the
greatest long-term dividends because it would come at the appropriate period
to enhance positive psychosocial development, thereby increasing the individual's chances of breaking out of the poverty cycle.

An example of such a multifaceted support program and its beneficial
ramifications could be suggested in terms of the specifics of the family of Mary
and Bill Crane and their children.

During the period when Bill and Mary Crane were going through rough
times together – he was drinking and she was sick, they were on welfare part
of the time, and they separated a few times, with Mary going home to
Mamma – there were young children and babies in the home.

Mary's affectionate interaction with their children and her nurturant personality may have helped cushion the effects on the children. There was no
problem of child abuse in this case, though several of the common correlates of
child abuse were present, perhaps partly because Mary had close relationships with a circle of family and friends.[11] But the level of tension and worry
in the household, the periodic fighting between parents, and the occasional
splitting up probably caused anxieties in the children and interfered with
their healthy development. Some of the children may have developed feelings
of guilt, or may have failed to develop autonomy and initiative, since there
was no way they could control what meant most to them – their parents and
family life. Clearly the risks to the children resulted not from any inadequacy
in Mary as a mother, but from the fact that many problems pressed in on the
family, making her less able to do the kind of mothering of which she was
otherwise capable.

Observations in this home and in many others showed that the quality and
quantity of mothering given to children was a barometer of how well or badly
things were going in the home at any given time. In most cases, minimal nur-
turing occurred only during periods of tension and upheaval in the home, and
thus had very little to do with a woman's adequacy or inadequacy as a
mother, very little to do with her valuing of or knowledge about being a nurturant mother. It seems clear that what was needed in those crucial years
was neither removal of the children from the home, nor parent education, but
a multifaceted support program for the household.

One can imagine a different scenario for the Cranes, based on a coordinated
program of intensive services and supports. If Bill had received pay more ade-

quate to the family's needs, or had been given assistance in finding the right kind of job, perhaps he would not have gone through a period of joblessness, changing jobs, and drinking; perhaps he would have felt more adequate as a husband and father, and therefore been somewhat more effective in these relationships. Extra income through a mechanism such as a guaranteed minimum income might have reduced the pressures and worries. And perhaps Mary could have received a small salary as a care-giver for her teenage sister.

Mary might have better satisfied her needs for social contacts and ego enhancement if she could have been involved in supportive interaction with other young mothers. Perhaps this could have taken the format of a playgroup for toddlers. It might even have been possible to organize a cooperative cottage-industry facility, in which the women could have produced some salable item (a craft, perhaps, or piecework for a factory) in a group setting, where their babies and young children could be brought along. Such a set-up might be quite attractive to women who need some income but cannot take on regular full-time work, partly because they do not want to put their young children into a day-care situation they regard as "institutional." Mary might also have eagerly participated in a mobile program bringing educational activities into homes with preschoolers.

Perhaps a home improvement grant would have enabled the Cranes to make their home a more safe, healthy, and convenient physical environment for youngsters. Adequate medical and dental services for all family members might have warded off later health problems, just as food stamps did help the family to eat reasonably well for a period. Various other supports and services might have been offered; though some might have been declined by the Cranes, who would have been actively involved in planning and decisions.

In all, this service package would have been designed by and for the entire household (including Mary's sister when she was living with them) and its entire complex tangle of problems and needs. The support program would not have been continued for more than a few years—just long enough to help the family avert or reduce some of the stresses and problems that can be particularly acute just when young children are most vulnerable. Later, Mary and Bill could well have managed on their own, as they have in fact done.

But in the meantime, the children would not have been negatively affected by the fact that their vulnerable years coincided with the years during which a young couple from a poverty-stricken background is also most vulnerable to economic, social, and emotional insecurity. The long-run beneficiaries are the children, who will become the next generation of adults.

Many aspects of such a multisupport program already exist in many communities: they should be encouraged, sufficiently funded, and coordinated vis-à-vis the individual family. Some coordinated programs for providing multiple supports to the young child's home environment have been tried on a pilot basis and for specific experimental or evaluative purposes.[12] But new ideas must continually be tried out, and successful pilot projects must be put into more widespread practice.[13]

10. Broadening Horizons

People who have grown up in rural poverty enter the adult world when they are in their middle or late teens. Often, however, they find themselves unprepared and unsuccessful at making their own way in the outside world. Consequently, they retreat to the home-haven. The knowledge that this refuge will always be open to them is a necessary security in the face of the high casualty rate they experience. The broadening of horizons can only be accomplished when there is a greater likelihood of satisfactory participation in the community. It may do little good to "expose" youngsters to the wonders of the outer world if the child sees them as belonging only to someone else's world. When restrictions and barriers are removed, horizons will almost automatically expand.

Young people need concrete help in realistically planning for their future and acquiring the variety of skills needed for standing solidly on their own. They need effective education, not just ten or twelve years of attendance in school. Some of the school-plus-employment combinations are particularly effective in this respect, and should be expanded. Basically, the goals of these programs are not so much a matter of stretching horizons as of helping young people reach the horizons they seek, helping them to deal effectively with the demands of adulthood—a stage they enter somewhat earlier than their middle-class agemates.

We can look more closely at the narrow horizons problem by examining one particular example, again from Mary Crane's family. Mary's sister Susan is seventeen, the mother of an infant, living in a somewhat tense situation with her parents, unmarried, and unsure.

Had Susan perceived real, reachable opportunities for herself in the broader community, and had she developed more effective ways of interacting with family and friends, at school and in the larger community, she might not have settled so young in life for narrowed horizons. It is possible that Susan became pregnant and kept her baby not out of ignorance of birth control, abortion, or adoption possibilities, but because she saw no other role in which she could succeed. One thing she could do to prove herself was to have a baby: becoming pregnant and giving birth was a public claim to competence. And Sue's mother, once over her initial anger about the pregnancy, encouraged Sue to keep the baby, hoping that this would make Sue grow up. (Possibly unsaid and unrealized was the fact that Sue's mother saw this new grandchild partly as her own child, as a chance to try again, as a child in whom she could place her hopes, now that her hopes for Susan seemed unlikely to be met.)

When the baby was born, Sue gained a whole bedroom just for herself and the baby – not only a physical gain of space, but an important symbol of her whole new definition and status. And there was a great deal of excitement and attention for both the new baby and for Sue. Her earlier problems were thus temporarily forgotten, sidestepped. But as the novelty of being a mother wore off, Susan's yearnings for friendship, love, and action with other teenagers surfaced again. She became restless at home, felt tied down by the baby, and was bewildered by her conflicting feelings toward the child.

In retrospect, one wonders if the signposts of trouble could have been spot-ted earlier. Pehaps there might have been other ways for Susan to escape from her unresolved childhood and teenage problems, other ways for her to earn status and recognition, other roles she could have filled, other means of showing competence.

Probably services and agencies and programs for all these needs were available within the community, but as often happens, people like Susan fall through the cracks – or hide in the cracks. By the time Susan was sixteen, becoming pregnant seemed, perhaps unconsciously, the only thing for her to do. At least it would release her from the frustrations of having to try to find a path for herself in the wider community, of having to stand on her own out there.

HELPING YOUNG PEOPLE PREPARE FOR THE WIDER WORLD. It is primarily because adult roles are taken on so soon afterwards that the later stages of childhood are critical in terms of people's horizons. This period is a watershed divide in their lives. And, importantly, late childhood and early adolescence is a period about which many of their parents feel particularly helpless, since the warm hugs, food treats, and verbal reassurances of "I love you" no longer seem appropriate or helpful. In many cases, parents are unable to help children prepare for entry into the larger world because the parents do not feel competent or confident in the interactional skills that facilitate successful participation in the world of schools, jobs, and community living. When the child was younger, the parent sent him off to school with the admonishment, "Now you behave yourself and don't cause trouble." Years later, as the grown child prepares to leave home, the parent's parting words are, "Remember, if things get too bad, you can always come home." Perhaps somewhere in be-tween these two points some effective assistance could come from community programs.

To help young people broaden their horizons, it is essential that early en-counters in the larger society be successful. One strategy to increase or insure success might be to provide a special program of specific training in interactive and practical adult-world skills. Small groups of young teenagers or preteens could be brought together in workshops to learn and practice ways of dealing with a boss, customer, social service worker, job counselor, teacher, and so on.

The program could be coupled with an existing youth job training program, and could be operated under the aegis of a community action agency (local antipoverty agency) or a community college. But the practical and interactive skills component would require some autonomy, so that it would not become diluted or diverted by the pressure in employment programs to meet a quota of job placements. Imaginative program design and careful planning stressing hands-on experiential training and keeping the needs, styles, and preferences of the adolescents uppermost would be essential. Assistance in conducting such a program could be sought from a variety of community resources. The instructors could include community employers, agency workers, and youth specialists. Young adults who had grown up in the community might be particularly effective as trainers, sharing the successes and difficulties of their encounters in the adult world. Role-playing sessions would enact job interviews, and dealings with service agencies and licensing bureaus. There could be actual experience in applying for Medicaid, getting a replacement birth certificate, obtaining working papers, a driver's license, or a Social Security card. There could also be sessions devoted to mental health and social skill topics such as how to release anger in a way that won't result in getting kicked out of school, losing a job, losing a girlfriend, or getting in trouble with parents or the law. Other sessions could deal with practical matters such as sex and birth control or nutrition—topics of natural interest and considerable importance for those who may be sexually active and searching for new models to follow, new roles to assume. (Particularly for girls approaching their childbearing years, awareness of the long-range importance of their nutritional health during prechildbearing adolescence could be stressed.)

Such a program would be designed to attract and accept a wide age range, say from twelve to twenty, with as little age separation as possible. The younger participants would be released from school and given school credit for their participation. Rather than wait until they have dropped out of school to participate in such a program, they could use the skills while they are still in school. The program might help them get more out of the remaining time they spend in school, or even encourage them to attend school more regularly or longer.

The extra effort to create and carry out such programs would pay extra dividends. The workshops would directly help young people develop skills their parents hadn't taught them, and thus increase their chances of successful early encounters with the outside world. As a side benefit, their adolescent years might be a little smoother because their newly developed skills could be applied to relationships with peers, girlfriends and boyfriends, and parents. They might be less motivated to leave their homes so early—and less likely to retreat to them so quickly after being knocked down in the first round.

If such programs helped make young adolescents more capable of successfully dealing with community interactional situations, there would be long-
term benefit in enabling them to believe that they *can* get along out there,
that their horizons *can* be broader.[14]

Summing Up

The struggle against adversity has long been a central theme in the history
of these stony, poor-soil hills—from the first white settlers who cleared the
land, through the sons, grandsons, and newcomers who tried to adapt
marginal farms to changing agricultural technology and modern marketing.
Struggle against adversity is still the dominant theme for residents who seek
to provide for their economic and social needs long after most farms have been
abandoned and the small rural communities have collapsed. There have
always been some individuals who have overcome the odds to win their
struggle, but even some of those may have been unduly scarred by the ordeal.
Many more have been beaten down by the struggle. Many are handicapped
almost from the start, and fall farther and farther behind as they continue.

In the late twentieth century, the forces and circumstances to which rural
people must adjust are different from those of earlier times. Today's hurdles
cannot successfully be overcome by the traditional virtues of working hard
and "making do." Furthermore, the new "community" to which people are in-
escapably connected is, for them, merely a rather loose conglomerate of institutions, agencies, and organizations, in which the traditional personal approach does not bring results.

The people have also changed. To a large extent, rural poor people are no
longer behind the times; their cultural values and consumption drives are
those of the wider society. By and large, the people of these rural enclaves of
poverty want to be accepted into the dominant community and society, to
become "like anybody else." But they are seldom able to achieve this goal, and
are often caught in the difficult position of having undersatisfied needs, unmet
goals, and feelings of deprivation compared to the society around them.

Because of this discrepancy, poor people have to make adjustments in their
behavior and personal surroundings, devising substitutes for what they lack,
relying on each other for help they cannot obtain in the community, project-
ing onto their children the hopes they once had for themselves, and insulating
themselves against the pain of further rejection and failure by lowering their
aspirations, hedging against disappointment, restricting their participation,
and reducing their commitment. In all aspects of life, these patterns of
behavior represent an attempt to adjust to an unrewarding life situation, and
the attempt itself places great stress on personal and social integration.

The behavioral patterns described in this book are mechanisms for adjusting to the difficult situation of continued poverty and marginality. However, these coping strategies are usually interpreted by others as evidence of character defects or faulty socialization, or as proof of deviant values. The struggles of individuals and families usually go unrecognized or misinter-preted. Dogged work brings only the demand that they work harder, or that more of them work. A decision to forgo certain material comforts for the sake of an occasional prestige item brings only condemnation for wasteful spen-ding. And individual initiative to forge one's own compromise solutions draws scorn from the community for living in an unacceptable manner.

The real tragedy of these small enclaves of marginality and poverty is that people are playing a game of life that has been structured in such a way that they are required to play but prevented from winning. Engulfed in an amor-phous urbanized community, they lack social-structural links to give them clear avenues of entry, and social distance is maintained by the force of strong negative stereotypes. Although most people attempt to play the game by the accepted rules, there is little reinforcement and positive reward for doing so. If they attempt to play the game differently, or to stop playing entirely, the penalties are severe. For most people, it is a discouraging and consuming struggle, often taking a psychological toll that makes them even less likely to be successful.

People caught in this bind can only survive by means of the adjustments they have forged, scraping along as best they can, keeping open their options to maneuver and carry on as they see fit in the circumstances. Taken as a whole, these adaptive mechanisms constitute a holding operation, a means of buying time while awaiting the development of a more favorable game situa-tion. Meanwhile, hopes are crushed, energies spent, and potential wasted.

From this perspective, it seems inescapable to conclude that what must be changed here is not the *people* who are poor and marginal, but the *situations* that make them so. If the negative situations that restrict and thwart people were removed and advantageous situations were substituted that enabled people to gain something recognizable from their efforts, society would not have to concern itself with trying to raise people's aspirations and broaden their horizons. If the game situations were restructured to allow some possibility of winning, people would play more eagerly and more successfully; and in playing more successfully, they would become more eager and suc-cessful people. Rural people emerging from poverty will, themselves, raise their aspirations; they will expand their own horizons. The responsibility of society at large is to change and improve the situations, to work to erase the primary causes of rural poverty. The secondary, derived causes, which are no more than adaptations to and results of the primary causes, will not require as much attention.

* * *

Entrenched economic poverty and psychosocial marginality need not con-tinue to blight America's rural hinterlands. This anthropological analysis of one specific case has demonstrated that better understanding of a situation can provide insight into ways of improving it. The book shows that rural poverty is a problem with many facets and many causes, that it is a self-perpetuating cycle; but this final chapter suggests that there are points at which the cycle could be broken.

Attempts to ameliorate the situation will only be effective, however, if they fit the specific context in which the problems exist. Solutions must be de-signed to produce this fit, tailored to meet the specific needs of different ages, sizes, situations, abilities, interests, and preferences. Just as there is no single, simple cause of rural poverty, so there can be no single, simple solution.

The development of specially designed, multifaceted approaches to eradi-cating rural poverty could benefit from additional social research in a variety of other locations. Research could help identify the particular needs and clarify the various causal factors operating in specific situations and in the general category of long-term, nonfarm rural poverty. The focus of such research on rural poverty (or on poverty anywhere, for that matter) should be on understanding how poor people perceive and cope with their cir-cumstances, not on demonstrating how poor people differ from some hypo-thetical middle-class model. It is important to understand poverty situations well before planning for their amelioration; it is important to understand the viewpoint of the intended beneficiaries before rushing in headlong with pro-grams. Anthropological research can help fill this need.

This study also indicates that any proposals developed to deal with non-farm rural poverty must leave several options open to rural people emerging from generations of poverty, for even in a tiny population there are significant differences among people. For some rural people, assistance in making a satisfactory transition into an urban environment may be desirable and/or necessary. But rural people must not be forced to move to cities as the only means of achieving economic security, must not be forced into cities as the only escape from the problems currently blighting rural areas. There must be, also, the option of improved situations for rural people where they are. Rural people should not be required to cut off their sustaining roots and ties in the rural area as the price for gaining a decent position in the wider society. Similarly, rural people should not be forced by unleashed marketplace deter-minants into becoming nomadic wanderers, following employment boomlets around the country or attempting always to find a depressed rural area where they can set down their trailer home. Our society *can* control and tame the economic forces that displace people. Our social scientists need not always be studying the casualties of historical processes. The manmade social and economic blight that grips much of the no-longer-agricultural regions of rural America should be subject to more control and cure than was the natural fungus blight that wiped out the chestnut trees of the northeastern hillsides.

Whatever solutions are worked out must build on the strengths that rural people already have. The people of rural poverty are clever at devising ingenious substitutes; they are determined to make do, on their own if possible; they help each other out, care for their disabled members, and maintain lifelong parent-child obligations of providing a home. The people of these rural poverty-stricken areas are extremely perceptive, as the quotations in this book should testify: they could certainly help design programs, solutions, and futures. They are committed to the belief that their children can share in the American Dream; and they urgently want to help their children gain a share of that dream.

Solutions will have to involve changes in society as a whole, and in the many particular communities where poverty-stricken populations remain enclaved on the margins. New opportunities for successful economic participation, new public attitudes, and new social bridges are needed. These can provide the means to make improvement possible. If these better situations become available, the people whose lives have heretofore been dominated by the tenacious blight of rural poverty will eagerly take advantage of them. The people of Chestnut Valley sometimes put a new twist on an old saying: "Where there's a way, there's a will."

Notes

Chapter 1

1. The observations recounted here were made over the course of several days in February 1971, and blended together to construct a realistic total day. In order to protect the anonymity of individuals being studied, family names and place names have been changed. Out of concern for the privacy of informants, identifying personal details have been omitted or altered. (See Chapter 2 for a fuller discussion of the ethical considerations of informant privacy.) The blurring of distinguishing aspects of Mary Crane and her family not only protects privacy, it also produces a family scene that is typical of many others in rural poverty.

The "day in a family" setting is a device Oscar Lewis used in his books (1961, 1966a, and especially 1962) and in his teaching as a vivid means of conveying, illustrating, and summarizing a large number of separate observations made in homes at various times. The device has been effectively used by others (e.g., Howell, 1973).

Chapter 2

1. For an eloquent demonstration of this position, see Lewis (1961, 1966a), the work of Robert Coles (e.g., 1971) and Rubin (1976).

2. I would argue, however, that a "culture of poverty" theory is not applicable as an explanation for similarities in observed behavior in this case – if indeed it is in any case. The culture of poverty theory neither fits nor explains the data. Readers interested in pursuing the debate over the theory are referred to Lewis (1966b) and to critics such as Valentine (1968) and Leacock (1971).

3. A similar position is clearly stated by Stack (1974, pp. 22–23) with respect to "pathology" in Black family structure.

4. For some interesting similarities in observed behavior patterns in urban poverty areas involving different regional, racial, or ethnic variables, see Liebow (1967), Hannerz (1969), Howell (1973), Stack (1974), and Valentine (1978). Some of the studies done in southern Appalachia show many similarities, and some interesting differences. See Weller (1965), Fetterman (1967), Gazaway (1969), Coles (1971), Loof (1971), and Schwarzweller (1971). A multidisciplinary study of a rural depressed area in Nova Scotia shows striking parallels: see Hughes (1960), Leighton (1965), and Stone (1966). Recent studies in Oregon point to pertinent similarities (Newton, 1977).

5. For example, in my own work as a consultant and trainer in poverty-related programs in various states, I have found that paraprofessionals working with low-income
families are struck as I am by the many similarities we find in widely separated poverty
situations. When I have used "A Day with Mary Crane" as a basis for group discussion, a number of workers have said Mary and her situation sound much like the
families they work with in their rural localities.

6. The government's official poverty counts show not only that poverty still exists,
but also that it has not steadily declined over the years. A significant decrease did occur through the 1960s, but progress since 1968 has been halting: in 1968, the government counted 25.4 million poor people; by 1973-74, about 23 million were poor; but by
1976, the figure had increased to 25 million. (See Rodgers, 1979, pp. 9, 19-20.)

It is important to note that, contrary to public impression, poverty is a particularly
severe problem in rural areas. In fact, the incidence of poverty is higher in rural
areas—roughly 25 percent, compared to 15 percent in urban areas and 12.5 percent in
the nation as a whole. While approximately 30 percent of the total U.S. population
was rural in 1970, approximately 40 percent of the poverty population was rural.

Chapter 3

1. For an overview of agricultural change in New York State, see Hedrick (1933)
and Gates (1969). A community study conducted in the Southern Tier region of the
state (Vidich and Bensman, 1958) identifies historical trends similar to those operating
in Chestnut Valley. Hurd (1879) presents a useful early history, showing population
trends.

Useful context for this historical study has come from the many pamphlets published
by the Cornell University Agricultural Experiment Station, New York State College of
Agriculture, Ithaca, New York. See especially: Warren and Livermore (1911),
Vaughan (1929), Melvin (1931), LaMont (1939), Hill (1943), Anderson (1954, 1958).

2. The historical approach to sociological analysis of the sweeping changes in rural
society is well illustrated by the Rural Life Studies of the United States Department of
Agriculture. The study of Landaff, New Hampshire (MacLeish, 1942) illustrates the
less compressed development period in the Northeast.

3. The soils are chiefly Lordstown, Mardin, or Volushia channery silt loam (United
States Department of Agriculture, 1965).

4. I am indebted to Professor Stanley Warren of the Cornell University College of
Agriculture for a discussion of the handicaps presented by soil and topography in different types and periods of agriculture.

5. Valuable source materials revealing patterns of acquiring farms include old diaries,
farm account books, and early newspaper articles. I am grateful to individuals who
shared such materials with me.

6. An elderly man vividly recalls his first sight of deer, around 1912. A Chestnut
Valley woman, writing a correspondence column for the county seat's newspaper in
1920, felt it newsworthy to report that a pair of deer had recently been seen.

7. See Warren and Livermore (1911).

8. Useful documentation comes from the newspapers of nearby small cities. Each
newspaper carried weekly columns from all the rural hamlets in its area. Documenting

farm turnover are many entries such as: "The [Jones] place has been sold to. . . ."; "The [Smith] heirs, all in Massachusetts, have sold the [Smith] farm to. . . ."; "Mr. and Mrs. [Green] have taken possession of the [Waters] place."

9. Conklin and Starbird (1958) note this as a general pattern for the state's low-income rural areas.

10. See Warren and Livermore (1911) and LaMont (1939).

Chapter 4

1. Studies conducted by rural sociologists suggest that there were antecedents for stratification in the late 1920s. In rural areas where agriculture had been seriously declining, there were significant differences in the standard of living and in participation in formal social organizations. (See Melvin, 1931, for example.) In later studies of several rural areas, Anderson (1954, 1958) found that unemployed people ranked lowest in participation in formal social activities and organizations.

2. Conklin and Starbird (1958), in an overview study of low incomes in rural New York State, identified these same two sources of the rural poverty population.

Chapter 5

1. The official definition of poverty is based on a figure that reflects income, household size, and current cost of living. The exact poverty level in a given year is set by the government according to a rather complex procedure, but it is essentially a gross income that would permit a family to obtain a minimally adequate diet if it spent one-third of its income on food.

Further explanation reveals the meagerness and arbitrariness of this definition. The basis for the poverty line is the cost of food. The minimal cost of adequate food for a family of a given size in any given year is figured by the U.S. Department of Agriculture at current market prices (actually using a 1965 index, updated every six months to reflect current Consumer Price Index). This figure represents the current cost of the "economy" or "thrifty" diet plan. Although the Department of Agriculture considers this "economy plan" diet to be nutritionally adequate only for "temporary, emergency use when funds are low," it is this cheaper diet, rather than the USDA's "basic low-cost plan" that is used in calculating the official poverty level.

The annual cost of the economy food plan is figured for each household size. This cost figure is then multiplied by 3, since government studies in 1955 showed that lower income families were spending about one-third of their income on food. The resultant figure represents the annual income a family would need to be able to purchase the economy diet (meeting temporary, emergency levels of nutritional adequacy). Any household with an income below this calculated level is officially poor, and every one above this level is officially not poor.

Various adjustments are made in calculating the poverty level: for farm families (who might not need to spend as much as one-third of their income on food) the poverty level is lower; for Alaska and Hawaii the level is higher; and for households headed by women, adjustments are made upward.

Using this formula, the official poverty level for a nonfarm family of four in 1970 was

$3,968 (this figure was derived from the 1970 cost of the economy diet, $1,323, multiplied by 3). In 1975, due to inflation, the poverty level for the same four-person family was $5,550. Any family of four below this income level was officially poor in that year. As of April 1980, the poverty line for a nonfarm family of four was $7,450.

There is growing awareness, even in government circles, that poverty cannot be adequately defined by absolute dollars per household, particularly when levels are set by such inadequate food-cost guidelines. Federal programs in the late 1970s often included as eligible not only people below the poverty line, but also those with slightly higher incomes, "up to 125 percent of poverty." Many people feel that if income is to be used as the basis of the definition, it should not be in absolute dollars but in dollars relative to the national median income at the time. A new definition of "low income" was included in the Housing and Community Development Amendments Act for 1979, dealing with the Farmers' Home Administration rural housing program: low income is defined as being at or below 80 percent of the median income of the area, as determined by the USDA (Rural Housing Alliance, *The RHA Reporter*, January 1980).

Definitions of poverty—the government's absolute definition and proposed relative definitions—are discussed in Rodgers (1979, pp. 17–38).

2. This pattern of avoiding management/supervisory positions is an interesting parallel to a pattern in the earlier farming period. Some men who had no flair for making farm-management decisions gravitated into the occupational niche of permanent farm laborers, and they remained hired hands for a lifetime, or else went into urban unskilled labor.

3. Roe (1973) conducted a comprehensive multidisciplinary study of the health status of women on welfare in some upstate New York communities. Her team found many longstanding medical and health problems that seriously affected employability and employment history of low-income women.

4. Some explanation of the food stamp program may be useful here. It was phased in nationally in 1969 and 1970, after pilot projects had demonstrated that it would be an improvement over the government's earlier food assistance program, the donated commodities program. For the period of this research, the food stamp program operated basically as follows.

A household certified as eligible is assigned a monthly food stamp allotment amount, determined by household size and composition, and by the cost of the USDA's "economy food plan." In 1974, for example, a family of four was allotted $142 worth of food stamps a month. To obtain the stamps, the recipient paid a purchase price based on the household's income relative to its size. In 1974, the family of four with an adjusted monthly income of $210 paid $59 for their $142 allotment of food stamps, whereas a four-person household with an income of $450 (maximum eligible) paid $118 for the same $142 worth of stamps.

The difference between the purchase price and the allotment amount is called the "bonus." In the first case, the bonus is $83; in the second case it is $24. The bonus is always greater for the household with lower per-capita income. The bonus represents the amount the government is paying into the household's food budget.

The participating family purchases its food stamps at a bank or other designated location once or twice a month, and spends the coupons on food items any time at any participating store. Food stamp purchase requirements, bonuses, and allotments have been revised upward regularly. In 1976, the four-person family with a $210 monthly net income paid $59, but received $166 worth of stamps (a bonus of $107).

In 1979, the food stamp program was changed to eliminate the cash purchase requirement. An eligible family now pays nothing, but collects a packet of coupons equivalent to the bonus level to which the household is entitled (still figured on the basis of household size, composition, and income). The cash that previously went toward purchasing stamps may now be spent directly on food – or on anything else. Those with no available cash can obtain the bonus food stamps, and thus can participate in the program.

Chapter 6

1. For an interesting and relevant study of spending decisions made by rural white poor people in Oregon, see Newton (1977). Her analysis of spending decisions provides concrete evidence that people allocate their meager economic resources rationally.

2. Perhaps it is worth noting here that this quoted passage, like all the others, is verbatim and unchanged. (In this case, the passage was tape-recorded because the informant was so articulate about money management and had so much to say on the subject.) These passages hardly fit the stereotyped notion of inability to defer gratifications or inability to plan for the future. Nor do they bear out the stereotypes that people who are poor cannot express themselves intelligently.

3. See Rubin (1976, pp. 199–200) for a description of this phenomenon among working-class people who grew up in poverty. Rubin also finds that the campers and boats people purchase are seldom used because the owners are too busy taking on extra jobs to pay for the items.

4. For a more complete description, see Fitchen (1977).

5. See Rubin (1976, pp. 161–67) for an interesting description and analysis of how working-class people responded to her query about what they'd do if they suddenly inherited a million dollars. In most cases, the answers were narrow and drab, confined mostly to, "I'd pay off all our debts."

Chapter 7

1. The sample was too small, and the time too short, to indicate whether this natural longevity built upon determination to "try one more time" is characteristic of the current generation of young adults. It would seem that the recent marriages of young people are just as tension-filled and rocky as the earlier married years of the previous generation. Whether today's young couples will stick it out remains to be seen. In any case, they seem no more divorce-prone than the rest of society, and possibly less so. Like their parents, young adults from the rural poverty enclaves believe in the importance of keeping the family intact for the sake of their children.

Parents tend to urge their grown children to marry their live-in mates, and to give a tenuous marriage one more try. However, the young adults are also a part of their own generation: they seem more accustomed to the fact of unwed motherhood, and they are not as concerned about divorce.

2. The high probability that both husband and wife had difficult childhoods is the

result of two factors: (1) the high incidence of family disruption in the preceding generation of rural low-income families, and (2) the pattern of socioeconomic endogamy, in which people from the rural depressed areas are likely to marry people of similar socioeconomic backgrounds.

3. This is in contrast to the more distinct lines and clear understandings between a young mother and her mother in the Black, urban families studied by Stack (1974). There, the very young mother might give over her first baby's care to her mother completely, and in so doing assign over the motherhood role, rights, and responsibilities. Although such an arrangement is not unknown in Chestnut Valley, it is rare, and did not occur during the decade of research.

Chapter 8

1. More of the younger mothers now appear to be breast-feeding their babies than was previously the case, but bottle-feeding seems still to predominate. The observed sample was too small for meaningful quantitative statements.

2. Specific documentation on the timetable of growing up was not obtained, nor was a sufficiently large number of individuals observed going through the successive stages to make definitive statements. Despite these shortcomings, the apparent patterns and timetables seem worth noting.

Chapter 9

1. As stated in Chapter 2, the few Chestnut Valley households who were not long-term poor and were not effectively included as neighbors were not among the families closely studied, for this is not a total-community study, but a study of rural poverty.

2. As the present cohort of people who were young children in 1969 reaches adulthood, it appears (although there are too few cases to be conclusive) that marriage partners are being drawn from a wider geographical area, including not only local neighborhoods but also nearby cities. Partners may come from families who previously did not know each other. Additionally, the selection of residential locations may now include a wider area, including the urban centers, in part because some young couples rent an apartment in the city or a trailer or house in another rural area, using cash assistance from social services if necessary, rather than living in their parents' back yard rent-free.

These new patterns exist alongside the more traditional patterns of mate selection and residence location. If the newer pattern increases, the kin-relatedness of the rural poverty neighborhood would correspondingly decrease. But at present, the kin pattern seems likely to continue because the older patterns are still strong. Furthermore, even those young adults who initially locate outside the home area tend to move back to it later.

Chapter 10

1. Similar racial prejudices were expressed by white, low-income urban residents in Howell's (1973) study in the Washington, D.C. area.

2. It should be noted that the absence of an intermediate-level social mechanism to pull together the multiplicity of parallel ties among individuals or families on one level and institutions or agencies on the other level is not unique to this setting or to its historical causes. Both suburbia and urban metropolis may suffer from the lack of built-in cohesive local-level units joining constituent individuals or families together vis-à-vis the large, amorphous community. But in the case of rural poor people, the situation is more serious because there are also economic, social, and attitudinal barriers to participation.

3. This attitude toward problems as unavoidable things that have to be put up with is apparently very common among poor people. I have found it mentioned or recognized by paraprofessionals working with low-income families in many settings – urban, rural, eastern, midwestern, Black, Puerto Rican, Mexican-American, and American Indian. I would not conclude, however, that this proves the existence of a "sense of hopelessness" or "fatalism" as part of a "culture of poverty." In fact, people seem to believe that problems – in general – are solvable. It's just that they see their own specific problems as unsolvable because they have had no experience to prove otherwise.

4. These hesitancies have been observed in the actions or inactions of many people as they stall and procrastinate after having finally agreed to try to get some help on a problem. When I accompanied individuals on their dreaded first visits to agencies – at their request only – their anxiety was reduced, and I gained insight into how help-seeking looks from the point of view of the seeker.

5. This same wait-and-see attitude was found in southern Appalachia (Weller, 1965).

Chapter 11

1. Conklin and Starbird (1958) saw this as a general pattern in the "abandoned farm areas" of New York State, and as the reason for the continuation of "chronically low incomes of nonfarm open-country residents" (p. 29). They foresaw the problem as likely to continue.

2. See, for example, Anderson (1954, 1958).

3. By both an absolute income standard (such as the government's present definition of poverty) and by a relative income standard (comparing income to the national median) the people of this study would be defined as poor. Even in their best periods, they remain within the income zone defined by the government as "under 125 percent of poverty." Townsend (1970, p. 225) proposed a definition of poverty that is particularly relevant here: "individuals and families whose resources, over time, fall seriously short of the resources commanded by the average individual or family in the community in which they live, whether that community is a local, national or international one, are in poverty."

4. No precise data were obtained on nutritional levels and medical status, but accumulated observations over the years point to a suspicious number of health problems, from mild to severe, that may have been caused, complicated, or prolonged by certain deficiencies in diet, poor sanitation, and other physical situations. Documentation of correlations between poverty and health in a similar population can be found in

Roe's (1973) study of health and nutritional status among poor women in upstate New York. Nutritional problems, dental problems, and various long-term disabilities such as diabetes were found to be common in the low-income sample she examined, and clearly contributed to the spotty employment histories and frequent unemployability that was found among the women. The study included careful medical examinations and lengthy medical histories of more than 450 women.

5. Concerning props for self-presentation, see Goffman (1959). Also of interest here are the striking similarities between economic management techniques found among rural New York's poor people and those reported for rural low-income Oregonians (Newton, 1977).

6. Kai Erikson's (1976) study of the psychosocial effects of the sudden loss of community in the Buffalo Creek Dam disaster provides an interesting analogy. It helps us to see what is lacking in places that have more gradually suffered a loss of community, if no substitute is provided. Among other results, he found a "loss of connection," a sense of separation from others and from the self, a difficulty in relating to others, each individual nursing his own hurts, tending his own business.

7. Several studies have shown the effects of inadequate local-level social structure in inhibiting the formation of a definition of the self. Gearing (1970, especially p. 148) illustrates the situation among Fox Indians in Iowa. Powdermaker (1939), in an early study of a southern community, shows that the brunt of frustrations encountered by Blacks in their participation in the wider community falls upon their marriage relationships.

The negative effects of a structural vacuum is analyzed in studies of eastern agricultural migrant workers (Friedland and Nelkin, 1971, and Nelkin, 1970), which reveal a "we-they" polarity. And in a depressed rural neighborhood in Nova Scotia, interdisciplinary studies revealed the negative social and psychological effects of inadequate local-level social structure (Hughes, 1960).

8. Leacock (1971, pp. 9–37) illustrates what she refers to as "structured discrimination" against lower-class pupils in the schools.

9. Excellent examples of the effects of stereotypes may be found in various parts of the Nova Scotia project on "Psychiatric Disorder and Sociocultural Environment" (Hughes et al., 1960, and Leighton, 1965). A related article (Stone et al., 1966) shows that far greater individual success is possible if a man can migrate beyond the reach of the stereotypes, for there he can obtain a good job and have the opportunity to prove himself as an employee.

The stereotypic perception of a marginal and poor neighborhood on the fringes of a larger community is illustrated in Vidich and Bensman (1958). The authors point out that the presence of the "shack people" serves an important social function for the larger community: a baseline, the very bottom standard for invidious comparison. Unfortunately, the authors appear to have swallowed whole the community's stereotypes about "the shack people," for they report that shack people respond only to immediate circumstances and reject or are ignorant of middle-class patterns and life styles (see especially pp. 69–71). Closer observation of the people, rather than reliance on community stereotypes, might have yielded a different explanation.

10. An interesting historical parallel here is that earlier in this century disasters such as barn fires were often the turning point that forced a marginal subsistence farmer to

go under, whereas a more successful farmer–operating on a cash basis, banking his profits, and protected by insurance–could rebuild and continue farming.

11. The same patterns are revealed in Howell (1973, p. 355). Some of his urban
white informants were described as "hard living"–indicative of a life style of intensity,
drama, and liquor that was the opposite of what they claimed to want. This pattern
resulted from their perception of the futility of striving for higher goals, and was "a way
of rebelling against the life circumstances one found himself in."

12. A sociopsychological study that reveals the important role of the failure syndrome in limiting job success is Goodwin (1972). Using quantitative methodology
based on questionnaires, Goodwin reached the same generalization that I have arrived
at by participant-observation. The phenomenon has also been observed by other traditional anthropological researchers: Liebow (1967) and Howell (1973).

13. This minimization of risks does not mean that people are generally cautious in all
things. It is risk of personal failure, risk of ego-damage, that they try to avoid when
possible. Risk of physical danger, on the other hand, is often undertaken, both know-
ingly and unknowingly, and may serve other psychological needs. Examples of risks
people commonly take, where risk could be reduced if desired, are quite obvious in connection with their use of vehicles. Babies and small children are seldom strapped into
car seats, but sit in laps or stand on the seat. Adults rarely use seat belts. Young boys
court danger doing stunts on bicycles, snowmobiles, and motorbikes. Their older
brothers and their fathers court physical danger and legal penalty in occasional bursts
of high-speed driving, in purposeful skidding on slippery roads, in driving occasionally
without a valid license, registration, or insurance.

14. The concept of psychological deficits derived from circumstances that inhibit or
truncate development at certain critical stages of early life comes from Erikson,
Childhood and Society (1963 edition, pp. 247–69). A relevant view of the etiology,
nature, and results of these deficits in a setting in Nova Scotia much like the one described here is found in Beiser (1965). An especially interesting work is *Appalachia's
Children* (Loof, 1971), which finds almost no emotional deprivation in infancy, but
significant problems of overly dependent personality disorders in children. Loof finds
children have satisfying relationships with their mothers and consequently are well
trained in relatedness, but are not trained well in acquiring controls over their ag-
gressive impulses.

Chapter 12

1. See Fitchen (1977).

2. Even the 1 percent loans available through Section 502 of the Farmers' Home Administration for providing a water supply, sewage disposal, bathrooms, central heating,
and so forth may not be within the grasp of people who simply cannot afford $700 for a
well and water system, no matter how low the interest or how spread-out the
payments. Some people simply cannot commit themselves to meeting payments regularly for up to thirty-three years.

3. By 1978, the province and mandate of the Department of Housing and Urban
Development had clearly been extended to include rural areas and small communities
in housing programs. At least on the level of demonstration projects, both Farmers'

Home Administration and HUD were making progress on low-income housing in rural areas. But significant housing assistance programs have been slow and meager in the rural areas, even by the government's own admission (Task Force on Rural and Non-Metropolitan Areas, 1978). Some loan regulations have been loosened, but increased flexibility on paper does not often translate into action, particularly when funding levels for the loan programs are consistantly far below need levels.

4. Rodgers (1979) evaluates past and current programs for overcoming poverty. He stresses full employment as the most important strategy, but also cites the need for a negative income tax to "provide a guaranteed liveable income to those unable to work" (p. 204). Williamson et al. (1975, p. 211) also conclude their comprehensive review of antipoverty strategies with the view that the negative income tax proposals, if enacted, would have "the greatest potential for a major impact on the extent of poverty and economic inequality in America."

5. For a comprehensive study of the effects on the family of the employment of the mother, see Feldman (1972). This study was based on a variety of research methodologies, including long-term studies as well as quantitative large-scale sampling, to investigate the interaction of work histories and family situations among low-income women in upstate New York communities.

6. At the end of 1979, the Carter administration, noting some of the special, unanswered needs of rural areas, announced its policy for rural America. (See The RHA Reporter, January 1980.) Carter proposed the creation of an Undersecretary of Agriculture for Small Community and Rural Development. This new branch of the USDA could be of great significance for rural Americans. It would identify and assess possible impacts that federal actions and decisions might have on rural areas. It would also provide an official advocate to help rural areas compete more successfully in the scramble for federal funds. This advocacy seems necessary because many federal funding allocation formulas discriminate against rural areas. For example, sparsely populated areas and rural counties that do not have a hospital may be effectively excluded from participation in a federally funded food assistance program, the Women, Infants and Children program (known as WIC). Other examples of funding discrimination against low-density areas are found in education aid formulas, where eligiblity for aid is based on percentages of low-income children in a school district (which may be lower in rural or consolidated districts than in inner-city districts).

New York State has established a specific official bureau to address the needs of rural areas.

7. In 1971, a high-level commission was appointed by the New York State Legislature to look into elementary and secondary education in the state. The commission (generally known as the Fleishmann Committee) came to the conclusion that "the biggest problem in the state is the high correlation between school success or failure and the student's socio-economic and racial origins. . . . [C]hildren from low-income and minority backgrounds fail in school in numbers which far exceed their proportion of the state's total population " (New York State Commission on the Quality, Cost and Financing of Elementary and Secondary Education, 1972, Vol. 1, p. 1.2). The commission report dismisses any possibility of different intellectual abilities correlating with socioeconomic status, stating that it had no "persuasive evidence" that a child's "innate ability correlates with family income, race, sex, parental occupation or ethnicity"

(Vol. 1, p. 1.29). The blame for low performance was laid squarely on the schools. "New York is not providing equality of educational opportunity to its students as long as the pattern of school success and school failure remains closely tied to a child's social origins" (Vol. 1, p. 1.2). The commission went on to say firmly, "the close parallel between school success and the child's socio-economic origin suggests that something is wrong with the way our educational system operates" (Vol. 1, p. 1.29).

8. Stack (1974, p. 71) emphasizes the same point with respect to low-income Blacks in an urban setting in the Midwest. "Statistical patterns do not divulge underlying cultural patterns. This confusion between statistics and cultural patterns underlies most interpretations of Black family life."

9. Erikson (1963 edition, p. 260) says, "The child's danger, at this stage, lies in a sense of inadequacy and inferiority."

10. Lazar et al. (1977, p. 27–31) evaluate a variety of preschool experiences, including Head Start and Home Start. They note the important long-range effects of increased parental involvement, although they admit that the precise effect has not been adequately measured. Unofficial evaluative comments by various personnel connected with local Head Start programs underscore the value of the home-centered components of the program.

11. A follow-up study (Elmer, 1967) of families of urban children who had been hospitalized with injuries resulting from abuse by parents indicates that child abuse by mothers is most likely to occur when the predisposing factors of emotional difficulties of mother, negative attitudes toward child, and lack of adequate social connections for mother are exacerbated in a situation of constant stress such as that fostered by poverty.

12. An effective demonstration project of this sort is reported in *A Second Chance for Families* (Jones, Neuman, and Shyne, 1976). This project, funded by the New York State Department of Social Services, "tested and demonstrated the effectiveness of intensive family services in averting or shortening placement" of children in foster care (p. 124). The evaluation found that a carefully planned program of intensive services tailored to the specific needs of the family was less costly but more beneficial to the child and his family than letting the family fend for itself in the community service network. Both the number of incidents of foster placement and the duration of placement were reduced in families that received the intensive coordinated family services.

13. Funding for such programs might be sought from a variety of sources and categories, including state monies for assisting children (such as, in New York State, the Division for Youth), regional development programs (such as the Appalachian Regional Commission, which includes this section of the state), and federal anti-poverty funds (through the Community Services Administration, formerly the Office of Economic Opportunity).

14. For this type program, private foundations and local employers might provide financial support. Public funds might come from local youth program monies, state youth funds (Division for Youth), and regional and federal grants (Appalachian Regional Commission and Community Services Administration).

Bibliography

Anderson, Walfred A.
1954   "Social Change in a Central New York Rural Community." Ithaca, N.Y.:
        Cornell University Agricultural Experiment Station. Bulletin 907.
1958   "Social Participation of Rural Nonfarm Adults." Ithaca, N.Y.: Cornell
        University Agricultural Experiment Station. Bulletin 928.
Beiser, Morton
1965   "Poverty, Social Disintegration and Personality." *The Journal of Social
        Issues.* Vol. XXI, no. 1, pp. 56–78.
Coles, Robert
1967   *Children of Crisis.* Boston: Atlantic-Little, Brown.
1971   *Migrants, Sharecroppers and Mountaineers*, Volume II of *Children of
        Crisis.* Boston: Atlantic-Little, Brown.
Conklin, Howard E. and Irving R. Starbird
1958   *Low Incomes in Rural New York State.* State of New York Interdepart-
        mental Committee on Low Incomes.
Elmer, Elizabeth
1967   *Children in Jeopardy: A Study of Abused Minors and Their Families.* Pitts-
        burgh: University of Pittsburgh Press.
Erikson, Erik H.
1950   *Childhood and Society.* (2nd edition, 1963). New York: W. W. Norton &
        Company.
Erikson, Kai T.
1976   "Loss of Community at Buffalo Creek." *American Journal of Psychiatry.*
        Vol. 133, no. 3, pp. 302–05.
Feldman, Harold et al.
1972   *A Study of the Effects on the Family Due to Employment of the Welfare
        Mother.* A Report to the Manpower Administration, U.S. Department of
        Labor.
Fetterman, John
1967   *Stinking Creek.* New York: E. P. Dutton.
Fitchen, Janet M.
1977   "Special Housing Problems of the Rural Poor." Washington, D.C.: Rural
        Housing Alliance.
Friedland, William H. and Dorothy Nelkin

1971   Migrant: Agricultural Workers in America's Northeast. New York: Holt, Rinehart & Winston.

Gans, Herbert
1962   The Urban Villagers. New York: Macmillan.
1970   "Poverty and Culture: Some Basic Questions about Methods of Studying Life-Styles of the Poor." In Townsend, 1970, pp. 146–64.

Gates, Paul W.
1969   "Agricultural Change in New York State." In New York History. Cooperstown: New York State Historical Association, pp. 115–41.

Gazaway, Rena
1969   The Longest Mile. Garden City, N.Y.: Doubleday.

Gearing, Frederick O.
1970   The Face of the Fox. Chicago: Aldine.

Goffman, Erving
1959   The Presentation of Self in Everyday Life. Garden City, N.Y.: Doubleday.

Goodwin, Leonard
1972   Do the Poor Want to Work? A Social-Psychological Study of Work Orientations. Washington, D.C.: The Brookings Institution.

Hannerz, Ulf
1969   Soulside: Inquiries into Ghetto Culture and Community. New York: Columbia University Press.

Hedrick, Ulysses Prentiss
1933   A History of Agriculture in the State of New York (1966 edition). New York: Hill and Wang.

Hill, F. F.
1943   Erin: The Economic Characteristics of a Rural Town in Southern New York. Ithaca: New York State College of Agriculture, Department of Agricultural Economics.

Howell, Joseph T.
1973   Hard Living on Clay Street. Garden City, N. Y.: Doubleday, Anchor.

Hughes, Charles C., M. A. Tremblay, R. N. Rapoport, and A. H. Leighton
1960   People of Cove and Woodlot: Communities from the Viewpoint of Social Psychiatry. New York: Basic Books.

Hurd, Duane H.
1879   History of Tioga, Chemung, Tompkins and Schuyler Counties, New York. Philadelphia: Everets & Ensign.

Jones, Mary Ann, R. Neuman, and A. W. Shyne
1976   A Second Chance for Families: Evaluation of a Program to Reduce Foster Care. New York: Child Welfare League of America.

LaMont, T. E.
1939   "State Reforestation in Two New York Counties: The Story of the Land and the People." Ithaca, N.Y.: Cornell University Agricultural Experiment Station. Bulletin 712.

Lazar, Irving et al.
1977   "The Persistence of Preschool Effects: A Long-Term Follow-up of Fourteen Infant and Preschool Experiments." Washington, D.C.: Department

of Health, Education, and Welfare.

Leacock, Eleanor Burke
1971   *The Culture of Poverty: A Critique.* New York: Simon & Schuster.

Leighton, Alexander H.
1965   "Poverty and Social Change." *Scientific American.* Vol. 212, no. 5, pp. 21–27.

Lewis, Oscar
1961   *The Children of Sanchez.* New York: Random House.
1962   *Five Families: Mexican Case Studies in the Culture of Poverty.* New York: John Wiley & Sons.
1966a   *La Vida: A Puerto Rican Family in the Culture of Poverty.* New York: Random House.
1966b   "The Culture of Poverty." *Scientific American.* Vol. 215, no. 4, pp. 19–25.

Liebow, Elliot
1967   *Tally's Corner: A Study of Negro Streetcorner Men.* Boston: Little, Brown.

Loof, David H.
1971   *Appalachia's Children: The Challenge of Mental Health.* Lexington: University of Kentucky Press.

MacLeish, Kenneth and Kimball Young
1942   *Landaff, New Hampshire: Culture of a Contemporary Rural Community.* USDA Bureau of Agricultural Economics, Rural Life Studies, no. 3.

Melvin, Bruce L.
1931   "The Sociology of a Village and the Surrounding Territory." Ithaca, N.Y.: Cornell University Agricultural Experiment Station. Bulletin 523.

Nelkin, Dorothy
1970   "A Response to Marginality: The Case of Migrant Farm Workers." Ithaca, N.Y.: New York State School of Industrial and Labor Relations, Cornell University. I. and L. R. Reprint Series, no. 282.

Newton, Jan
1977   "Economic Rationality of the Poor." *Human Organization.* Vol. 36, no. 1, pp. 50–61.

New York State Commission on the Quality, Cost and Financing of Elementary and Secondary Education
1972   *Report of the Commission.* Vol. 1.

Powdermaker, Hortense
1939   *After Freedom: A Cultural Study in the Deep South.* New York: Viking Press.

President's National Advisory Commission on Rural Poverty
1968   *Report of the Commission.*

Rodgers, Harrell R., Jr.
1979   *Poverty Amid Plenty.* Reading, Mass.: Addison-Wesley.

Roe, Daphne A.
1973   *Health and Nutritional Status of Working and Non-Working Mothers in Poverty Groups.* Report to the Manpower Administration, U.S. Department of Labor.

Rubin, Lillian Breslow
   1976   *Worlds of Pain.* New York: Basic Books.
Rural America, Inc.
        Rural America (a monthly publication). Washington, D.C.
Rural Housing Alliance – Rural America
        The RHA Reporter. Washington, D.C.
Schwarzweller, Harry K., J. S. Brown, and J. J. Mangalam
   1971   *Mountain Families in Transition: A Case Study of Appalachian Migration.*
        University Park, Pa.: Pennsylvania State University Press.
Stack, Carol B.
   1974   *All Our Kin: Strategies for Survival in a Black Community.* New York:
        Harper & Row.
Stone, I. Thomas, D. C. Leighton, and A. H. Leighton
   1966   "Poverty and the Individual." In Fishman, Leo, ed., *Poverty Amid Af-*
        fluence. New Haven: Yale University Press.
Townsend, Peter, ed.
   1970   *The Concept of Poverty: Working Papers on Methods of Investigation and*
        Life-Styles of the Poor in Different Countries. London: Heinemann.
United States Department of Agriculture
   1965   *Soil Survey, New York.* Soil Conservation Service.
United States Department of Housing and Urban Development
   1978   "Report of the Task Force on Rural and Non-Metropolitan Areas."
Valentine, Bettylou
   1978   *Hustling and Other Hard Work.* New York: The Free Press.
Valentine, Charles A.
   1968   *Culture and Poverty: Critique and Counter-Proposals.* Chicago: University
        of Chicago Press.
Vaughan, Lawrence M.
   1929   "Abandoned Farm Areas in New York." Ithaca, N.Y.: Cornell University
        Agricultural Experiment Station. Bulletin 490.
Vidich, Arthur and Joseph Bensman
   1958   *Small Town in Mass Society: Class, Power and Religion in a Rural Com-*
        munity. Princeton, N.J.: Princeton University Press.
Warren, G. F. and K. C. Livermore
   1911   "An Agricultural Survey." Ithaca, N.Y.: Cornell University Agricultural
        Experiment Station. Bulletin 295.
Weller, Jack E.
   1965   *Yesterday's People: Life in Contemporary Appalachia.* Lexington: Univer-
        sity of Kentucky Press.
Williamson, John B. et al.
   1975   *Strategies Against Poverty in America.* New York: John Wiley & Sons.

Index